rororo sprachen
Herausgegeben von
Ludwig Moos

Falsche Freunde sind besonders tückisch. Die False Friends, jene Worte oder Wortpaare, die im Deutschen und Englischen gleich oder fast gleich aussehen und zudem in vielen Fällen täuschend ähnlich klingen, aber eine andere Bedeutung haben, sind zähe Begleiter. Ihre raffinierteren Tarnungen entlarven selbst professionelle Sprachbenutzer oft nicht. "More False Friends", der Folgeband zu "False Friends" (rororo sprachen 8492), nimmt es mit ihnen auf. Ein konsequentes Übungsprogramm vom Fehler-Ausgang bis zur Fehler-Korrektur führt zum einwandfreien Gebrauch – von True Friends.

Prof. Hartmut Breitkreuz, M. A., lehrt auf dem Fachgebiet Englisch (Methodik und Didaktik des Fremdsprachenunterrichts und Angewandte Linguistik) an der Pädagogischen Hochschule Heidelberg.

ERRORS

Hartmut Breitkreuz

More False Friends

Tückische Fallen des deutsch-englischen Wortschatzes

Zeichnungen
Mathias Hütter

rororo
Rowohlt

Originalausgabe
Veröffentlicht im Rowohlt Taschenbuch Verlag GmbH,
Reinbek bei Hamburg, Januar 1992

Umschlagillustration Gerd Huss
Umschlagtypographie Büro Hamburg/Peter Wippermann
Satz Times und Helvetica (Linotronic 500)
Gesamtherstellung Clausen & Bosse, Leck
Printed in Germany
1780-ISBN 3 499 19172 5

For my two Mothers

Irmgard Breitkreuz † née Hett and Edith Breitkreuz née Hett

Marienwerder
Hildburghausen
Rodach

Gelsenkirchen-Buer

St. Petersburg/Florida

INHALT

VORWORT 9

False Friends-Zeichen und -Typen 11
Fehler-Zeichen und -Typen 11

TEIL I: Tückische Fallen des deutsch-englischen Wortschatzes 13

DIFFICULT FALSE FRIENDS:
False Friends-Paare A–U 15

Tests 1–4: FALSE FRIENDS TRAPS 46
Lösungen 1–4: TRUE FRIENDS 47

TEIL II: Tückische Fallen des deutsch-englischen Wortschatzes 149

PARTICULARLY DIFFICULT FALSE FRIENDS:
False Friends-Paare A–Z 151

TERRIBLE TWINS 150
Test 5: TERRIBLE TWINS (mit Lösungen) 184

TRICKY OVER-/UNDER-COMPOUNDS 186
Test 6: TRICKY OVER-/UNDER-COMPOUNDS (mit Lösungen) 240

CONFUSIBLES 243
Test 7: CONFUSIBLES (mit Lösungen) 282

PSEUDO-ANGLICISMS 284
Test 8: PSEUDO-ANGLICISMS (mit Lösungen) 326

FINAL TEST I and Answer Sheet 328
FINAL TEST II and Answer Sheet 331

False Friends-Übersicht 334

Literaturhinweise 337

FALSE FRIENDS-INDEX 340

VORWORT

Der vorliegende zweite False Friends-Band eröffnet dem Leser Einblick in "neue" Bereiche eines faszinierenden Gebiets der Fehlerkunde. Kurz-Einführungen zu jedem Kapitel ebnen den Weg für die Beschäftigung mit bestimmten False Friends-Typen wie den *Terrible Twins*, *Confusibles* oder *Pseudo-Anglizismen*.

False Friends zeichnen sich im wesentlichen durch ihre verführerische Ähnlichkeitswirkung aus, die zu Fehlern führen kann, vom Fremdsprachenbenutzer aber häufig nicht wahrgenommen wird. Das gilt insbesondere für die *Difficult False Friends*, die hauptsächlich auf fehlerhaften Gebrauch von Fremdwörtern zurückgehen. Die sprachlichen Fehlleistungen beim Umgang mit Fremdwort-Paaren wie *Allüren ≠ allure*, *eventuell ≠ eventual*, *Fraktion ≠ fraction*, *prägnant ≠ pregnant* oder *Rezept ≠ receipt* können im Einzelfall durchaus überraschen, sind aber in den Griff zu bekommen. Der hier beschrittene Weg reicht bei jedem False Friends-Paar von der Bewußtmachung möglicher Fehler im False Friends-Dreieck, Fehlertherapiestufe mit Klärung der Bedeutung und Gebrauch in typischem Kontext über die Zusammenfassung im False Friends-Viereck bis zur eigenen Anwendung in dem kurzweilig gehaltenen Teil *False Friends in Context*.

Der zweite Teil dieses Buchs stellt vier False Friends-Sondertypen in den Mittelpunkt: *Terrible Twins*, *Tricky Over-/Under-Compounds*, *Confusibles*, *Pseudo-Anglicisms*. Der thematisierte Aufbau dieses Bands entspricht den unterschiedlichen Fehlertypen, die sich hinter dem Sammelbegriff False Friends verbergen. Einige Beispiele für Terrible Twins stehen stellvertretend für diese Fehler-Untertypen der False Friends: Bei *electric/electrical* unterscheidet das Englische zwischen 'an *electric* blanket' und 'an *electrical* fault'; bei *classic/classical* trennt es bedeutungsmäßig zwischen 'a *classic* case' und '*classical* music', und bei dem Adjektiv-Paar *economic/economical* besteht eine Aufteilung zwischen 'the *economic* situation' und 'an *economical* heating system'.

Gerne entledige ich mich der angenehmen Pflicht, einigen *native speakers* meinen Dank für die erfahrene sprachliche Beratung im Zuge der Bearbeitung abzustatten:

Peter Bews, B. A., für fundierte Kritik und Anregungen

Dr. Paul Foster, M. A., für verläßliche Klärung von Detailfragen und stilistische Sicherheit

Dr. J. Tudor Morris, M. A., für Präzisierungen landeskundlicher Aspekte und sprachliches Augenmaß

John Robinson, B. A., für die aufmerksame Durchsicht eines Teil-Manuskripts

C. Ross Martin, B. A., für seinen Einsatz bei Fragen des sprachlichen Feinschliffs

Peter Catchpole, B. A., für die Beurteilung eines Großteils der Dialogisierungen.

Auch einigen weiteren, hier nicht aufgeführten Personen gilt mein Dank. Bei Fragen des deutschen Sprachgebrauchs half die Sprachberatungsstelle der Dudenredaktion (Bibliographisches Institut) manche Nuance abklären. Zum Abschluß spreche ich allen Beteiligten nochmals meinen herzlichen Dank aus – das gilt auch *und vor allen* für meine Frau.

Last but by no means least sei dem Leser die Lektüre des Einleitungsteils LERNEN IM FALSE FRIENDS-BEREICH (S. 11–18) des ersten False Friends-Bands (rororo Sprachen 8492) als *warming up* empfohlen.

Heidelberg, im August 1991 *Hartmut Breitkreuz*

False Friends-Zeichen und -Typen

False Friends-Zeichen	Zeichen-Erklärung	False Friends-Beispiele	False Friends-Typ
≠	ist nicht bedeutungsgleich, entspricht nicht	aktuell ≠ actual Chef ≠ chef mondän ≠ mundane Rezept ≠ receipt	voller False Friend, totaler False Friend, echter False Friend
◑	ist nur teilweise bedeutungsgleich, entspricht nicht immer	Basis ◑ basis fatal ◑ fatal komisch ◑ comic intensiv ◑ intensive	teilweiser False Friend, partieller False Friend, unechter False Friend, 'halbwahrer' False Friend

Fehler-Zeichen und -Typen

Fehler-Zeichen	Zeichen-Erklärung	False Friends-Fehlerbeispiele	False Friends-Fehlertyp
*	**Fehlerstern:** das folgende Wort ist ein False Friend.	* cylindric * smoking * talkmaster * twen	Terrible Twin } echte Pseudo-Anglizismen
(*)	**Fehlerstern in Klammern**: je nach Bedeutung liegt ein True Friend oder False Friend vor.	(*) affect(n.) (*) old-timer (*) slip	} teilweise Pseudo-Anglizismen

TEIL I

DIFFICULT FALSE FRIENDS

KURZ-EINFÜHRUNG

Was sind Difficult False Friends?

Zu den schwierigen Falschen Freunden zählen hauptsächlich deutsch/englische Wortpaare, bei denen es sich beim deutschen Wortpartner um ein *Fremdwort* handelt. Deutsche Fremdwörter verführen in besonderer Weise zu dem falschen Schluß, daß ein gleichgeschriebenes oder ähnlich aussehendes Wort im Englischen die richtige Entsprechung sei. Im Fremdwort-Bereich sind Fehlschlüsse dieser Art häufig anzutreffen, wie False Friends-Paare vom Typ **Akkord ≠ accord**, **Allüren ≠ allure**, **Konfession ≠ confession**, **Konkurrenz ≠ concurrence**, **sensibel ≠ sensible** oder **Stipendium ≠ stipend** ausweisen. Die mögliche Bandbreite der *sog. Fremdwort-False Friends* ist bisher nicht verläßlich erfaßt; daher muß sich der Fremdwort-Benutzer auf viele 'böse Überraschungen' im Englischen einstellen.
Andererseits zieht nicht jedes Fremdwort einen False Friend nach sich. Die (Fremd-)Wortpaare **dogmatisch/dogmatic**, **Effekt/effect**, **immens/immense**, **Konfrontation/confrontation**, **Priorität/priority**, **Sequenz/sequence** stellen *True Friends* dar, die zeigen, daß es auch 'ganz normale Entsprechungen' gibt.

AKKORD ≠ accord

accord [əˈkɔ:d] → **AKKORD**

piece-work etc. ← (= **Akkord**arbeit)

Akkord: (1) Akkord(arbeit): piece(-work)
(2) in combinations such as '**piece**-work rates'
(3) (Musik**akkord** etc.) chord [kɔ:d] (also fig.)

(1) "Ich habe den ganzen Winter im **Akkord** gearbeitet," sagte die Frau und zeigte auf die Rasierapparate.
"I've been on **piece**-work throughout the winter," said the woman pointing at the shavers.
(2) "Der **Akkord**lohn ist gut, aber die Arbeitsbedingungen schlecht", beklagte sich einer der Arbeiter.
"**Piece**-work rates are good, but the working conditions are bad," one of the workers complained.
(3) Nachdem der Pianist die einleitenden **Akkorde** gespielt hatte, stimmte der Chor ein.
After the pianist had played the introductory **chords**, the choir joined in.
"Der Schluß**akkord** der Symphonie muß noch geschrieben werden", endete der Bericht des Journalisten.
"The last **chord** of the symphony has yet to be written," was how the journalist's report ended.

Note: einen **Akkord** anschlagen;
eine Erinnerung wachrufen = strike a **chord**
"Kohl's speeches in East Germany strike **chords** among middle-of-the-road people," wrote an *Observer* commentator.
but: Stimmbänder = vocal chords (or vocal cords)
James Bond star Sean Connery had a wart removed from his **vocal chords**; he denied having throat cancer.

accord: (1) Übereinkunft, Zustimmung (formal)
(2) in Verbindungen wie 'of one's own **accord**', 'with one **accord**'

(1) The Geneva **accord** led to the final peace talks.
Die Genfer **Übereinkunft** führte zu den endgültigen Friedensgesprächen.
As yet there has been no **accord** between the Soviet Union and the United States on destroying chemical weapons.
Bisher gibt es keine **Zustimmung** zwischen der Sowjetunion und den Vereinigten Staaten zur Zerstörung chemischer Waffen.
(2) Some of the Kurds left Turkey of their own **accord**.
Einige Kurden verließen die Türkei aus eigenem **Antrieb**.
A rolling police roadblock was set up, but the drunk driver stopped of her own **accord**.
Es wurde eine Auto-Straßensperre der Polizei gebildet, aber die betrunkene Fahrerin hielt aus freien **Stücken**.
With one **accord** the youths stood up and left the church.
Die Jugendlichen standen **geschlossen** auf und verließen die Kirche.

'**Akkord**'
(1) **Akkord**arbeit
(2) '**Akkord-**'
(3) (Musik- etc.) Akkord

(1) **piece**-work
(2) in combinations such as '**piece**-work rates'
(3) chord (also fig.)

≠

(1) Übereinkunft, Zustimmung (formal)
(2) in Verbindungen wie 'aus eigenem **Antrieb**', 'aus freien **Stücken**', '**geschlossen**'

1) accord
2) in combinations such as 'of one's own **accord**', 'with one **accord**'

FALSE FRIENDS IN CONTEXT

Chinese Rock

British Rock Star: ... Walking through a Hong Kong factory I watched hundreds of Chinese doing ________ (1) -work listening to rock music.
Producer: And what was so impressive about it?

British Rock Star: There was nothing wrong in listening to rock music. But then I heard the opening ________ (2) of *Love*, my international hit.
Producer: Is that true? It's a scandal!
British Rock Star: I made enquiries about the origin of the 'Chinese' version of my hit and was led into the Canton Disco in downtown Hong Kong.
Producer (alarmed): We're on a visit here. Did you make a scene?
British Rock Star: No, but they introduced me to the local disc-jockey and asked him to record a few ________ (3) of the 'Chinese' version of my hit *Love*. When I told him who I was, he was taken by surprise.
Producer: So what did you do?
British Rock Star: I told the disc jockey to hand over the Cantonese version of *Love* immediately which he did. He even told me my hit had been re-recorded by the local pop singer Yi Ying.
Producer: Listen what I'll do. While the Hong Kong record company produces thousands of *Love* records on ________ (4) rates I'll walk in and claim our rights on Chinese rock. Hong Kong falls under the New York ________ (5) on rock music!

SOLUTION

(1) piece-work (2) chords (3) chords (4) **piece**-work rates (5) New **York accord**

AKTION ◑ action

action [ˈækʃn]

AKTION

(Kampagne, Unternehmen)

campaign [kæmˈpeɪn] **etc.**

AKTION: (1) (Kampagne, Unternehmen etc.) campaign, drive etc.
(2) in combinations such as 'aid **programme**', 'rescue **operation**'
(3) (politische Säuberungs**aktion**) purge [pɜːdʒ]

(1) Die **Aktion** für behinderte Kinder war wieder ein großer Erfolg.
The **campaign** for handicapped children was once again a great success.
"Dies ist eine **Aktion** gegen das Rauchen in der Schule", kündigte der Direktor am Ende der Schul-Morgenfeier an.
"This is a **drive** against smoking in schools," announced the headmaster at the end of the morning assembly.
(2) Nach den Überflutungen im Sudan ließ die Regierung eine Hilfs**aktion** anlaufen.
After the flooding in the Sudan the government launched an aid **programme**.
Das Robbensterben macht eine neue Rettungs**aktion** erforderlich.
The death of the seals calls for a new rescue **operation**.
(3) Der Geheimdienst beteiligte sich an der politischen Säuberungs**aktion**.
The secret service joined in the **purge**.

action: (1) Tat
(2) Handeln, Eingreifen
(3) Klage (jur.), (Gerichts-, Disziplinar-) Verfahren
(4) (Arbeitskampf-)Maßnahmen

(1) This new idea was quickly put into **action**.
Diese neue Idee wurde schnell in die **Tat** umgesetzt.
(2) Quick **action** has helped to save Nicola, a newborn baby with a heart defect.
Schnelles **Handeln** half, Nicola, ein neugeborenes Baby mit einem Herzfehler, zu retten.

"The Tube driver's prompt **action** averted a Tube disaster," said the spokesman.
"Das sofortige **Eingreifen** des U-Bahn-Fahrers wendete ein U-Bahn-Unglück ab", sagte der Sprecher.
(3) A group of parents has threatened sit-ins and legal **action** over the appointment of a new liaison teacher.
Eine Elterngruppe hat mit Sitzstreiks und einer **Klage** wegen der Ernennung eines neuen Verbindungslehrers gedroht.
After the ship's collision the captain may also face disciplinary **action**.
Nach dem Schiffszusammenstoß muß der Kapitän auch mit einem Disziplinar**verfahren** rechnen.
(4) Ferry travellers heading for Calais were delayed for more than two hours because of industrial **action** by French seamen.
Fähren-Reisende in Richtung Calais hatten wegen Arbeitskampf**maßnahmen** französischer Seeleute mehr als zwei Stunden Verspätung.

Note: **action** committee = **Aktions**komitee
action group = (Bürger-, Eltern- etc.) Initiative
but: libel **action** = Verleumdungs**klage**
Lord Aldington in the most costly **libel action** in British history won £1.5 million in damages.
Compare: There are, however, cases in which **Aktion** and **action** overlap.
Such an **action** could have serious consequences.
Solch eine **Aktion** könnte ernste Folgen haben.

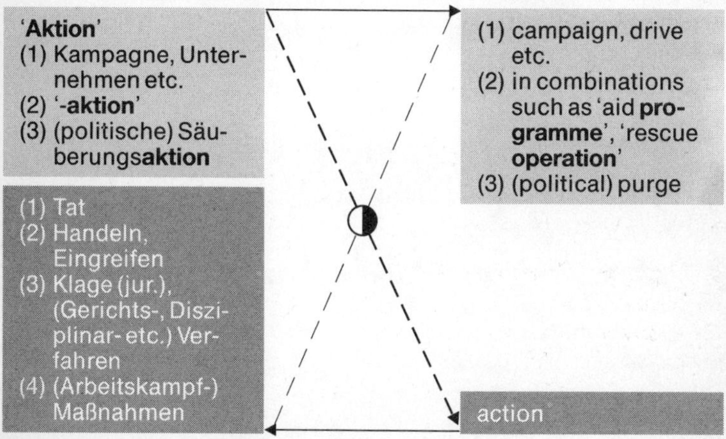

FALSE FRIENDS IN CONTEXT

No Fuss about Furs

Top Model Yasmin: . . . and Brigitte Bardot makes no fuss about her love of animals.
Model Suzie: She's quite right. It's unnecessary and cruel to kill animals just to make a profit from their furs.
Top Model Yasmin: That's why I've launched a ________ (1) to persuade women not to buy clothes made of fur.
Model Suzie: I'll wear fake fur to support your ________ (2).
Top Model Yasmin: Thank you, Suzie. But it's far more important to stop the fur industry. Quick ________ (3) is needed.
Model Suzie: Hm. Why not stop the fur industry by legal ________ (4)?
Top Model Yasmin: I don't know. At the moment much of our anti-fur ________ (5) rests with the Lynx pressure group.
Model Suzie: And what kind of quick ________ (6) do you have in mind?
Top Model Yasmin: The Lynx pressure group is collecting furs from women who no longer want to wear them. It intends to burn £ 1 million worth of fur as a protest at the end of next month.

SOLUTION

(1) campaign/drive (2) campaign/drive (3) action (4) legal **action**
(5) anti-fur **campaign** (6) action

This is a campaign against smoking in public...

AKTUELL ≠ actual

actual ['æktʃʊəl]

AKTUELL
(gegenwärtig; das neueste etc.)

current ['kʌrənt] **etc.**

AKTUELL:	(1) (gegenwärtig, jetzig, von heute) current
	(2) (von augenblicklichem Interesse) topical
	(3) (nach dem neuesten Stand) up-to-date
	(4) (das letzte, das neueste) latest
	(5) (derzeitig, augenblicklich) present
	(6) (modisch) fashionable
	(7) (neuerlich) recent

(1) Die **aktuelle** politische Situation sollte allen Aktionären eine Warnung sein.
The **current** political situation should be a warning to all shareholders.
(2) Im Augenblick ist die Umweltverschmutzung ein **aktuelles** Thema.
At the moment environmental pollution is a **topical** subject.
(3) Der Geschäftsführer legte den **aktuellen** Bericht des Unternehmens vor.
The manager presented the company's **up-to-date** report.
(4) Die **aktuellen** Zahlen zeigen keine Verbesserung der Wirtschaft.
The **latest** figures show no improvement of the economy.
(5) Die **aktuellen** Zinsen sind um ein Prozent gesunken.
Present interest rates have dropped by one per cent.
(6) Helle Farben sind wieder **aktuell**.
Light colours are **fashionable** again.
(7) Die **aktuelle** Entwicklung in der Sowjetunion muß genau beobachtet werden.
Recent developments in the Soviet Union have to be watched closely.

Note: nicht mehr **aktuell** sein = be no longer **relevant/important**
The Iron Curtain **is no longer important** today.
aktuell sein = be of interest (to)
The threat of a nuclear war **is of interest to** countries in the Middle East.

actual: (1) Adj.: wirklich, tatsächlich; eigentlich
(2) Adv.: eigentlich; überhaupt

Note: 'actually' is in many cases a filler which remains untranslated.

(1) The **actual** circumstances of the murder were quite different.
Die **wirklichen** Umstände des Mords waren ganz anders.
Epstein's bronze sculpture *Social Consciousness* was shown for the first time in **actual** size in Philadelphia in 1953.
Epsteins Bronze-Plastik *Soziales Gewissen* wurde erstmals in **tatsächlicher** Größe in Philadelphia 1953 gezeigt.
"What interests me is the debate going on beneath the **actual** issues. It's a debate about values, about things like wealth, progress and growth," Prince Charles said.
"Was mich interessiert, ist die Diskussion unterhalb der **eigentlichen** Probleme. Es ist die Diskussion über Werte, über Dinge wie Wohlstand, Fortschritt und Wachstum", sagte Prinz Charles.
(2) It has been maintained the so-called homeless are **actually** tramps who do not want a home.
Es ist behauptet worden, daß die sog. Obdachlosen **eigentlich** Landstreicher sind, die keinen festen Wohnsitz wollen.
My husband's left me. I **actually** don't know what to do now.
Mein Mann hat mich verlassen. Ich weiß **überhaupt** nicht, was ich jetzt tun soll.

'aktuell'
(1) gegenwärtig, jetzig, von heute
(2) von augenblicklichem Interesse
(3) nach dem neuesten Stand
(4) das letzte, das neueste
(5) derzeitig, augenblicklich
(6) modisch
(7) neuerlich

(1) current
(2) topical
(3) up-to-date
(4) latest
(5) present
(6) fashionable
(7) recent

≠

(1) Adj.: wirklich, tatsächlich; eigentlich
(2) Adv.: eigentlich; überhaupt

(1) adj.: actual
(2) adv.: actually

FALSE FRIENDS IN CONTEXT

Little Snoring and Great Snoring

Presenter: Surfers do it standing up. In contrast, Prince Charles, Winston Churchill, Leo McKern and many others do it or did it while sleeping. Our ________ (1) subject today is *snoring*. With me is Dr. Ashton, an expert at one of Britain's sleep centres. What is the ________ (2) situation in this field?
Dr. Ashton: Snoring can damage your health. If someone snores heavily, they can ________ (3) stop breathing for nearly 30 seconds. It can cause heart disease. And it can be lethal.
Presenter: An ________ (4) report on the Sleep Syndrome shows the social disadvantages of snoring. Marriages are ruined, jobs lost and even murders committed. A ________ (5) court case revealed that a man hit his room-mate over the head with a fire extinguisher and smothered him with a pillow because he had been kept awake for seven weeks on end. Is snoring really so bad?
Dr. Ashton: The ________ (6) study estimates that two-thirds of all men and 50 per cent of females over 45 are regular snorers. They should see a chest specialist.

Presenter: By the way, *Little Snoring* and *Great Snoring* really exist – they are not names of Indian chiefs, but the names of two villages in Norfolk.

SOLUTION

(1) **topical** subject (2) **present** situation (3) actually (4) **up-to-date** report (5) **recent** court case (6) **latest** study

ALLÜREN ≠ allure

allure [əˈljʊə]

ALLÜREN
(= Gebaren, Gehabe)

airs [eəz] **etc.**

ALLÜREN: (1) (Gebaren, Gehabe) airs, airs and graces
(2) (ausgefallenes Benehmen) (eccentric) behaviour

(1) Prinzessin Diana ist eine angenehme Persönlichkeit, die keine **Allüren** hat.
Princess Diana is a pleasant personality who does not give herself **airs**.
Gesellschaftliche **Allüren** sind zu einem Mittel auf der Erfolgsleiter in der Lokalpolitik geworden.
Social **airs and graces** have become a means to climbing the ladder to success in local politics.
(2) Solche ausgefallenen **Allüren** zeichnen künftige Olympiasieger nicht aus.
Such eccentric **behaviour** isn't the mark of future Olympic champions.

allure: (1) Anziehungskraft, Faszination
(2) Reiz, Verlockung

(1) Ihre Verehrer schrieben Lobgedichte auf ihre geheimnisvolle **Anziehungskraft** und verglichen sie mit der Garbo.
Her worshippers wrote poems in praise of her dark **allure**, comparing her with Garbo.
Many girls are attracted to the job of stewardess by the **allure** of foreign travel.
Viele Mädchen werden vom Stewardess-Beruf durch die **Faszination** von Reisen in fremde Länder angelockt.
(2) It was the irresistible **allure** of the Niagara Falls that kept the Swedish tourists looking at them.
Es war der unwiderstehliche **Reiz** der Niagara-Fälle, deren Anblick die schwedischen Touristen in den Bann schlug.
The **allure** of meeting the Swedish girl again nearly overwhelmed im.

Die **Verlockung**, das schwedische Mädchen wiederzusehen, überwältigte ihn fast.

Note: lure = Lockmittel
The **lure** of sex was so strong for the prison officer to become an IRA accomplice – disrupting his family life and costing him his career.

Compare: **Allure** (= Anziehungskraft, Reiz) is mostly the **positive** attraction of s. o. or sth., whereas **lure** (= Lockmittel) is often the **negative** attraction of s. o. or sth.

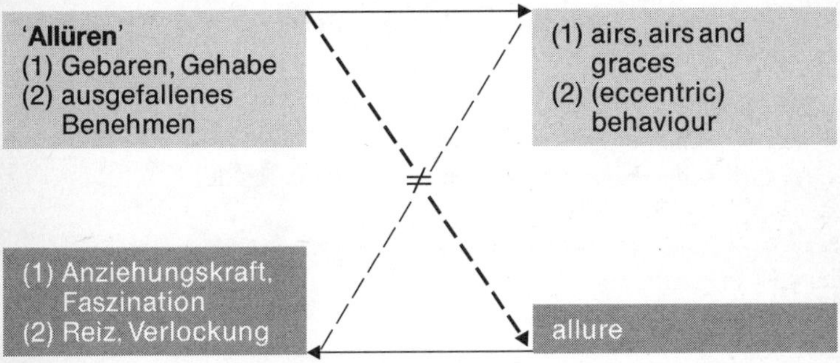

FALSE FRIENDS IN CONTEXT

Road to an Ode: Music and Verse

Radio Presenter (during family listening time): Have you ever heard of a real princess having a part-time job with a travel agency? If not, I'd like to introduce you to Princess Zohra Ghazi who gives herself few royal ________ (1).
Princess: Hello.
Radio Presenter: Tell us about your royal background first.
Princess: I'm a princess of the Afghan royal house. In the 1978 revolution 19 members of my family were shot in the royal palace in Kabul. I'm the only surviving member of the royal family.
Radio Presenter: You're married now to a famous cellist. Does the ________ (2) of music inspire your relationship?
Princess: It certainly does. But my husband doesn't put on ________ (3)

as great musicians often do. Musicians like him have to work far too hard. I support him as far as possible, but I won't play second fiddle.

Radio Presenter: What do you do in your spare time?

Princess: I write a little. The ________ (4) of the former royal palace still inspires my verse.

Radio Presenter: That's a nice surprise for our listeners.

SOLUTION

(1) airs and graces (2) allure (3) airs (4) allure

AMBULANZ ◑ ambulance

ambulance ['æmbjʊləns] ·························

AMBULANZ
(Unfallklinik etc.)

out-patients' department etc.

AMBULANZ: (Unfallklinik; poliklinische Station für ambulante Behandlung) out-patients' department; out-patients' clinic; emergency ward

Die **Ambulanz** mußte Überstunden machen, weil viele Verletzte immer noch von dem Flugzeugunglück eintrafen.
The **out-patients' department** had to work overtime because many injured people kept arriving from the plane crash.
"Wir konnten all die neuen Patienten in unserer **Ambulanz** nicht behandeln", sagte der diensthabende Arzt. "Viele mußten in andere Krankenhäuser umgeleitet werden."
"We couldn't treat all the new patients in our **emergency ward**," said the doctor on duty. "Many had to be diverted to other hospitals."

ambulance: (1) Krankenwagen, Sanitätsauto
(2) '**Rettungs**-', '**Notfall**-' (Fahrzeug anderer Art) (in combinations)

(1) The **ambulance** went to the overturned lorry and took the injured driver to hospital.
Der **Krankenwagen** fuhr zu dem überschlagenen Lastwagen und brachte den verletzten Fahrer ins Krankenhaus.
During the rush-hour an **ambulance** couldn't go on because of an accident, and the patient had died when the **ambulance** arrived at the hospital.
Während der Hauptverkehrszeit konnte ein **Sanitätsauto** wegen eines Unfalls nicht weiterfahren, und der Patient war bereits gestorben, als das **Sanitätsauto** im Krankenhaus eintraf.
(2) All the **ambulances** from the Croydon area were ordered to the burning hotel at once; even a helicopter was used as a flying **ambulance**.
Alle **Rettungsfahrzeuge** aus dem Gebiet von Croydon wurden sofort

zu dem brennenden Hotel beordert; sogar ein Hubschrauber wurde als fliegendes **Rettungsfahrzeug** eingesetzt.
The British Red Cross sent an **ambulance** helicopter to help the Armenian people after the earthquake disaster.
Das britische Rote Kreuz schickte einen **Rettungs**hubschrauber, um dem armenischen Volk nach der Erdbebenkatastrophe zu helfen.
His parents had to fly their son home by **air ambulance** after a swimming accident on a Greek holiday island.
Seine Eltern mußten ihren Sohn mit einem **Notfall-Flugzeug** nach einem Schwimmunfall auf einer griechischen Ferieninsel nach Hause fliegen lassen.

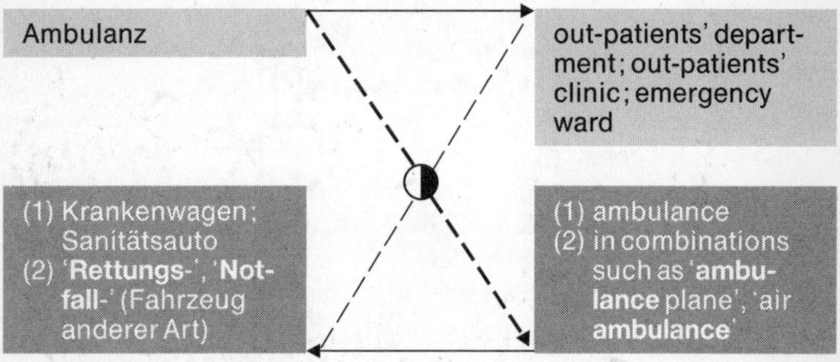

FALSE FRIENDS IN CONTEXT

The After-Effects of Gas-Sniffing

Mrs McGillis: Did you see that ________ (1) go down the road and turn into the fields?
Mrs McFarlane: Yes, I wonder what happened.
Mrs McGillis: Well, I saw them carry a man to the ________ (2) and then rushed him to the ________ (3) at the hospital.

* * *

Mrs McFarlane (looking through next day's local paper, *The Morning Courier*): "A teenage boy caught gas-sniffing by a policeman ran out of a shed across some fields – and dropped dead. The ________ (4) came too late. A police spokesman said the teenager was caught by PC Ronald McNeil looking into some fuel containers."

SOLUTION

(1) ambulance (2) ambulance (3) out-patients' department (4) ambulance

APART ≠ apart

apart [əˈpa:t] ············ ▶ **APART**

attractive etc. ◀—— (auffallend; geschmackvoll etc.)

APART: (1) (auffallend, reizend) attractive, charming
(2) (ungewöhnlich) unusual, striking
(3) (besonders) remarkable, distinctive
(4) (besonders reizvoll) charming, delightful
(5) (geschmackvoll) in perfect taste, stylish, smart

(1) Für ihr Alter ist Joan Collins eine **aparte** Frau.
For her age Joan Collins is an **attractive** woman.
Kennst du sie nicht? Sie ist eine ganz **aparte** Person.
Don't you know her? She's quite a **charming** person.
(2) Die neuen Hüte der alten Dame sehen jedesmal **apart** aus.
The old lady's new hats always look **unusual**.
Durch ihr **apartes** Aussehen gewann Raquel Welch stets viele Bewunderer.
Her **striking** appearance always won Raquel Welch many admirers.
(3) Das ovale Gesicht der Gräfin hatte **aparte** Züge.
The countess's oval face had **remarkable** features.
Wenn sie zum Essen ausgeht, legt sie auf **aparte** Abendgarderobe Wert.
Whenever she goes out to dinner, she makes a point of putting on **distinctive** evening clothes.
(4) Ich fand die Art, wie sie es gemacht hat, ganz **apart**.
I found the way she did it really **charming**.
Eine Frau dieses Alters mit einem solch **aparten** Gesicht habe ich noch nie gesehen.
I've never met a woman of that age with such a **delightful** face.
(5) Unsere Empfangsdame ist stets **äußerst apart** gekleidet.
Our receptionist always dresses **in perfect taste**.
Die Herzogin von York sah **apart** in dem grünen Anzug und dem schwarzen Hut aus.
The Duchess of York looked **stylish** in a green suit and black hat.
Mein Chef hat eine ungewöhnlich **aparte** Wohnung in Pimlico.
My boss has an unusually **smart** flat in Pimlico.

apart: (1) prep.: apart (from): außer, neben; beiseite
(2) (in combinations such as 'be **apart**', 'live **apart**'; 'fall **apart**'): **getrennt** sein, **getrennt** leben; **auseinanderfallen** etc.

(1) **Apart from** her unemployment benefit Mrs. Smallbone has no income.
Außer der Arbeitslosenunterstützung hat Mrs. Smallbone kein Einkommen.
Joking **apart** I don't believe a word of it.
Spaß **beiseite**! Ich glaube nicht ein einziges Wort.
(2) Liverpool has two cathedrals, both on the same road and only half a mile **apart**.
Liverpool hat zwei Dome, die beide in derselben Straße sind und nur eine halbe Meile **auseinanderliegen**.
The Johnsons have been living **apart** since her affair with their gardener.
Die Johnsons leben seit ihrer Affäre mit ihrem Gärtner **getrennt**.

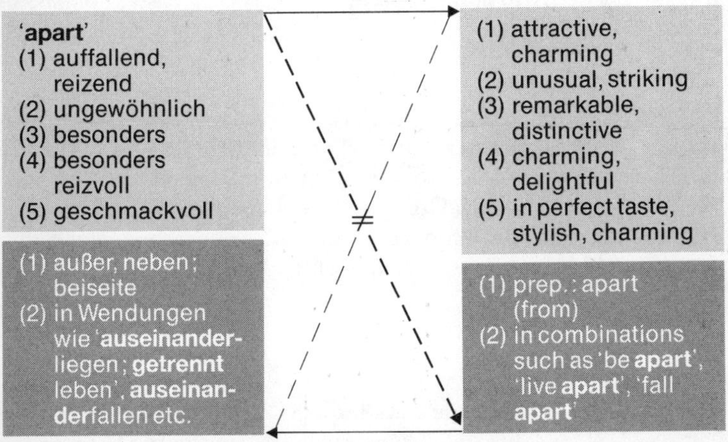

How to Win a Rich Heiress

Court Scene 1 (at the Old Bailey)
Judge: ... and you fell desperately in love with the rich, ________ (1) property heiress?
Accused (David Mander): I met Judy when I worked as a barrow boy and then turned to crime to keep her.
Judge: Why was that?
Accused: Judy came from a well-to-do family and I wanted to offer her a life-style beyond my means.
Judge: So you carried out a series of armed robberies including the armed robbery on the Post Office in North London?
Accused: Yes. ________ (2) from that I had to divorce my first wife. I didn't want to live ________ (3) from Judy, now my second wife. So we moved into a ________ (4) West End flat at Ivor Court. Judy liked to wear ________ (5) designer clothes and go on expensive holidays in Nepal and Barbados...

* * *

Court Scene 2 (at the end of the trial)
Judy: ... Your Highness, I married David in jail after his arrest, but I can't face years ________ (6) all on my own. It would ruin my life. (Sobbing) I married David for love, and I intend to stick by him.
Judge (at the end of the court procedures): ... I hereby sentence the accused to 15 years imprisonment. Court adjourned.

SOLUTION

(1) attractive/charming (2) apart from (3) live **apart** (4) smart/ delightful (5) **stylish** designer clothes (6) years **apart**

ARTIST ≠ artist

artist [ˈɑ:tɪst] → **ARTIST**

artiste [ɑ:ˈti:st] → (Jongleur, Clown etc.)

ARTIST: (1) (Jongleur, Clown etc.; Zirkus- etc. **Artist**) (circus) artiste
(2) (Darsteller, Künstler) performer (on radio, TV); (variety) artiste

Note: The French spelling **artiste** still exists in modern English, but is now gradually being replaced by the English spelling **artist** (used for a professional **performer**).

(1) Viele Menschen waren von Charlie Chaplins Vorstellung in *Der Landstreicher* begeistert; er war ein begnadeter **Artist**.
Many people were enthusiastic about Charlie Chaplin's performance in *The Tramp*. He was a gifted **artiste**.
Sie bewunderte die Zirkus**artisten** in der Manege, aber sie mochte ihren Lebensstil nicht.
She admired the circus **artistes** in the ring, but she disliked their way of life.
(2) Chaplins Eltern waren Music-Hall-**Artisten**.
Chaplin's parents were music-hall **performers**.
Als professionelle Varieté-**Artisten** treten Jim und Mandy fast jede Woche in Radio-Sendungen und auf der Bühne auf.
As professional variety **artistes** Jim and Mandy appear in radio shows and on stage almost every week.

artist: (1) (Kunst-)Maler, Künstler
(2) Künstler (z. B. als Pianist)

(1) **Artists** don't like being totally dependent on sponsorship.
Maler sind nicht gerne völlig von Gönnern abhängig.
Like an abstract **artist**, the Czech Jana Bokova used her cameras to create an atmosphere.
Wie ein abstrakter **Künstler** hat die Tschechin Jana Bokova Kameras verwendet, um die Atmosphäre einzufangen.

(2) Several other **artists** took the judges' fancy, among them the pianist Andrew West and the viola player Jane Atkins.
Mehrere andere **Künstler** fielen den Preisrichtern positiv auf, darunter der Pianist Andrew West und die Viola-Spielerin Jane Atkins.

Note: woman artist = Künstlerin
The Hayward Annual presented the works of some **women artists** such as Wendy Taylor, Sandra Blow, Mary Kelly in the context of a mixed show.

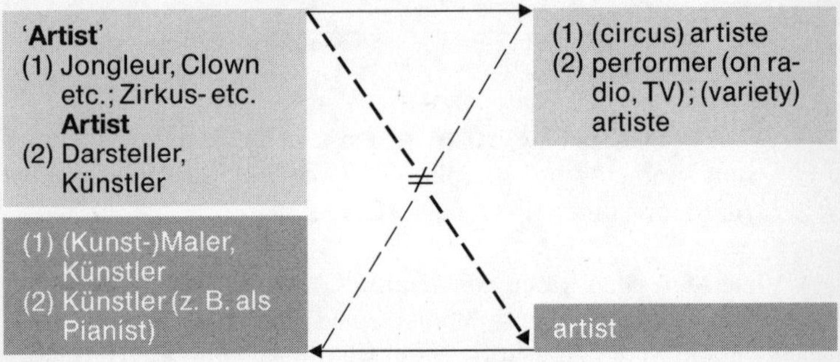

FALSE FRIENDS IN CONTEXT

What do you Want to be?

Mark: ... At first I had an interest in art and wanted to become an ________ (1). But now I've changed my mind. I'm going to join a circus.
Jack: But what are you going to do in the circus? You wouldn't even make it as a sword dancer.
Mark: Listen, I'm going to be a trapeze ________ (2).
Jack: You what? (Looking up and down at Mark) You're much too tall for a trapeze ________ (3).
Mark: That's the idea. I'll be the tallest trapeze ________ (4) in the world.

SOLUTION

(1) artist (2) artiste (3) artiste (4) artiste

BASIS ◑ basis

basis ['beɪsɪs],
(pl.) **bases** ['beɪsi:z] ········ → **BASIS**

base [beɪs],
(pl.) **bases** ['beɪsɪz] ← (Stützpunkt; Standquartier etc.)

BASIS: (1) (Stützpunkt; Abschußbasis) base
(2) (Standquartier, auch fig.) base
(3) (Grundlinie etc.) base
(4) (Fuß, Sockel) base

(1) "Wir müssen in einigen Sekunden zur **Basis** zurückkehren, da wir nur drei Meilen von der Grenze entfernt sind", kündigte der Chefpilot an.
"We've got to return to **base** in a few seconds, as we're only three miles from the border," announced the chief pilot.
"Unsere Bodentruppen haben eine ideale Abschuß**basis** für die Raketen", kommentierte einer der Offiziere in der Flugkanzel.
"Our ground troops have got an ideal **base** for their rockets," commented one of the officers in the cockpit.
(2) Die Bergsteiger kehrten nach 12 Stunden zum **Basis**lager zurück.
The climbers returned to their **base** camp after 12 hours.
Die Kinder sind mein ganzes Leben, und ich möchte, daß sie wissen, eine sichere und angenehme **Basis** zu haben.
The children are my whole life and I want them to know they have a secure and happy **base**.
(3) "Die **Basis** des Dreiecks ist länger als jede der beiden anderen Seiten. Beweist es", forderte der Mathe-Lehrer seine Schüler auf.
"The **base** of the triangle is longer than each of the two other sides. Prove it," the maths teacher told his pupils.
(4) Die **Basis** der Säulen ist vom Wasser unterspült worden. Es muß sofort etwas unternommen werden.
The **base** of the columns has been undermined by water. Something has to be done at once.

Note: Vorratslager, Nachschublager = supply **base**
During the fighting our supply **base** was also destroyed.

basis: (1) Basis, Grundlage
(2) Grundprinzip; Hauptbestandteil

(1) British building societies make every effort to arrange their mortgages on an endowment **basis**.
Die britischen Bausparkassen unternehmen jede Anstrengung, ihre Hypotheken auf Erb**basis** zu vereinbaren.
"At the moment we can't see any **basis** for further cooperation with your company," he said, concluding his remarks.
"Im Augenblick sehen wir keine **Grundlage** für eine weitere Zusammenarbeit mit Ihrem Unternehmen", schloß er seine Ausführungen ab.
(2) Trust and mutual respect form the **basis** of living together.
Vertrauen und gegenseitige Achtung bilden das **Grundprinzip** des Zusammenlebens.

Note: shop floor = (die Arbeiter, die Belegschaft an der) Basis
The union leaders negotiated under pressure from the **shop floor**.

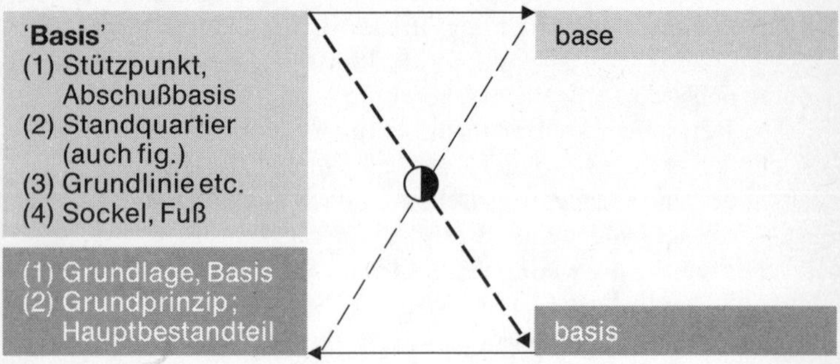

FALSE FRIENDS IN CONTEXT

Saving the Ozone Layer

First Tory MP: Have you heard of the Prime Minister's attempt to save the ozone layer?
Second Tory MP: How will he do it? He isn't a world policeman!

First Tory MP: He's given scientists the financial ________ (1) for a research project. This makes him the man of the hour!
Second Tory MP: I don't understand what is planned.
First Tory MP: Well, Britain's going to set up a big research ______ (2) in the Antarctic. It's been revealed there's a temporary ________ (3) camp out there already.
Second Tory MP: Is that why he's called a world-wide conference on environmental problems?
First Tory MP: Yes, otherwise we'll be faced with a global emergency. What we need is a general ________ (4) of agreement to stop the use of harmful chlorofluorocarbon, CFC, gases in aerosols and fridges.

SOLUTION

(1) basis (2) research **base** (3) **base** camp (4) basis

CHEF ≠ chef

chef [ʃef]

CHEF

(Vorgesetzter)

boss etc.

CHEF(IN): (1) boss
(2) chief (mainly in combinations such as '**chief** editor')

(1) Ich kann nicht einfach einige Stunden von der Arbeit wegbleiben; mein **Chef** würde mir sofort die Papiere geben.
I can't simply stay away from work for a few hours. My **boss** would sack me at once.
(2) Es ist jemand am Apparat, der den **Chef**redakteur zu sprechen wünscht.
There's someone on the phone wanting to speak to the **chief** editor.
Die Feuerwehr-**Chefs** werden für einen eintägigen Streik stimmen sowie dreitägige Arbeitsniederlegungen auf Flughäfen.
Fire **chiefs** are to vote for a one-day strike and for three-day stoppages at airports.

Note: In BE '**chief**' is mainly used in compound nouns; otherwise it means 'Häuptling'. This is different in AE:
Lee Brown, who became the new **chief** for public safety, assured he had a plan to fight crime in New York City.
Compare: Polizeipräsident = **chief** constable
but: **Chef**arzt = senior consultant
Personal**chef** = personnel manager

chef: (1) Oberkoch, Küchenchef
(2) '**-koch**' (in combinations)

Note: The English term **chef** is short for the French **chef de cuisine**. In English **chef** is used only of a man; a woman in the same position is a **cook**.

(1) "I'm sorry, our **chef** is busy preparing the meal with the other cooks," the waiter remarked to the new guest.

“Leider ist unser **Küchenchef** gerade damit beschäftigt, das Essen mit den anderen Köchen zuzubereiten”, teilte der Kellner dem neuen Gast mit.
(2) The Gatwick Wena Hotel is looking for a breakfast **chef** and a banqueting **chef**, the advertisement ran.
Das Gatwick Wena Hotel sucht einen Frühstücks**koch** und einen Bankett**koch**, lautete die Anzeige.

Note: head **chef** = **Chef**koch, Küchen**chef** (in better restaurants etc. only)
master **chef** = Meister**koch**
“BBC **master chef** Glynn Christian will be demonstrating ideas for quick meals,” said the announcer, introducing the programme.

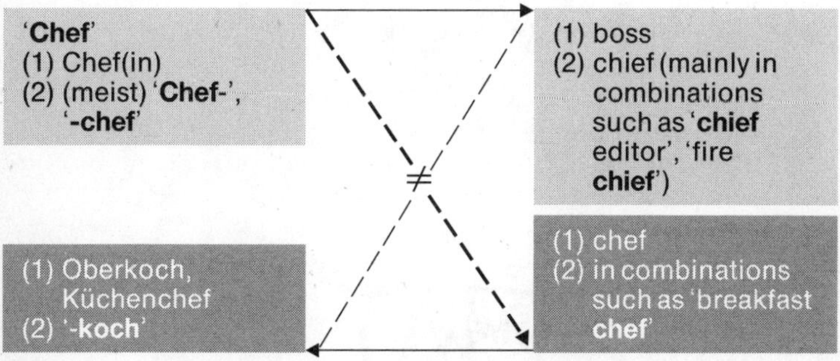

FALSE FRIENDS IN CONTEXT

The Consequences of Cooking

Major: One of our men has been killed.
General: What do you mean?
Major: People are saying that the soldier who killed him saved the lives of the entire division.
General: How is that possible?
Major: He shot the ________ (1)!

General: That’s one problem solved then, but the other is that I’ve got to inform the police ________ (2)...

SOLUTION

(1) chef (2) police **chief**

An Old Pun

The other day our old ________ (3) walked into the old hotel kitchen and came up with the old joke:
"He was a good ________ (4), as good ________ (5) go. And as good ________ (6) go, he went."

SOLUTION

(3) boss (4) chef (5) chefs (6) chefs

DELIKAT ◑ delicate

delicate ['delɪkət]

DELIKAT
(köstlich, lecker etc.)

delicious [dɪ'lɪʃəs] **etc.**

DELIKAT: (1) sehr wohlschmeckend, köstlich, lecker: delicious
(2) (äußerst) zurückhaltend, (sehr) behutsam: careful, gentle
(3) (aus)erlesen, fein: excellent, exquisite, select

(1) Das Essen war wieder **delikat** zubereitet.
Once again the meal was **delicious**.
Unsere walisischen Gäste mochten den **delikaten** Obstsalat.
Our Welsh guests liked the **delicious** fruit salad.
(2) Die Damen waren von der **delikaten** Art angetan, wie unser Gastgeber mit der Ungehörigkeit des Vortragenden umging.
The ladies were pleased with the **gentle** way our host treated the speaker's rudeness.
(3) Ich muß schon zugeben, es war ein **delikater** Wein von **delikatem** Geschmack.
I have to admit it was a **select** wine with an **exquisite** taste.

delicate: (1) heikel, schwierig
(2) feingliedrig, grazil
(3) schwächlich
(4) zart, fein

(1) "What about the money we need?" the manager pressed on. "It won't be easy to solve this **delicate** problem."
"Wie steht es mit dem Geld, das wir benötigen?" drängte der Geschäftsführer weiter. "Es wird nicht leicht sein, dieses **heikle** Problem zu lösen."
(2) Her piano teacher admired her **delicate** fingers and her **delicate** figure when she played the piano.
Ihr Klavierlehrer bewunderte ihre **feingliedrigen** Finger und ihre **grazile** Figur, als sie Klavier spielte.
(3) Hazel was too **delicate**; she wasn't strong enough to survive the operation.

Hazels Gesundheit war zu **schwächlich**; sie war nicht stark genug, um die Operation zu überstehen.
(4) When they parted, she gave him a **delicate** kiss.
Als sie sich trennten, gab sie ihm einen **zarten** Kuß.
Mary had spent months **delicately** embroidering the table-cloth.
Maria hatte Monate darauf verwendet, die Tischdecke **fein** zu bestikken.

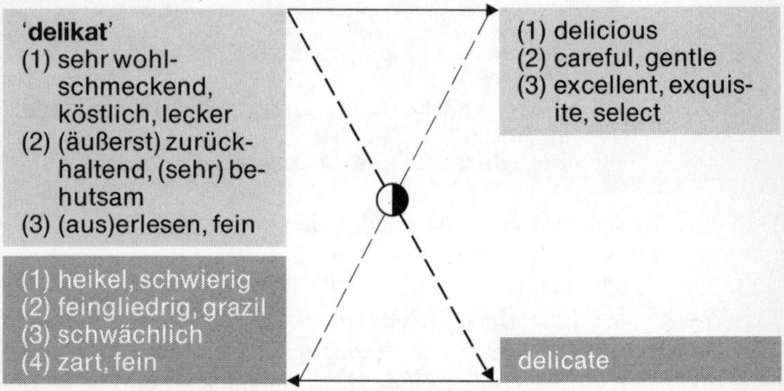

FALSE FRIENDS IN CONTEXT

Five Young Sherlocks

TV Reporter (interviewing five boys about their real-life adventure): It is a ________ (1) matter to put a dangerous criminal behind bars again. How did you manage to track him down?
Nick Spender (15): On the way home from school we passed the old shed where we always go and play in summer.
Stephen Moore (14): At lunchtime I had prepared some ________ (2) fruit salad and taken it to the shed by the river.
Nicholas Newman (14): When we saw a stranger coming out of the shed, we went into action. As I passed him I asked the time and I noticed the two black initials *B. W.* ________ (3) inscribed on the white face of his ________ (4) watch. This reminded me of a description of an escaped prisoner I'd heard on the local radio.
James Reid (13): Then I left the others to make a 999 call at home. I dropped the ________ (5) hint we had spotted a shabby, limping

stranger with the initials *B. W.* It turned out later they stood for *B*rian *W*admore – the wanted man.
Charles Ridley (15): The other four members of our gang split into two to shadow the stranger as he walked along the riverbank.
James Reid: We hid in the bushes until the police cars arrived. The policemen arrested the escaped prisoner at once.
TV Reporter: It's amazing what our five young Sherlocks did. And how did you like your real-life adventure?
Stephen Moore: It was a lot more exciting than playing football.

SOLUTION

(1) **delicate** matter (2) **delicious** fruit salad (3) **delicately** inscribed
(4) **excellent** watch (5) **careful** hint

FALSE FRIENDS TRAPS TEST 1

DIFFICULT FALSE FRIENDS

1.a. Sandra liked Bertrand's paintings, but she disliked his ________, espccially at parties (**Allüren ≠ allure**).
1.b. "The ________ of the beautiful scenery still inspires my paintings," the artist admitted (**Allüren ≠ allure**).
2.a. If the computer firm ________ finds out you did not turn up for work last Friday, he'll sack you at once (**Chef ≠ chef**).
2.b. The new ________ gave a broad selection of recipes (**Chef ≠ chef**). He is a trained ________ (**Chef ≠ chef**).
3.a. As the couple sat in a Montmartre pavement cafe, an ________ sketched her (**Artist ≠ artist**).
3.b. "Buy me a ticket for this afternoon," my sister asked him. "I'd like to see the circus ________ (**Artisten ≠ artists**)."
4.a. "________ influences appear to be making you more confident and energetic," the psychologist observed (**aktuell ≠ actual**).
4.b. Miniskirts are the ________ fashion for girls (**aktuell ≠ actual**).
5.a. It's Sunday today. I'm afraid we've got to take you to the ________ of the University Hospital (**Ambulanz ◑ ambulance**).
5.b. The Duchess of York ordered her snowcat to be turned into an ________ after learning I was suffering from food poisoning (**Ambulanz ◑ ambulance**).
6. The ________ (**Aktion**) for Handicapped Children was a tremendous success.
7. It was pleasant at the seaside hotel. Helen enjoyed the ________ (**delikat**) fish dishes at dinner time.
8. "We've been on ________ (**Akkord**) for seven years and now they want to get rid of us without a social plan," the workers protested.
9. After three hours of emergency action the army helicopters returned to ________ (**Stützpunkt**).
10. For many male admirers Joan Collins is still ________ (**apart**) on stage – at least during her first London appearance after 11 years.

ANSWER SHEET: TRUE FRIENDS TEST 1

DIFFICULT FALSE FRIENDS

1.a. Sandra liked Bertrand's paintings, but she disliked his (**eccentric**) **behaviour**, especially at parties.
1.b. "The **allure** of the beautiful scenery still inspires my paintings," the artist admitted.
2.a. If the computer firm **boss** finds out you did not turn up for work last Friday, he'll sack you at once.
2.b. The new **chef** gave a broad selection of recipes. He is a trained **chef**.
3.a. As the couple sat in a Montmartre pavement cafe, an **artist** sketched her.
3.b. "Buy me a ticket for this afternoon," my sister asked him. "I'd like to see the circus **artistes**."
4.a. "**Current** influences appear to be making you more confident and energetic," the psychologist observed.
4.b. Miniskirts are the **latest** fashion for girls.
5.a. It's Sunday today. I'm afraid we've got to take you to the **out-patients' department** of the University Hospital.
5.b. The Duchess of York ordered her snowcat to be turned into an **ambulance** after learning I was suffering from food poisoning.
6. The **campaign** for Handicapped Children was a tremendous success.
7. It was pleasant at the seaside hotel. Helen enjoyed the **delicious** fish dishes at dinner time.
8. "We've been on **piece-rate** for seven years and now they want to get rid of us without a social plan," the workers protested.
9. After three hours of emergency action the army helicopters returned to **base**.
10. For many male admirers Joan Collins is still **attractive** on stage – at least during her first London appearance after 11 years.

DESSERT ≠ desert

desert [ˈdezət]

DESSERT
(= Nachtisch)

dessert [dɪˈzɜ:t] **etc.**

DESSERT:	(1) (Nachtisch) dessert
	(2) in combinations such as '**dessert** wine'
	(3) sweet (course); pudding

(1) Als **Dessert** gibt es heute Obst und Käse. Ich bin sicher, daß ihr das mögt.
There's fruit and cheese for **dessert** today. I'm sure you'll like it.
(2) Aber es fehlen noch die **Dessert**löffel und die -gabeln. Ich hole sie.
But there aren't any **dessert** spoons or forks. I'll get them.
Probieren Sie einen unserer **Dessert**-Weine, und Sie werden verstehen, warum sie sich so viel Ansehen erworben haben.
Sample any of our **dessert** wines, and you'll know why they've earned such a good name.
(3) "Möchten Sie etwas zum **Dessert**?" fragte uns die Kellnerin.
"Would you like a **sweet (course)**?" the waitress asked us.
"Was gibt's heute als **Dessert**?" fragte ihr Mann. "Apfelkuchen mit Vanillesauce", antwortete sie.
"What's for **pudding** today?" her husband asked. "Apple-pie and custard," she replied.

Note: Pudding = blancmange (German '**Pudding**' is another False Friend)

desert:	(1) Wüste
	(2) '**Wüsten-**' (in combinations)

(1) A man searching for opals in the Australian **desert** was found alive after surviving on nothing but water for 45 days.
Ein Mann, der in der australischen **Wüste** nach Opalen suchte, wurde lebend aufgefunden, nachdem er 45 Tage lang sich von nichts anderem als Wasser ernährt hatte.

(2) The **desert** sun hit the back of her neck like a flaming torch.
Die **Wüsten**sonne traf ihren Nacken wie eine brennende Fackel.
A storm in the southwest of England recently coated the Plymouth area with **desert** sand from the Sahara.
Ein Sturm im Südwesten Englands überzog vor kurzem das Gebiet um Plymouth mit **Wüsten**sand aus der Sahara.

Note: **desert** island = einsame Insel
In her dreams Jenny wanted to live on a **desert island** in the South Pacific.

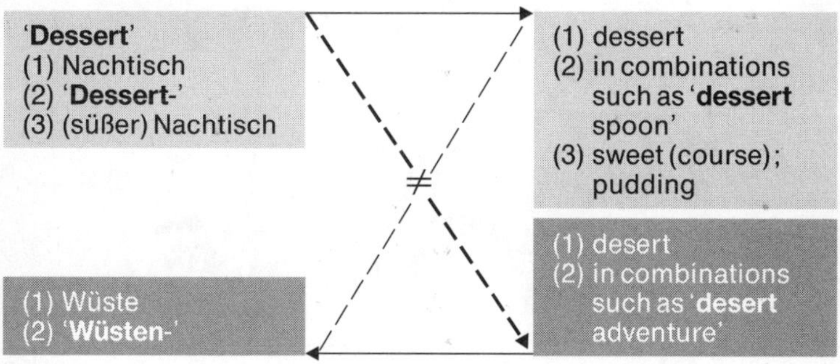

FALSE FRIENDS IN CONTEXT

An Optical Illusion

Alan: Do you remember when our art teacher told us he had been to a hot ________ (1)?
Sheila: Of course I do. What about it?
Alan: I don't think he has ever travelled to a ________ (2).
Sheila: How do you know?
Alan: You see, I drew a camel in the ________ (3) with a little chap on it, eating a banana for ________ (4). I showed him my drawing. The little chap was Beau Peep of the Foreign Legion in one of his ________ (5) adventures.
Sheila: You mean, the comic drawing was taken from a Beau Peep cartoon strip?
Alan: Exactly. Our art teacher looked at it, shook his head and said he couldn't make out what it was.

Sheila: Anyone can see what it is even if he's never been there. He didn't even recognize it was a comic cartoon with the little chap, Beau Peep.

SOLUTION

(1) hot **desert** (2) desert (3) in the **desert** (4) dessert (5) **desert** adventures

DEZENT ◑ decent

decent [ˈdi:snt] → **DEZENT** (unaufdringlich etc.) ← **discreet** [dɪˈskri:t] **etc.**

DEZENT: (1) (unaufdringlich) discreet
(2) (zurückhaltend, taktvoll) unobtrusive, restrained
(3) (gedämpft, abgetönt) soft, subdued
(4) (fein, zart) subtle

(1) Am Ende ihrer Morgentoilette nahm sie noch ein **dezentes** Parfum.
After her morning wash she put on a **discreet** perfume.
(2) Seine **dezente** Art gefiel den Damen auf der Party.
His **unobtrusive** manners went down well with the ladies at the party.
Sein **dezentes** Verhalten kam bei den Damen an.
The ladies were impressed by his **restrained** behaviour.
(3) Bei **dezenter** Beleuchtung tanzte das Paar zu **dezenter** Musik bis in die frühen Morgenstunden.
In **subdued** lighting the couple danced to **soft** music until the small hours.
(4) In ihrer Kleidung bevorzugt Prinzessin Diana **dezente** Farben.
Princess Diana prefers **subtle** colours in her dress.

decent: (1) anständig, richtig (koll.)
(2) rechtschaffen, ehrbar
(3) 'schön' (ironisch)

(1) John has always earned a **decent** salary.
John hat stets ein **anständiges** Gehalt gehabt.
I had my first **decent** meal after a week in the jungle.
Nach einer Woche im Dschungel bekam ich meine erste **richtige** Mahlzeit.
(2) We're **decent** country folk and have lived here for generations.
Wir sind **rechtschaffene** Leute vom Lande und leben hier schon seit Generationen.
(3) "Acid House parties will quickly die a **decent** death," my friend added ironically.

"Acid House Parties werden schnell einen **schönen** Tod sterben", fügte mein Freund ironisch hinzu.

'**dezent**'
(1) unaufdringlich
(2) zurückhaltend, taktvoll
(3) gedämpft, abgetönt
(4) fein, zart

(1) discreet
(2) unobtrusive, restrained
(3) soft, subdued
(4) subtle

(1) anständig, richtig (koll.)
(2) rechtschaffen, ehrbar
(3) 'schön' (ironisch)

decent

FALSE FRIENDS IN CONTEXT

Smartening up one's Act

Magazine Reporter: The jury accused you of 'advertising for sex' by the way you were dressed.
Sheila: That's untrue. All I was wearing was an ________ (1) mini-skirt and a white blouse. I'm a ________ (2) girl from a Catholic family trying to live a ________ (3) life.
Magazine Reporter: What did you do on the night in question?
Sheila: I had been to the cinema for a late-night show. On my way home I stopped at a cafe to get a ________ (4) meal. It was about two o'clock in the morning.
Magazine Reporter: What happened?
Sheila: As I left my car someone grabbed me from behind putting a knife to my throat. It was dark and misty, so the lights in the car park were ________ (5) and no one could see what happened. I had to do what my attacker wanted.
Magazine Reporter: What's your reaction to the jury's verdict?
Sheila: I believed there were ________ (6) people on the jury to protect me. I'm shocked, particularly about the female members of the jury. I hope they'll die a ________ (7) death.

SOLUTION

(1) unobtrusive (2) decent (3) decent (4) decent (5) subdued
(6) decent (7) decent

ENGAGIERT ◑ engaged

engaged [ɪn'geɪdʒd] ··· **ENGAGIERT** (= innerlich überzeugt etc.)

committed [kə'mɪtɪd] **etc.**

ENGAGIERT: (1) (innerlich überzeugt) committed (to sth.)
(2) (aktiv beteiligt) involved (in sth. or with s. o.)
(3) (am Theater etc. verpflichtet) taken on (or engaged)
(4) (mit einer Arbeit beauftragt) commissioned (to do sth.)

(1) Sie ist stets eine **engagierte** Christin gewesen.
She has always been a **committed** Christian.
Mutter Teresa **engagierte sich** viele Jahre **für** die Kranken und Sterbenden in Kalkutta.
Mother Teresa was **committed** for many years **to** helping the sick and dying in Calcutta.
(2) "Ich staune, wie stark du dich in der Politik **engagiert** hast. Hoffentlich geht das gut", warnte ein wohlgesonnener Freund.
"I'm surprised how **involved** you have become **in** politics. I hope it works out," a well-meaning friend warned him.
"Billy war immer beim Kinder-Fernsehen **engagiert**", erinnerte sich sein Freund.
"Billy had always been **involved with** children's TV," his friend recalled.
(3) The bank has **taken on/engaged** a new director general in order to increase profits.
Die Bank hat einen neuen Generaldirektor **engagiert**, um den Gewinn zu erhöhen.
(4) Der Künstler wurde **engagiert**, um die Königin zu malen.
The artist was **commissioned to** paint the Queen.

Note: eine **engagierte** Persönlichkeit = an **active** personality
sehr für den Verein **engagiert** sein = **devote** a lot of energy **to** the club
engagiert arbeiten an = put a lot of work into (sth.)
The team **put a lot of work into** the project.

engaged: (1) verlobt
(2) (Telefon) besetzt
(3) beschäftigt, in Anspruch genommen

(1) Jonathan has got **engaged** to a Swedish girl. But his parents are not at all happy about it.
Jonathan hat sich mit einem schwedischen Mädchen **verlobt**. Aber seine Eltern sind darüber überhaupt nicht glücklich.
(2) "Mike's number has been **engaged** for the last two hours. I wonder who he's speaking to," Maureen told her mother.
"Mikes Telefon ist schon die letzten zwei Stunden über **besetzt**. Ich hätte gerne gewußt, mit wem er spricht", sagte Maureen zu ihrer Mutter.
(3) Professor Dixon couldn't come to the meeting, as he was otherwise **engaged**.
Professor Dixon konnte nicht an der Sitzung teilnehmen, da er anderweitig **in Anspruch genommen** war.

Note: She had **engaged** the wrong gear = Sie hatte den falschen Gang eingelegt.
Compare: She was **engaged/taken on** to play a major role in Shakespeare's *As You Like It*.
The architect was **commissioned to** re-plan a part of the city.
In the first sentence **engaged** is synonymous with **take on**. In this particular instance German **engagiert** and the two verbs given overlap. **Commissioned** in the sense of **engagiert** cannot usually be applied to hiring an actress, but is relevant to the undertaking of larger transactions as in the second sentence.

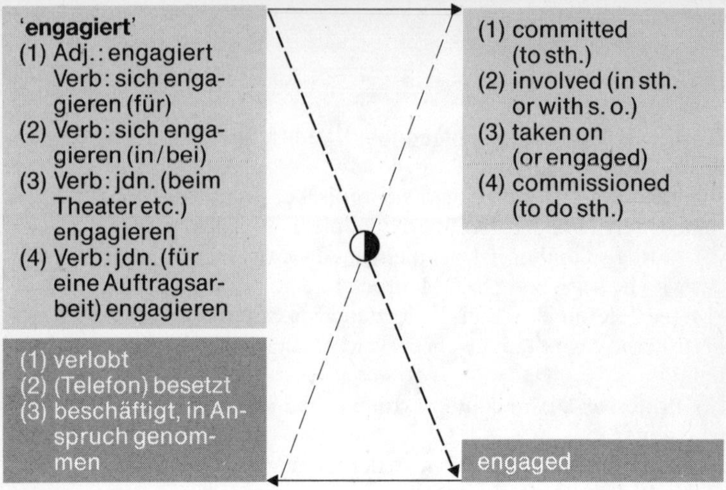

FALSE FRIENDS IN CONTEXT

The Wrong Question

Graham: Is it true you're ________ (1)? Tell me who the lucky girl is.
Colin: Well, it's like this . . . (A pause follows)
Graham: What's wrong? You don't sound very ________ (2) to the ideal of marriage. I put a straight question, so give me a straight answer.
Colin: Well, it's the girl's mother.

SOLUTION

(1) engaged (2) committed

The Wrong Answer

Salesman: I've been ringing your boss nearly all day, but his number was always ________ (3). So I came along to see what was wrong.
Personal Assistant: I'm sorry about that. The boss is otherwise

________ (4) just now and mustn't be disturbed. Can he give you a ring when he wakes up?

SOLUTION

(3) engaged (4) engaged

EVENTUELL ≠ eventual

eventual [ɪ'ventʃuəl]

EVENTUELL

(= vielleicht etc.)

possible etc.

EVENTUELL: (1) (vielleicht etc.) adj.: possible
(2) (möglicherweise etc.) adv.: possibly, perhaps, maybe
(3) **may/might** in affirmative sentences
(4) **any...may/might** in questions or negative sentences

(1) "Hat dieses Medikament **eventuelle** Nebenwirkungen?" fragte die Patientin den Arzt.
"Are there any **possible** side-effects with this drug?" the patient asked the doctor.
"**Eventuelle** Fragen werden am Schluß beantwortet", kündigte der Redner an.
"Any **possible** questions will be answered at the end," the speaker announced.
(2) Kannst du mich **eventuell** heute abend am Flughafen abholen?
Could you **possibly** meet me at the airport tonight?
"Ich gehe nächste Woche **eventuell** in ein Wohltätigkeitskonzert", erwähnte meine Tante auf dem Nachhauseweg.
"**Perhaps** I'll go to a charity concert next week," my aunt mentioned on the way home.
Eventuell kaufen wir nächstes Jahr ein neues Auto.
Maybe we'll buy a new car next year.
(3) Großbritannien muß **eventuell** die Rheinarmee wegen der politischen Veränderungen in Mitteleuropa abziehen.
Britain **may** have to withdraw its Rhine Army because of the political changes in Central Europe.
Dies führt **eventuell** zu verbesserten Beziehungen zu einigen östlichen Ländern.
This **might** lead to improved relations with some Eastern countries.
(4) "Über **eventuell** auftretende Schlafstörungen in den ersten Tagen brauchen Sie sich keine Sorgen zu machen", beruhigte sie der Hausarzt.
"You needn't worry about **any** sleep problems that **may** occur during the first few days," the family doctor reassured her.

Warum sollte **eventuell** übriggebliebenes Geld nicht auf das Konto eingezahlt werden?
Why not pay **any** money that **might** be left over into the account?

eventual: (1) Adj.: letztendlich; schließlich
(2) Adj.: als Folge von, sich ergebend (aus)
(3) Adv.: (eventually) schließlich, am Ende

(1) The Labour Party accepts the goal of an **eventual** monetary union of Europe.
Die Labour-Partei akzeptiert das Ziel einer **letztendlichen** monetären Einheit Europas.
Michael Gross' **eventual** win of a gold medal at the Olympics in 1988 was well deserved.
Michael Gross' **schließlicher** Gewinn einer Goldmedaille bei der Olympiade 1988 war hoch verdient.
(2) Jeannie put his **eventual** infidelity down to his mid-life crisis.
Jeannie wertete seine Untreue **als Folge** seiner Midlife-Krise.
His **eventual** death was a shock for the family all the same.
Sein **sich daraus ergebender** Tod war trotzdem für die Familie ein Schock.
(3) **Eventually** the holiday-makers realized there was a terrible problem at the border.
Schließlich merkten die Urlauber, daß ein schreckliches Problem an der Grenze entstanden war.
His wife will **eventually** feel less bitter towards him.
Seine Frau wird **am Ende** weniger Bitterkeit ihm gegenüber empfinden.

eventuell

(1) adj.: possible
(2) adv.: possibly, perhaps, maybe
(3) **may/might** in affirmative sentences
(4) **any...may/might** in questions or negative sentences

≠

(1) Adj.: letztendlich; schließlich
(2) Adj.: als Folge von, sich ergebend (aus)
(3) Adv.: schließlich, am Ende

(1) + (2) adj.: eventual
(3) adv.: eventually

Heading for the Finishing Line

Bride (talking to one of her neighbours after the wedding reception): It was amazing, wasn't it? We were all safely inside the church, but with no sign of the best man. We were all awaiting his _______ (1) arrival, but he didn't turn up.
Neighbour: And the bridesmaids were in place, but still no sign of the best man.
Bride: I wondered what the minister would do. So _______ (2) the Reverend Clarke had to go ahead without him.
Neighbour: I know, and you had already said "I will" when the best man _______ (3) walked through the church door – twenty minutes late blaming his car. I couldn't believe it.
Bride: Neither could I. _______ (4) we were getting ready for the wedding photos. Again the best man was missing, so we were stuck for some time awaiting his _______ (5) return. I couldn't have _______ (6) forgiven him for not being on our wedding photos.
Neighbour: Incidentally, at the champagne wedding breakfast he offered to take you _______ (7) to the airport. But I told him you were going on your honeymoon and didn't want to face your first marriage crisis because of him.

SOLUTION

(1) **eventual** arrival (2) eventually (3) eventually (4) eventually
(5) **eventual** return (6) possibly (7) perhaps/possibly

EXISTENZ ◑ existence

existence

EXISTENZ
(= Lebensgrundlage)

livelihood

EXISTENZ: (1) livelihood, living
(2) in combinations such as '(new) life', '(own) business'

(1) Seit der Schließung von 229 Bergwerken zwischen 1965 und 1971 in Großbritannien lebten die Bergleute in Sorge, ihre **Existenz** zu verlieren.
Since the closure of 229 pits between 1965 and 1971 in Britain coal miners have lived in fear of losing their **livelihood**.
Nach dem letzten Kriege glaubten viele Auswanderer, sich in den Vereinigten Staaten eine gesicherte **Existenz** schaffen zu können, aber die Wirklichkeit sah anders aus.
After the last war many emigrants believed they could make a good **living** in the United States, but the reality was different.
"Das Leben mit dir war stets ungesichert. Jetzt müssen wir eine gesicherte **Existenz** anstreben", betonte seine Frau mit Nachdruck.
"Life with you has always been precarious. We've got to look for a secure **livelihood** now," his wife insisted.
(2) Mr. Frawley verließ Ashford, um sich in London eine neue **Existenz** aufzubauen.
Mr. Frawley left Ashford to begin a **new life** in London.
Es gibt eine ganze Reihe staatlicher Hilfen für **Existenz**gründungen.
There are all kinds of government grants for those who want to set up their **own businesses**.

Note: **Existenz**angst = fear for the future
Lots of people in Eastern Germany **fear for the future** in the present situation of high unemployment.

existence: (1) Dasein
(2) Leben
(3) Bestehen

(1) It infuriated me that this fellow wouldn't acknowledge my **existence**.
Es machte mich wütend, daß dieser Kerl von meinem **Dasein** keine Notiz nehmen wollte.
Many people who are out of work have a hard struggle for **existence**.
Viele Arbeitslose führen einen harten Kampf ums **Dasein**.
(2) Many Puerto-Ricans lead a miserable **existence** in one of New York's suburbs.
Viele Puertoricaner führen ein trostloses **Leben** in einer der Vorstädte New Yorks.
(3) It was the first time his polo team had won the Unipart Prince of Wales Trophy in its three-year **existence**.
Es war das erste Mal, daß sein Polo-Team den Unipart-Prince-of-Wales-Preis in dessen dreijährigem **Bestehen** gewonnen hatte.

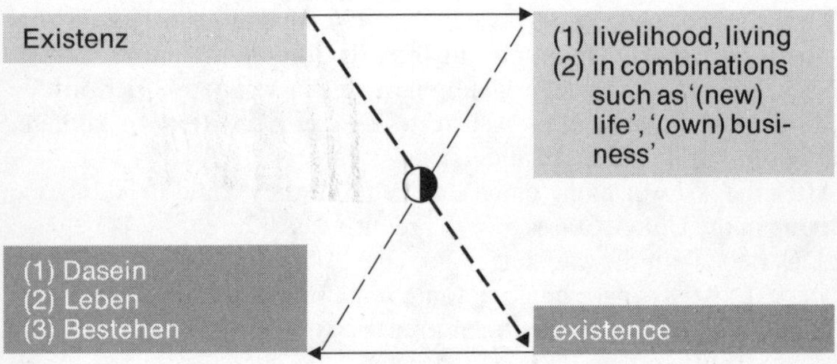

FALSE FRIENDS IN CONTEXT

It All Depends

Judge: You drove into a group of pedestrians and endangered their ________ (1). This is a serious offence. I'm afraid I shall have to ban you from driving for three years.
Defendant: But, your Lordship, my ________ (2) depends on being able to drive.
Judge: So does theirs.

SOLUTION

(1) existence (2) livelihood

FAMOS ≠ famous

famous

FAMOS
(großartig etc.)

wonderful etc.

FAMOS: (1) (mehr emotional wertend) wonderful, splendid, marvellous
(2) (mehr sachlich wertend) great, fine, excellent

(1) Meine Freundin fand diese Idee einfach **famos**.
My girlfriend found my idea simply **wonderful**.
Der arabische Scheich dachte, daß er die **famose** Yacht kaufen sollte.
The Arab sheik thought he ought to buy the **splendid** yacht.
Dein Plan klingt **famos**, und ich werde ihn unterstützen.
Your plan sounds **marvellous** and I'll support it.
(2) Der Briefmarkensammler war von der **famosen** Sammlung begeistert.
The stamp collector was enthusiastic about the **fine** collection.
Er ist ein **famoser** Bursche. Wir wollen ihn zu unserer nächsten Party einladen.
He's a **great** guy. Let's invite him to our next party.
Mein Freund ist ein **famoser** Bergsteiger; ich bin sein Begleiter.
My friend is an **excellent** climber and I'm his companion.

famous (for): berühmt (wegen, für)

"That painting is from Picasso's **famous** Rose Period," my friend remarked.
"Das Gemälde stammt aus Picassos **berühmter** Rosa Periode", bemerkte mein Freund.
Stanley Matthews, England's **most famous** footballer, was one of the few sportsmen to be knighted by the Queen.
Stanley Matthews, Englands **berühmtester** Fußballspieler, war einer der wenigen Sportler, die von der Königin geadelt wurden.
Kentucky is **famous for** its good quality bourbon.
Kentucky ist **wegen** seines hervorragenden Bourbon **berühmt**.

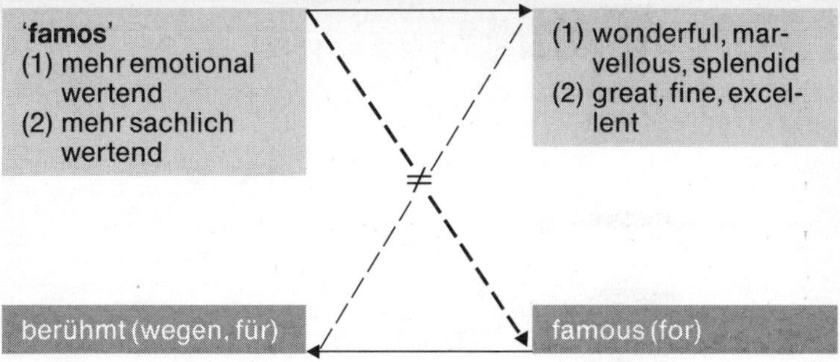

FALSE FRIENDS IN CONTEXT

The Hymn of Survival: I'm Still Here

Theatre Critic: Even during his lifetime Sir Laurence Olivier was the most ________ (1) actor in Britain. I can't see anyone who can reach him.
Producer: In my view Eartha Kitt is the exception. For her age Eartha is still a ________ (2) actress.
Theatre Critic: She's been called the sexiest old age pensioner ever to qualify for a free bus pass. She became ________ (3) in the fifties being very much ahead of her time.
Producer: ... and she's still ahead in the game of love. Eartha would flirt on stage with a boy young enough to be her grandson by saying, "You're 22. How would you like to be 62 before the night's over?"
Theatre Critic: Apart from making it fashionable for the woman to be the sexual predator, she's also ________ (4) for running the first one-woman show in Britain.
Producer: This endearing woman is at her best when she sings what became her personal anthem, Stephen Sondheim's ________ (5) hymn of survival – "*I'm Still Here.*"

SOLUTION

(1) most **famous** actor (2) a **wonderful** actress (3) became **famous**
(4) **famous** for (5) **fine** hymn of survival

FATAL ◑ fatal

fatal ['feɪtl]

FATAL

(= unangenehm; verhängnisvoll etc.)

awkward ['ɔ:kwəd] **etc.**

FATAL: (1) (äußerst unangenehm, peinlich) awkward, embarrassing, unfortunate
(2) (verhängnisvoll) disastrous [dɪ'za:strəs]

(1) Wie war ihr Bruder nur in diese **fatale** Lage geraten, fragte sich Laura immer wieder.
How had her brother got into this **awkward** situation, Laura kept asking herself.
Es war ein **fataler** Fehler, seine frühere Frau auf die Cocktailparty einzuladen.
It was an **embarrassing** lapse to invite his former wife to the cocktail party.
Der **fatale** Konflikt in Nordirland könnte sich zu einer größeren Auseinandersetzung zwischen Kirche und Staat ausweiten.
The **unfortunate** conflict in Northern Ireland could escalate into a major clash between Church and State.
(2) Plötzlich wußte sie die Antwort. Es war die **fatale** Finanzkrise seiner Firma, die alles ausgelöst hatte.
Suddenly she knew the answer. It was the **disastrous** financial crisis of his firm that had caused everything.

fatal: (1) tödlich; todbringend
(2) '**Todes-**' (in combinations)

(1) Everything seemed senseless. His girlfriend's **fatal** riding accident had changed his life.
Alles erschien sinnlos. Der **tödliche** Reitunfall seiner Freundin hatte sein Leben verändert.
How did the passengers on the plane behave during the **fatal** minutes?
Wie verhielten sich die Passagiere im Flugzeug während der **todbringenden** Minuten?
(2) The **fatal** shot was fired at short range.
Der **Todes**schuß wurde aus nächster Nähe abgegeben.

Note: **Fatal** often implies the person is already dead.
Lethal mostly indicates that something (i. e. poison) or the use of an object (i. e. a weapon) could result in death.
a **lethal** weapon = eine **tödliche** Waffe
a **lethal** overdose = eine **tödliche** Überdosis
Wendy, a teenage girl, had a **lethal** dose of alcohol – five times over the drink-drive limit.

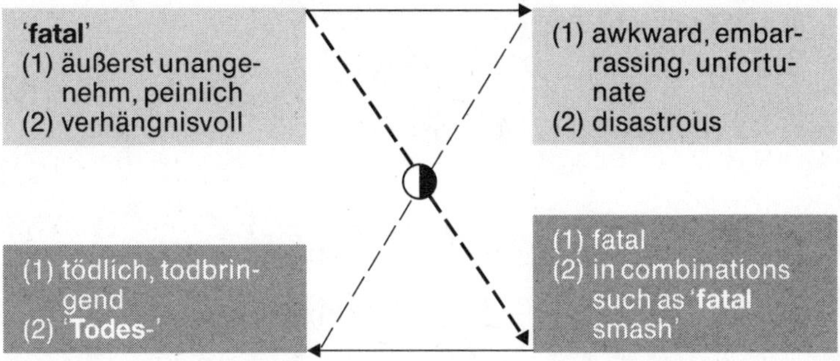

FALSE FRIENDS IN CONTEXT

An Australian Balloon Safari

In spite of the balloon disaster in the Australian desert in which 13 passengers died experts still consider ballooning to be one of the safest sports in the world. However, Australia's hot-air balloonists are faced with an ________ (1) situation.
Air Safety Expert (from Adelaide): You were an eyewitness of the ________ (2) balloon accident. Could you describe the ________ (3) minutes after the take-off?
German Tourist (on Toddy's Balloon Safari in the Australian desert): The four balloons left the same launching site near Alice Springs minutes apart. I was in the first one. Suddenly the last balloon came up quite fast under the third.
Air Safety Expert (to another balloonist): What did you notice after the ________ (4) collision?
English Tourist: A flame appeared at the top of the lower balloon and it started to lose height. It completely lost its shape before hitting the ground.

Air Safety Expert: How did the people in the basket of the ________ (5) balloon react?

Canadian Tourist: The pilot seemed to be the first to realize something ________ (6) had happened. He was desperately trying to blast hot air into the balloon. The people in the basket didn't panic, but shortly before the ________ (7) crash some tried to leap to safety.

SOLUTION

(1) unfortunate (2) fatal (3) embarrassing (4) disastrous (5) fatal
(6) disastrous (7) fatal

FRAKTION ≠ fraction

fraction ['frækʃn]

FRAKTION

parliamentary party etc. — (Partei-**Fraktion** etc.)

FRAKTION: (1) (Partei-**Fraktion** im Parlament) parliamentary party, (parliamentary) group
(2) (political) group, faction

(1) Die **parlamentarische Fraktion** der Grünen verließ unter Protest die Plenarsitzung
The **parliamentary group** of the 'Greens' left the plenary session under protest.
Margaret Thatcher erhielt mehr als die Hälfte der Stimmen ihrer **Fraktion**, trat aber aus Enttäuschung als Premierministerin zurück.
Margaret Thatcher received more than half of the votes from her **parliamentary party**, but stepped down in disappointment as Prime Minister.
(2) Die Euro-Tories, offiziell bekannt als die Europäische Demokratische **Fraktion**, unterstützen die Schaffung einer europäischen Zentralbank.
The Euro-Tories, formally known as the European Democratic **Group**, support the creation of a European central bank.
Seit den frühen siebziger Jahren setzt die Rote-Armee-**Fraktion** den Stadtguerillakrieg fort.
Since the early 1970s, the Red Army **Faction** continues to carry on urban guerilla warfare.

Note: Splittergruppe = **faction**
In 1972, Captain 'Willie' Orr made a reckless bid to re-unite and lead the splintering **factions** of Unionism.

fraction: (1) Bruchteil
(2) Bruch (math.)

(1) For a **fraction** of a second he didn't pay attention, so his opponent knocked him out.
Er paßte den **Bruchteil** einer Sekunde nicht auf. Auf diese Weise schlug ihn sein Gegner k. o.

"Unfortunately, the fraud cases we uncover are only a **fraction** of the cases that exist," he told the reporters.
"Leider stellen die Betrugsfälle, die wir aufdecken, nur einen **Bruchteil** der vorhandenen Fälle", erzählte er den Reportern.
(2) "How do we reduce a **fraction**?" asked the maths teacher.
"Wie kürzen wir einen **Bruch**?" fragte der Mathematiklehrer.
"In sentences such as 'She won two-thirds of the money' a hyphen is used with **fractions** in English," she maintained.
"In Sätzen wie 'She won two-thirds of the money' wird im Englischen bei **Brüchen** ein Bindestrich gebraucht", behauptete sie.

Note: **breach** of contract = Vertrags**bruch**
break, go to pieces = zu **Bruch** gehen
but: fracture = Knochen**bruch**
quarry = Stein**bruch**

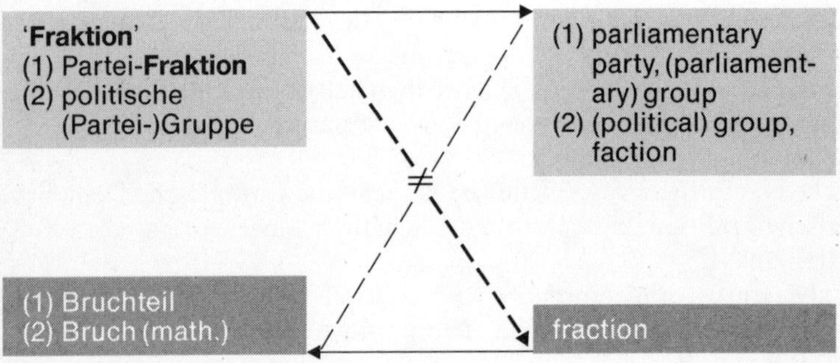

FALSE FRIENDS IN CONTEXT

Red Carpet Treatment

Labour's Shadow Chancellor: I wonder why the Labour Party ________ (1) of MEPs (= **M**ember of the **E**uropean **P**arliament) has been invited to drinks by the British Ambassador to Belgium.
Labour Party Politician: You're quite right. This hasn't happened once in the past decade.
Labour's Shadow Chancellor: What's even more surprising, the Labour Party ________ (2) of MEPs and myself have also been invited to Frankfurt and Paris.

Labour Party Politician: Western European governments are realizing that a future Labour government will be a pro-European force.
Labour's Shadow Chancellor: After many years Labour is back. The Tories have only a ________ (3) of their former following.
Labour Party Politician: What you haven't taken into consideration is the role of the Euro-Tory ________ (4) and the influence of the leader of the European Parliament's dominant socialist ________ (5), Jean-Pierre Cot. Much Labour thinking still lags far behind its European partners.
Labour's Shadow Chancellor: The politics of the 1990s are taking on a new dimension. Look at the shifting scene in Eastern Europe. In Poland a hotel worker earns only a ________ (6) of the £1,320-a-month he's offered at a small hotel in West Germany such as the Hotel Edelweiss where we stayed last week.

SOLUTION

(1) Labour Party **group** (2) Labour Party **group** (3) fraction
(4) Euro-Tory **group** (5) socialist **group/party** (6) fraction

GENIAL ≠ genial

genial [ˈdʒiːnjəl]

GENIAL
(großartig, vollendet)

ingenious [ɪnˈdʒiːnjəs] etc.

GENIAL: (1) (von Dingen: großartig, vollendet) ingenious, brilliant
(2) (von Personen: hervorragend begabt) (full) of genius; inspired

(1) Der Computer ist bestimmt eine der **genialsten** Erfindungen des 20. Jahrhunderts.
The computer is definitely one of the most **ingenious** inventions of the 20th century.
Im Jahre 1861 hatte Philipp Reis eine **geniale** Idee. Er erfand den Fernsprecher, einen Vorläufer des modernen Telefons.
In 1861 Philipp Reis had a **brilliant** idea. He invented the telephone transmitter, a forerunner of the modern telephone.
(2) Im Rückblick war Pablo Picasso ein **genialer** Künstler.
In retrospect, Pablo Picasso was an artist **full of genius**.
Obwohl polnisch von Geburt, wurde Joseph Conrad einer der **genialsten** Romanschriftsteller der englischen Literatur.
Although Polish by birth, Joseph Conrad became one of the most **inspired** novelists in English literature.

Note: **genial** begabt sein = be a natural genius; be gifted with genius
ein Problem **genial** lösen = solve a problem like a genius
but: ein **genialer** Einfall = an **inspired** guess

genial: (1) freundlich, herzlich
(2) angenehm
(3) (Klima etc.) wohltuend, mild

(1) The nurse gave the new patient a **genial** smile.
Die Krankenschwester sah den neuen Patienten mit einem **freundlichen** Lächeln an.
When I entered, I was **genially** received by the Lord Mayor.
Als ich eintrat, wurde ich **herzlich** vom Oberbürgermeister empfangen.

(2) The final talks between the delegations took placc in a **genial** atmosphere.
Die Abschlußgespräche zwischen den Delegationen fanden in **angenehmer** Atmosphäre statt.
(3) The **genial** climate of that Mediterranean region helped to restore her health.
Das **wohltuende** Klima dieser Mittelmeer-Region trug dazu bei, ihre Gesundheit wiederherzustellen.

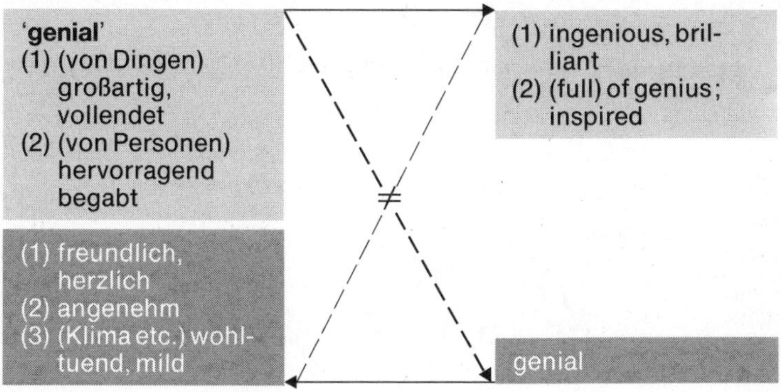

FALSE FRIENDS IN CONTEXT

The Crate Escape – A Modern Attitude?

Home Affairs Reporter: The bakers of Britain work very hard, but if the crate escape goes on at the present rate they'll end up in the red.
Director of the Federation of Bakers, answering with a ________ (1) smile on his face: The staggering number of crates stolen is costing British bakers at least £ 6 million a year. It's no laughing matter for us.
Home Affairs Reporter: After the incredible disappearance of more than a million supermarket trolleys it's now the bread crate 'escape' from supermarkets and delivery rounds. How do you account for that?
Director of the Federation of Bakers: People will take away anything nowadays. In fact, shoppers have found many ________ (2) ways of using stolen property including lobster pots to stand on while watching football matches. Outrageous as it is, but it's really ________ (3) what people do with them.

Home Affairs Reporter: I wonder why people think it's such a ________ (4) idea to go for bread crates, there are beer crates too.
Director of the Federation of Bakers: We've considered charging a 50 p deposit, but that wouldn't be a very effective deterrent as the crates cost £ 4 each. In future we'll advise bread companies to only use crates for deliveries.

SOLUTION

(1) **genial** smile (2) **ingenious** ways (3) ingenuous (4) **brilliant** idea

GRAZIÖS ≠ gracious

gracious [ˈgreɪʃəs]

GRAZIÖS
(= anmutig etc.)

graceful [ˈgreɪsfʊl]

GRAZIÖS: (anmutig etc.) graceful

Die Primaballerina bewegte sich **graziös**; die Zuschauer klatschten.
The prima ballerina moved about **gracefully**; the spectators applauded.
“Steffi Graf hat die **graziösesten** Beine im Damentennis”, kommentierte die französische Zeitung *Libération*.
“Steffi Graf has the most **graceful** legs in women’s tennis,” commented the French paper *Libération*.

Note: ehrenvoll, mit Anstand = **graceful** (mainly in sport)
After my defeat I prepared to make a **graceful** exit.
Talking of sportsmanship, England is a country that has shaken itself free of the ability to lose **gracefully**.

gracious: (1) freundlich, gütig, liebenswürdig
(2) huldvoll, ergeben
(3) kultiviert

(1) Dr. Runcie, the Archbishop of Canterbury, was most **gracious** to everyone at the reception.
Dr. Runcie, der Erzbischof von Canterbury, war auf dem Empfang zu jedermann sehr **freundlich**.
All the brave knight got from his queen was a **gracious** smile.
Alles, was der tapfere Ritter von seiner Königin erhielt, war ein **gütiges** Lächeln.
‘The forgotten royal’, Princess Alexandra, is a truly **gracious** lady who needs sympathy in her family crisis.
‘Die vergessene Angehörige der königlichen Familie’, Prinzessin Alexandra, ist eine wirklich **liebenswürdige** Dame, die in ihrer familiären Krise Mitgefühl benötigt.
(2) Queen Elizabeth **graciously** waved to the crowd on the way to the opening of Parliament.

Königin Elisabeth winkte der Menge **huldvoll** auf dem Wege zur Parlamentseröffnung zu.
(3) The **gracious** drawing rooms still speak of the faded grandeur of Victorian society.
Die **kultivierten** Salons zeugen noch immer von dem verblichenen Glanz der viktorianischen Gesellschaft.

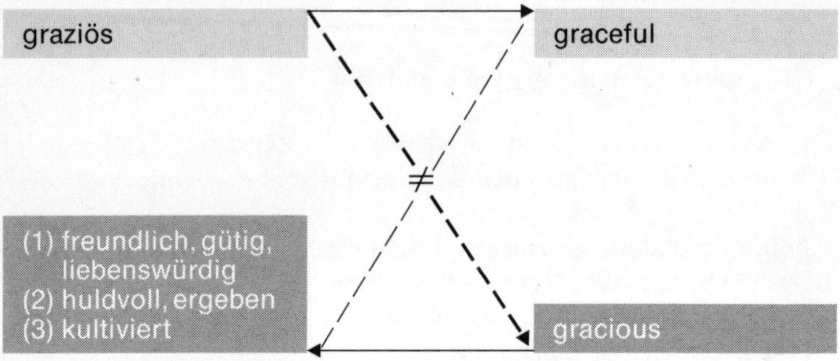

FALSE FRIENDS IN CONTEXT

Design for Living

Dan: I wonder why you're so keen on ballet performances and on *Carmen* in particular.
Lady Jane: I've always taken an interest in classical music and the ballet. I love the ________ (1) movements of the ballet dancers. But I'm also very keen on classical music.
Dan: I didn't realize you were given to ________ (2) living to such an extent. What do your friends say?
Lady Jane: Of course, this has caused a certain amount of talk among my friends. But after a glass or two they are ________ (3) enough to acknowledge my good taste in classical music and the ballet.
Dan: So you wake in the morning with a Bach sonata on your lips.
Lady Jane, smiling at the ________ (4) compliment: Come on, Dan. It was you who said that!

SOLUTION

(1) graceful (2) gracious (3) gracious (4) gracious

HUMAN ◑ human

human [ˈhjuːmən]

HUMAN

humane [hjuːˈmeɪn] **etc.** (menschenfreundlich)

HUMAN: (1) (menschenfreundlich) humane
(2) (anständig, rücksichtsvoll) considerate

(1) Amnesty International fordert die **humane** Behandlung aller politischen Gefangenen.
Amnesty International demands the **humane** treatment of all political prisoners.
Diese Idealisten kämpfen für eine **humanere** Gesellschaft.
These idealists are fighting for a more **humane** society.
(2) Unser Chef behandelt uns gewöhnlich sehr **human**.
Our boss is usually very **considerate** towards us.

human: (1) menschlich
(2) '**Menschen**-' (in combinations)

(1) **Human** life can be destroyed by **human** error, said the professor of physics, summing up his talk.
Das **menschliche** Leben kann durch **menschliches** Versagen zerstört werden, faßte der Physik-Professor seinen Vortrag zusammen.
(2) Who would have thought our personnel manager was such a poor judge of **human** character?
Wer hätte gedacht, daß unser Personalchef ein solch schlechter **Menschen**kenner ist.

Note: humans = die Menschen (also human beings)
The virus is closely related to the one that attacks **humans**.
but: crowd (of people) = **Menschen**menge
kidnapping = **Menschen**raub

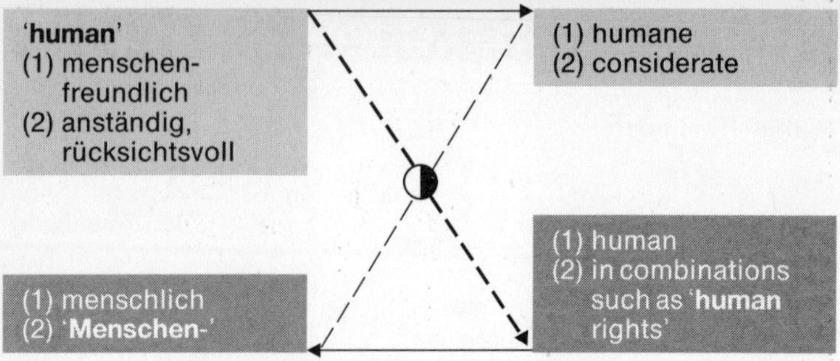

FALSE FRIENDS IN CONTEXT

Barking Up the Wrong Tree

Daily News Reporter: Even today postmen do seem to have a particular problem. Why do dogs enjoy biting them?
Post Office Official: First of all, our postmen behave like ________ (1) beings and not like dogs. They alert dogs when they put post through the letter boxes. While a dog goes wild and attacks, a postman reacts in a ________ (2) way.
Daily News Reporter: Now the Post Office is considering arming postmen with a new 'weapon'. What is it?
Post Office Official: The new device called the Dazer is an ultrasonic hand-held squealer. It emits a high-pitched blast, which is beyond the range of ________ (3) hearing. It can stop dogs at 15 feet to prevent bodily attacks.
Daily News Reporter: Of course postmen have my greatest sympathy. But how urgent is the ________ (4) need to stop attacks by dogs?
Post Office Official: Postal staff in Britain suffer from more than 6,000 attacks by dogs every year. We intend to equip all postmen and women with the Dazer. But there's also a snag: the Dazer has no effect on deaf dogs. Not everything is perfect, even in a more ________ (5) world.

SOLUTION

(1) **human** beings (2) in a **humane/considerate** way (3) **human** hearing (4) **human** need (5) more **humane** world

FALSE FRIENDS TRAPS TEST 2

DIFFICULT FALSE FRIENDS

1.a. Smoking can cause ________ diseases (**fatal ◑ fatal**).
1.b. The cult of youth is one of the causes of the ________ decline of British industry (**fatal ◑ fatal**).
2.a. Smelly feet are a ________ hygiene problem, even for a happy marriage (**human ◑ human**).
2.b. At its last conference Amnesty International demanded more ________ treatment for political prisoners in Third World countries (**human ◑ human**).
3.a. "We can't tolerate a traitor in our own ________," exclaimed the party leader (**Fraktion ≠ fraction**).
3.b. Those gathered were only a ________ of the hundreds of thousands of Britons affected (**Fraktion ≠ fraction**).
4.a. ________ I'll go to the concert on Saturday, but I haven't decided yet (**eventuell ≠ eventual**).
4.b. ________ sold for scrap, the ship was abandoned in the River Humber (**eventuell ≠ eventual**).
4.c. She put his ________ infidelity down to a mid-life crisis (**eventuell ≠ eventual**).
5.a. Above all, the billionaire liked the ________ colours in some of Gainsborough's landscape paintings and decided to buy one at the next auction (**dezent ◑ decent**).
5.b. It turned out the Russian refugee had never earned a ________ living (**dezent ◑ decent**).
6. The Germans Einstein, Hahn and Heisenberg were ________ (**genial**) pioneers of modern physics.
7. Don't you know? Most inhabitants of the Swiss village owe their ________ (**Existenz**) to modern tourism.
8. Peter Shilton, the 33-year-old England goalkeeper, was fitter, faster and more ________ (**graziös**) than any other player on the field.
9. The Avon Foundation poetry course is always hosted by ________ (**famos**) lecturers and ________ (**berühmt**) poets.
10. Visitors to Dubai can be taken on overnight trips into the ________ (**Wüste**) where supper and ________ (**Dessert**) will be eaten under a velvet sky.

ANSWER SHEET: TRUE FRIENDS TEST 2

DIFFICULT FALSE FRIENDS

1.a. Smoking can cause **fatal** diseases.
1.b. The cult of youth is one of the causes of the **disastrous** decline of British industry.
2.a. Smelly feet are a **human** hygiene problem, even for a happy marriage.
2.b. At its last conference Amnesty International demanded more **humane** treatment for political prisoners in Third World countries.
3.a. "We can't tolerate a traitor in our own **parliamentary party**," exclaimed the party leader.
3.b. Those gathered were only a **fraction** of the hundreds of thousands of Britons affected.
4.a. **Perhaps** I'll go to the concert on Saturday, but I haven't decided yet.
4.b. **Eventually** sold for scrap, the ship was abandoned in the River Humber.
4.c. She put his **eventual** infidelity down to a mid-life crisis.
5.a. Above all, the billionaire liked the **subtle** colours in some of Gainsborough's landscape paintings and decided to buy one at the next auction.
5.b. It turned out the Russian refugee had never earned a **decent** living.
6. The Germans Einstein, Hahn and Heisenberg were **ingenious** pioneers of modern physics.
7. Don't you know? Most inhabitants of the Swiss village owe their **livelihood** to modern tourism.
8. Peter Shilton, the 33-year-old England goalkeeper, was fitter, faster and more **graceful** than any other player on the field.
9. The Avon Foundation poetry course is always hosted by **excellent** lecturers and **famous** poets.
10. Visitors to Dubai can be taken on overnight trips into the **desert** where supper and **dessert** will be eaten under a velvet sky.

KAUTION ◑ caution

caution [ˈkɔːʃn] ……… **KAUTION** (Miet**kaution** etc.)

deposit [dɪˈpɒzɪt] **etc.**

KAUTION: (1) (Miet**kaution**) (returnable) deposit
(2) (gerichtlich verfügte Sicherheitsleistung) bail
(3) (Vertrags**kaution**) deposit

(1) Die Miet**kaution** für die neue Wohnung betrug 650.– Pfund. Da Janet diesen Betrag nicht zahlen konnte, ließ man sie nicht einziehen.
The **deposit** for the new flat was £ 650.00. As Janet couldn't pay this sum, they didn't let her move in.
Sie bestand darauf, daß die Miet**kaution** auf einem gesonderten Konto verzinslich angelegt wird.
She insisted on the **deposit** being paid into a separate interest-paying account.
(2) Der Angeklagte wurde gegen 20000 Pfund **Kaution** freigelassen.
The accused was released on £20,000 **bail**.
(3) "Bei Vertragsunterzeichnung müssen Sie eine **Kaution** von 500 Pfund leisten", gab der Makler an.
"On signing the contract you'll have to pay a £ 500 **deposit**," the estate agent stated.

Note: Anzahlung = deposit
"Before we book the flight for you, we'll need a £ 70 **deposit**," the travel agent explained.
Flaschen**pfand** = bottle **deposit**
but: Sparkonto = **deposit** account

caution: (1) Vorsicht, Umsicht
(2) Warnung; Verwarnung (meist jur.)

(1) The police stopped our car and advised us to drive with **caution** because of the possibility of flooding.
Die Polizei hielt unser Auto an und riet uns, wegen möglicher Überschwemmungen mit **Vorsicht** weiterzufahren.
Caution is essential in assessing nervous diseases.

Umsicht ist wesentlich bei der Beurteilung von Nervenkrankheiten.
(2) The Argentine soccer players had already received 19 **cautions** before the World Cup Final.
Die argentinischen Fußballspieler hatten schon 19 **Verwarnungen** vor dem Weltmeisterschaftsendspiel erhalten.

Compare: In England heißt die gerichtlich verfügte Sicherheitsleistung **bail**, in Schottland jedoch **caution**.
In Großbritannien kennt man eine rückzahlbare Mietsicherheit (Miet**kaution**) wie etwa in Deutschland nicht.

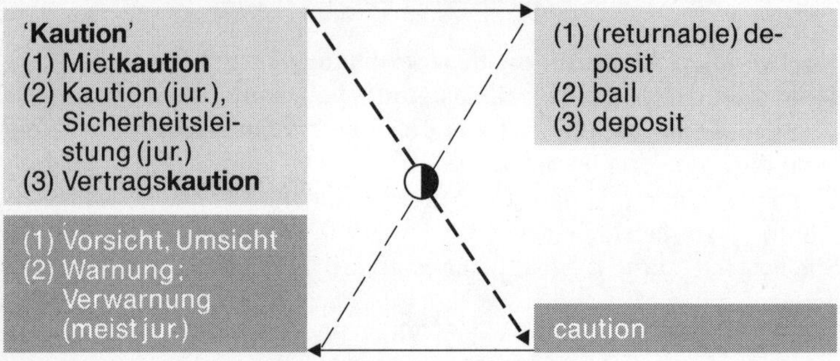

FALSE FRIENDS IN CONTEXT

Time to Zero in

Julie: There's an interesting finance scheme in today's paper.
Simon (somewhat alarmed): If you are thinking of buying a new car and the equipment for satellite TV, I have to put in a word of ________ (1) because we simply wouldn't be able to make ends meet.
Julie: Look at the finance offer by Vauxhall for a Nova Star car! Their 0% finance scheme is based on a 12 months' repayment period. No interest charges at all! There's only a 40% minimum ________ (2).
Simon: Forget it. That's more than £2,500. I'm afraid we haven't got that in the bank at the moment.
Julie: But there's also a 7.9% finance offer with only a £99 minimum ________(3) and a repayment period of 48 months. It's a real bargain.
Simon (reading): The Nova Star has central locking, sunroof and tinted glass. Plus six months' road tax free! Let's do it then.

Julie: What about having satellite TV in our home as well?
Simon: Enough is enough.
Julie: This is your lucky day, Simon. The police stopped you last week on the way home and now they have let you off with a ________ (4). You're a lucky man!

SOLUTION

(1) word of **caution** (2) deposit (3) deposit (4) caution

KONFESSION ≠ confession

confession [kən'feʃn]

denomination [dɪ,nɒmɪ'neɪʃn]

KONFESSION
(= religiöses Bekenntnis)

KONFESSION: (religiöses Bekenntnis) denomination

Welcher **Konfession** gehören Sie an, der anglikanischen oder baptistischen (d. h. ev.-freikirchlichen)?
Which **denomination** do you belong to, Anglican or Baptist?
Die **Konfession** der meisten Franzosen ist katholisch.
The **denomination** of most Frenchmen is Catholic.

confession: (1) Geständnis
(2) Beichte
(3) Bekenntnis

(1) The murderer's **confession** came late, but did not surprise the defence.
Das **Geständnis** des Mörders kam spät, aber nicht als eine Überraschung für die Verteidigung.
The Guildford Four were bullied by the police into making false **confessions**.
Die Vier von Guildford wurden von der Polizei so unter Druck gesetzt, daß sie falsche **Geständnisse** ablegten.
(2) The priest heard the youths' **confessions**.
Der Priester nahm den Jugendlichen die **Beichte** ab.
(3) In 1954, Thomas Mann rounded off his literary work with *The* **Confessions** *of Felix Krull*.
Im Jahre 1954 rundete Thomas Mann sein literarisches Schaffen mit *Die* **Bekenntnisse** *des Hochstaplers Felix Krull* ab.
"There is no need to complicate things with an unnecessary **confession**," the marriage guidance counsellor advised her.
"Es besteht kein Anlaß, die Dinge durch ein unnötiges **Bekenntnis** zu komplizieren", riet ihr die Eheberaterin.

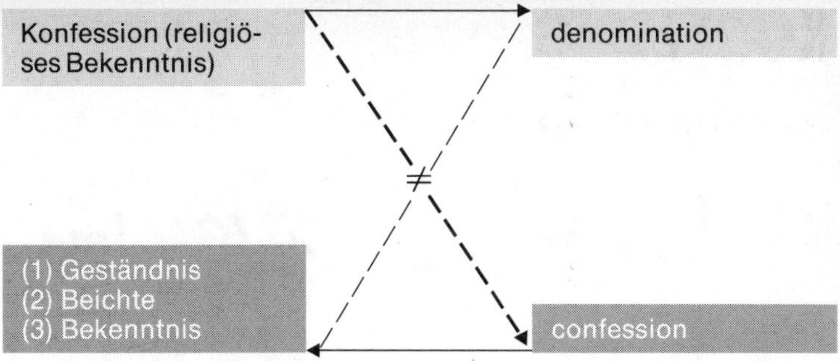

FALSE FRIENDS IN CONTEXT

Double Talk

Social Affairs Correspondent: Aren't the ________ (1) in Dwyfor and Ceredigion mixing up church and politics in this case?
Rev. Thomas: Not at all. We're against our parishioners breaking the Fourth Commandment. We're against people in mid-Wales visiting a pub on Sunday.
Social Affairs Correspondent: In referenda, all other Welsh districts voted for Sunday opening; the new Licensing Act had allowed this since the Sixties.
Rev. Thomas: One thing leads to another. Teledate Ltd. is now offering a telephone service encouraging so-called ________ (2) calls regarding Sunday drinking and other matters. These calls are a modern form of the old ________ (3) box and could easily lead to blackmail. Look at the Guildford case. The Unlucky Four were forced to make false ________ (4) and had to spend almost 15 years in jail.
Social Affairs Correspondent: But don't you know what's happening in your districts on Sundays?
Rev. Thomas: No. But if you mean people of various ________ (5) joining the local Conservative Club mainly for a drink on Sunday, it is their right to do so. I like a drink myself, but not in a pub on Sunday. The 1881 Licensing Act is not an archaic law, it's an act based on the Bible.

SOLUTION

(1) denominations (2) **confession** calls (3) **confession** box (4) false **confessions** (5) denominations

KONKURRENZ ≠ concurrence

concurrence [kən'kʌrəns] .... KONKURRENZ

competition [ˌkɒmpɪ'tɪʃn] **etc.**

KONKURRENZ: (1) competition
(2) in combinations such as '**rival** firm', '**competitive** prices', '**professional** jealousy'

(1) Es herrscht starke **Konkurrenz** durch die Japaner auf den meisten europäischen Märkten.
There is keen **competition** from the Japanese in most European markets.
Ein Fünftel der Restaurants spürten stärkere **Konkurrenz** von den Gaststätten, behauptete das Handelsblatt.
One fifth of restaurants felt greater **competition** from public houses, the trade journal argued.
(2) Eine **Konkurrenz**firma aus Frankreich bietet im Augenblick in England eine Reihe von interessanten Produkten an.
A **rival** firm from France is offering a number of interesting products in England at the moment.
Was die Marktsituation verschlimmert, sind die **Konkurrenz**preise, die unter den englischen Preisen liegen.
What aggravates the situation in the market is the **competitive** price which is below English prices.
"Ich bin gegen **Konkurrenz**neid in jeder Form", behauptete der junge Unternehmer.
"I'm against **professional** jealousy in any form," the young entrepreneur maintained.

Note: Die **Konkurrenz** schläft nicht = Our competitors do not sleep.
Dieser Wagen ist in seiner Klasse **konkurrenz**los = This car is unrivalled in its class.
Schönheits**konkurrenz** = beauty **contest**

concurrence: (1) Zusammentreffen (of events, views etc.)
(2) Übereinstimmung, Einverständnis

Note: **concurrence** is a more formal word.

(1) No one could explain the strange **concurrence** of events in the Caribbean Sea.
Niemand konnte das merkwürdige **Zusammentreffen** der Ereignisse in der Karibik erklären.
(2) The United Nations gave its formal **concurrence** to the sending of Swedish peace forces to Beirut.
Die Vereinten Nationen gaben das formelle **Einverständnis** für die Entsendung der schwedischen Friedenstruppe nach Beirut.

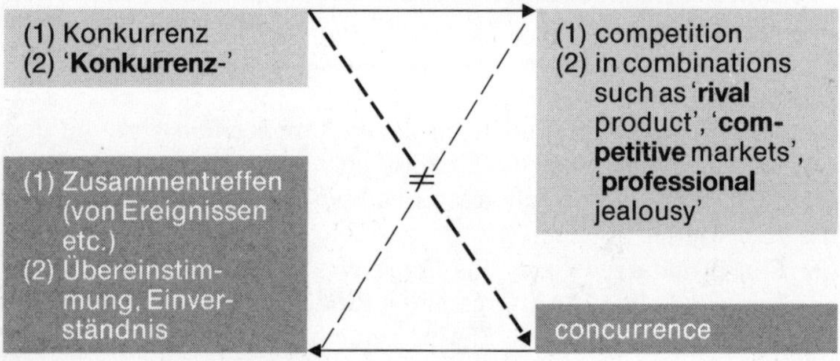

FALSE FRIENDS IN CONTEXT

Top of the High Street League

Business Expert: The Sainsbury family has always resisted the temptation to smear its name. Is that a ________ (1) of events or one of the tricks of the trade?
Lord Sainsbury: Behind it is what I call gentlemanly behaviour and not a ________ (2) of economic factors.
Business Expert: Only last year your food stores in Britain made £ 403 billion. That was £ 168 million ahead of Marks and Spencer. Your food stores top the high street league table. Aren't you afraid of the ________ (3)?
Lord Sainsbury: First of all, we're running a retail business. ________ (4)

jealousy in the high street is ruthless. ________ (5) firms are out to steal ideas, no matter what it costs.
Business Expert: Sainsbury is now Britain's biggest drinks retailer marketing its own wines and whiskies. Aren't you moving too fast?
Lord Sainsbury: That's a question I'll not answer because of the ________ (6). But I'd like to make one thing clear. We're not offering whisky tasting festivals for everyone.

SOLUTION

(1) **concurrence** of events (2) **concurrence** of factors (3) competition
(4) **professional** jealousy (5) **rival** firms (6) competition

KONSEQUENT ◑ consequent

consequent ['kɒnsɪkwənt] ············▾

KONSEQUENT

(unbeirrbar; logisch folgernd etc.)

consistent [kən'sɪstənt] **etc.** ▴

KONSEQUENT: (1) (ohne innere Widersprüche) consistent(ly)
(2) (unbeirrbar, zielstrebig) unremitting(ly)
(3) (logisch folgernd, logisch vorgehend) logical(ly)

(1) Die meisten meiner Parteifreunde sind **konsequente** Verfechter der Wirtschaftspolitik der Regierung.
Most of my colleagues in the party are **consistent** supporters of the government's economic policy.
Der Häftling lehnte es **konsequent** ab, irgend etwas zu sagen, ehe er mit seinem Rechtsberater gesprochen hatte.
The prisoner **consistently** refused to say anything, before he had talked to his legal adviser.
(2) Durch Können und **konsequentes** Training schaffte Steffi Graf den Gewinn des Grand-Slam-Titels 1988.
Her ability and **unremitting** training won Steffi Graf the Grand Slam in 1988.
(3) Der Polizeieinsatz vom heutigen Tage war eine **konsequente** Entscheidung nach den Unruhen am letzten Wochenende.
Today's police operation was a **logical** decision after the riots last weekend.
Leider hatte er das Problem nicht **konsequent** zu Ende gedacht.
Unfortunately he hadn't thought out the problem **logically**.

consequent: (1) Adj.: (consequent) daraus resultierend; in der Folge; (consequent on/upon sth.) als Folge, im Ergebnis
(2) Adv.: (consequently) daher, infolgedessen
(3) Verb: (be consequent on) eine Folge sein von

(1) A very wet summer has led to a poor harvest and a **consequent** increase in grain prices.
Der regenreiche Sommer führte zu einer schlechten Ernte und **in der Folge** zu einem Anstieg der Getreidepreise.

Continuous government pressure on the management of the Underground to reduce costs, and the **consequent** reduction in manpower have affected safety standards.
Der fortgesetzte Druck der Regierung auf die U-Bahn-Führung, die Kosten zu verringern, und der **daraus resultierende** Personalabbau wirkten sich nachteilig auf die Sicherheitsmaßnahmen aus.
Consequent upon the increase of trade, wealth spread throughout the country.
Als Folge der Zunahme des Handels breitete sich Wohlstand im ganzen Lande aus.
(2) My friend had an accident on the motorway and **consequently** had to spend a fortnight in hospital.
Mein Freund hatte auf der Autobahn einen Unfall und mußte **infolgedessen** 14 Tage im Krankenhaus bleiben.
(3) The dismissal of the Chancellor of the Exchequer **was consequent on** the recent scandal.
Die Entlassung des Finanzministers **war eine Folge** des kürzlichen Skandals.

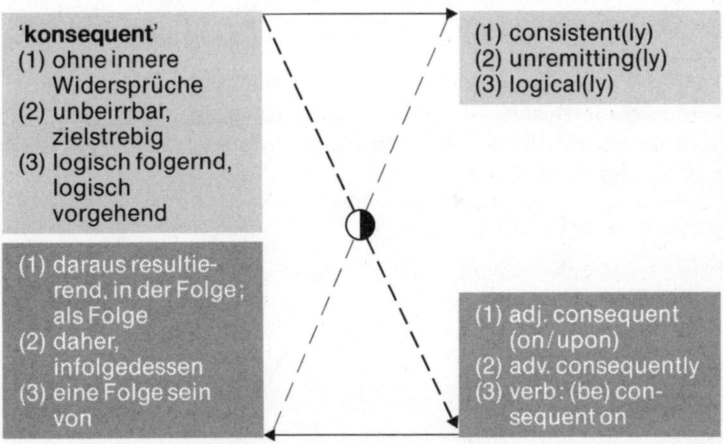

FALSE FRIENDS IN CONTEXT

Beating the Taxman

Owner of Longleat House: This is one of the grandest Elizabethan houses in Britain and it belongs to our family.
Caewlin (his 15-year-old son and the next heir): Was that what you wanted to tell me when you phoned the school?
Owner of Longleat House: I've got to be ________ (1) about this matter. You're the next Longleat heir.
Caewlin: I still don't understand.
Owner of Longleat House: I'm getting old now and I'm ________ (2) in my desire to beat the taxman. Large parts of the estate will be handed over to you. If I leave it any longer, the capital transfer tax will be enormous. ________ (3), Longleat, one of Britain's stately homes, will remain in the family for at least another two generations.
Caewlin: But I'm still at school...
Owner of Longleat House: You are to inherit the historic Longleat House. My father did the same with me when I was in my early twenties.
Caewlin: What has the taxman got to do with me?
Owner of Longleat House: If I die, you've got to pay tax. ________ (4), with rising tax rates and horrific capital income tax after my death, handing Longleat over to you is the right thing to do *now*.
Caewlin: O. K. Let's beat the taxman then.

SOLUTION

(1) logical (2) unremitting (3) consequently (4) consequently

KONTROLLIEREN ◑ control

control [kən'trəʊl] ····· **KONTROLLIEREN**

check etc. ←—— (= überprüfen)

KONTROLLIEREN: (1) (überprüfen) check
(2) (nochmals kontrollieren) double check
(3) (sorgfältig überprüfen) inspect
(4) (regelmäßig mit wissenschaftlichen Methoden prüfen) monitor

(1) "**Kontrollieren** Sie die Haltbarkeitsdaten auf allen Nahrungsmitteln!" riet der Fernsehansager.
"**Check** sell-by dates on all foods!" advised the TV announcer.
"Wissenschaftler haben einen neuen Test entwickelt, um Nahrungsmittel wegen Salmonellen-Vergiftung schneller zu **kontrollieren**", fuhr er fort.
"Scientists have developed a new test to **check** food quicker for salmonella poisoning," he went on.
Bitte **kontrolliere**, ob die Zündflamme ausgegangen ist.
Please **check** in case the pilot light has gone out.
(2) "Wir haben das ganze Gebäude abgesucht – und um ganz sicher zu sein, haben wir auch das Flugzeug **nochmals kontrolliert**, konnten aber keine Bombe finden", bestätigte der Kommissar.
"We searched the whole building – and to be absolutely sure – we even **double checked** the plane, but couldn't find a bomb," the police superintendent confirmed.
(3) British Rail kann nicht alle Bahnlinien regelmäßig **kontrollieren**.
British Rail cannot **inspect** all its railway lines regularly.
(4) Empfindliche Computer **kontrollieren** den Fortschritt der Patienten während der Herzoperationen.
Sensitive computers **monitor** patients' progress during heart operations.

control (o. s.): (1) sich zusammenreißen, sich beherrschen
(2) in den Griff bekommen
(3) überwachen, regeln

(1) Billy tried to **control** his temper, but didn't manage to.
Billy versuchte **sich zusammenzureißen**, aber es gelang ihm nicht.
Her teacher asked Sheila to **control herself**, but she went on giggling.
Ihre Lehrerin bat Sheila **sich** zu **beherrschen**, aber sie kicherte weiter.
(2) "The only way out is to **control** the crisis through research into salmonella," maintained the Farmers Union chief.
"Der einzige Ausweg ist, die Krise durch Salmonellen-Forschung **in den Griff** zu **bekommen**", behauptete der Chef der Bauerngewerkschaft.
(3) Bristol police had **controlled** the traffic all day, but there was no trace of the van with the diamonds.
Die Polizei von Bristol hatte den ganzen Tag den Verkehr **überwacht**, aber es gab keine Spur von dem Lieferwagen mit den Diamanten.

Note: controlled = beherrscht
The ballet at the Theatre Royal puts great emphasis on ground work with jumps at their most exciting and splendidly **controlled**.

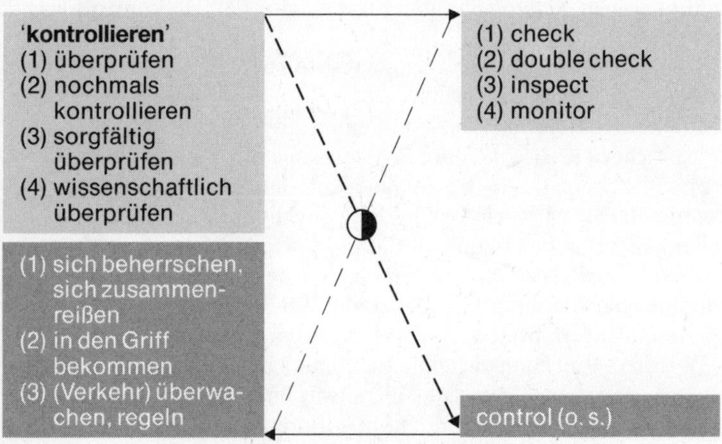

FALSE FRIENDS IN CONTEXT

Young and Unconcerned

"Steve . . .," his mother pleaded for the third time, but he didn't listen. "________ (1) yourself, Steve," his mother told him a minute later. "People are beginning to look at you."
After the inspector had ________ (2) the tickets, someone tapped her on the shoulder from behind.
"Can't you ________ (3) that boy? He's kicked me twice, and now he's torn off my wig!"
(Mother looking round into an angry face) "Oh, what a relief! I thought he had scalped you," she said getting off the bus.

SOLUTION

(1) control yourself (2) checked (3) control

KONZEPT ◑ concept

concept [ˈkɒnsept]

KONZEPT

(erster Entwurf etc.)

rough draft, rough copy etc.

KONZEPT: (1) ([erster] Entwurf, Roh**konzept**; Stichworte) rough draft; rough copy; first draft; notes
(2) (Konzept, fig.) plan, idea(s)

(1) "Warum gibst du den Aufsatz im **Konzept** ab? So kann ich ihn nicht lesen", unterbrach der Lehrer den Schüler.
"Why are you handing in the **rough draft/first draft** of your essay? I can't read it in this form," the teacher interrupted the pupil.
"Ich habe meine Rede nach meinem **Konzept** gehalten; das endgültige **Konzept** habe ich noch nicht", bekannte der Redner.
"I have delivered my speech from my **notes**; the final **draft** is not ready yet," the speaker confessed.
"Am Ende der Klausur müssen das **Konzept** und die Reinschrift abgegeben werden", betonte der aufsichtsführende Prüfer.
"At the end of the test you've got to hand in your **rough copy** and your fair copy," the supervising examiner emphasized.
(2) "Wir wollten die gegnerische Mannschaft gleich am Anfang überraschen, aber dieses **Konzept** ging leider nicht auf", gab der Trainer vor der Presse zu.
"We had wanted to take the opposing team by surprise right at the beginning but unfortunately this **plan** did not work," our coach admitted to the press.
"Die neuen Unruhen in Nord-Irland passen mir überhaupt nicht ins **Konzept**", ließ Ian Paisley durchblicken.
"The latest riots in Northern Ireland do not fit in with my **ideas** in the least," Ian Paisley intimated.

Note: aus dem **Konzept** bringen = get s. o. rattled, put s. o. off his stride, upset s. o.
aus dem **Konzept** kommen = lose one's thread
but: **Konzept**papier = scribbling paper, note paper

concept: (1) (Allgemein-, Gesamt-)Begriff, Vorstellung
(2) Konzeption

(1) “I agree with you here. But your **concept** of society and your **concept** of freedom are unacceptable for me,”, argued my opposite number.
“Ich stimme Ihnen hier zu. Aber Ihr Gesellschafts**begriff** und Ihr Freiheits**begriff** sind für mich unannehmbar”, bestritt mein Gegenüber.
Your **concept** of democracy is radically different from mine.
Ihre **Vorstellung** von Demokratie unterscheidet sich grundlegend von meiner.
(2) The Chancellor of the Exchequer’s new budget was described as brilliant in **concept** and brilliant in delivery.
Der neue Haushalt des Schatzkanzlers wurde als brillant in der **Konzeption** und brillant in der Vortragsweise beschrieben.

Note: conception = Empfängnis (eines Kindes)
but: He has no **conception** of space = Er hat keine Raum-**Vorstellung**.
Compare: As expected, Prince Charles was in favour of the ‘new village’ **concept/plan (idea)** between Kettering and Market Harborough which would maintain the community character.
The pair of False Friends may overlap in meaning. **Concept** here refers to the general or theoretical aspects of a ‘new village’, whereas **Konzept** in the sense of **plan** or **idea** hints at the practical aspects of the village project such as ‘low-cost homes for the local people’.

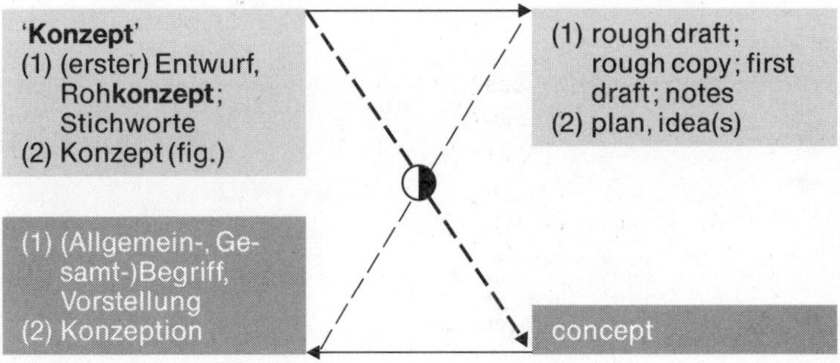

FALSE FRIENDS IN CONTEXT

A TV Revolution?

Live-in Lover: Sky Television is being offered for only £4.49 a week. They're introducing a new ________ (1) never before experienced in Britain.
Girlfriend: Really? What's new about it?
Live-in Lover: The new ________ (2) is satellite TV by subscription. What's more, for £4.49 a week you get all the satellite equipment and dish installed and this includes all maintenance and programme charges.
Girlfriend: There must be a catch somewhere. How does it differ from the normal TV channels?
Live-in Lover: Their overall ________ (3) is to offer four new channels – Sky One, Sky Movies, Sky News and Eurosport – plus access to four other satellite channels including MTV, the 24-hour music station – and Children's Channel.
Girlfriend: Excellent. That fits in with my ________ (4) of educating our children at home, that is by watching the school programme on Children's Channel.
Live-in Lover: Wait a minute! You don't mean to say you're pregnant, do you?
Girlfriend: Yes, darling. I've been thinking out a ________ (5) as to educate our children this morning. I'm expecting twins.
Live-in Lover: That's better than any TV revolution. It's the most wonderful revolution in our lives! Darling, let's get married first.

SOLUTION

(1) concept (2) concept (3) concept (4) idea (5) plan

MENÜ ≠ menu

menu [ˈmenju:] ····· **MENÜ**

set meal etc. ——— (= Tagesgedeck)

MENÜ: (1) (Tagesgedeck) set meal; set lunch, set dinner
(2) (**Menü**vorschlag) table d'hôte [ˌtɑ:blˈdəʊt] (in first-class restaurants etc.)

Note: **Table d'hôte** is "a meal consisting of a set number of courses, served at a fixed price" (see Greenbaum / Whitcut, p. 697), normally for hotel guests.

(1) "Sie können heute zwischen vier **Menüs** wählen", kündigte der Kellner an.
"You can choose between four **set meals** today," announced the waiter.
"Ich nehme das Mittags**menü**; es kostet nur vier Pfund", sagte der eine Tourist zu dem anderen.
"I'm going to have the **set lunch**. It only costs £4," said one tourist to the other.
Das **Menü** bestand aus vier Gängen und war sein Geld wert.
The **set dinner** consisted of four courses and was good value for money.
(2) In *Country Club Hotels* kann man zwischen einem **Menü** im großen Hotel-Restaurant oder einem Essen in der Bar am Swimmingpool wählen.
In *Country Club Hotels* you can choose either a **table d'hôte** dinner in the main hotel restaurant or a meal in the poolside bar.

menu: Speisekarte

No sooner had the old ladies sat down than the head waiter brought them the **menu**.
Kaum hatten die alten Damen sich gesetzt, da brachte der Oberkellner schon die **Speisekarte**.
It took the old ladies a long time to read the **menu**, and even then they couldn't decide what to order.

Es dauerte ziemlich lange, bis die alten Damen die **Speisekarte** gelesen hatten, und auch dann konnten sie sich nicht entscheiden, was sie nehmen wollten.

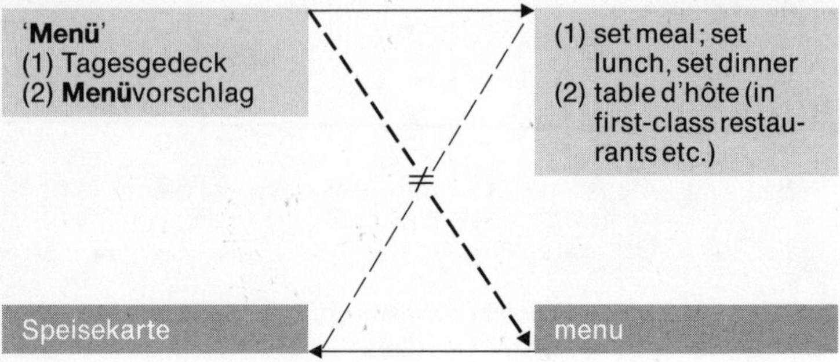

FALSE FRIENDS IN CONTEXT

Junk Food Appetizers

Fat Woman: I'm fed up with dieting, especially with having to count all the calories.
Junk Food Adviser: You don't need to if you stick to the Junk Food Diet. You can put together your own ________ (1) as long as you stick to your calorie level. That's our recipe for success.
Fat Woman: There's another thing. I don't want to read all your diet booklets and recipe leaflets and I haven't the time to go to health food stores.
Junk Food Adviser: You don't have to. We've got a much better system. Our ________ (2) can be bought at all supermarkets. What's more, Junk Food Diet prices are always lower at supermarkets than at health food stores. And don't forget, you won't find our ________ (3) on the ________ (4) of restaurants or hotels. So why bother to go there?

SOLUTION

(1) set meal (2) set meals/set dinners (3) set lunches/set dinners
(4) menu

MONDÄN ≠ mundane

mundane [ˌmʌnˈdeɪn] ··· **MONDÄN**

elegant etc. ··· (= betont elegant etc.)

MONDÄN: (extremely) elegant, fashionable, (very) chic, stylish

In den letzten Jahren hat sich Joan Collins zu einer ganz **mondänen** Frau entwickelt.
In the last few years Joan Collins has turned into an extremely **elegant** lady.
Als Weltstar pflegte sie nur in **mondänen** Hotels zu übernachten.
As a superstar she would only spend the night in **stylish** hotels.
Aber sie lehnte es ab, einem bestimmten **mondänen** Klub in Monaco beizutreten.
But she rejected the idea of joining a certain **fashionable** club in Monaco.
Sie bevorzugte es, sich auf den Filmfestspielen von Cannes **mondän** gekleidet zu zeigen.
She preferred to be seen **fashionably** dressed at the Cannes Film Festival.
In dem neuen Film tragen alle Frauen **mondäne** Modellkleider.
In the latest film all women wear **chic** designer clothes.

mundane: (1) langweilig
(2) alltäglich, banal

(1) He turned off the radio. **Mundane** speeches of this sort always put him off at once.
Er stellte das Radio ab. **Langweilige** Reden dieser Art vergraulten ihn sofort.
(2) The professor was not interested in **mundane** matters. He had other things to see to now.
Der Professor war an den **alltäglichen** Dingen nicht interessiert; er hatte sich jetzt um andere Dinge zu kümmern.
After months in space the shock of a return to reality is profound for an astronaut. He must now address himself to **mundane** pursuits, like his front lawn or his shed in the garden.

Nach Monaten im Weltraum sitzt der Schock der Rückkehr in die Realität bei einem Astronauten tief. Er muß sich jetzt **banalen** Beschäftigungen zuwenden, wie dem Rasen vor dem Haus oder dem Schuppen im Garten.

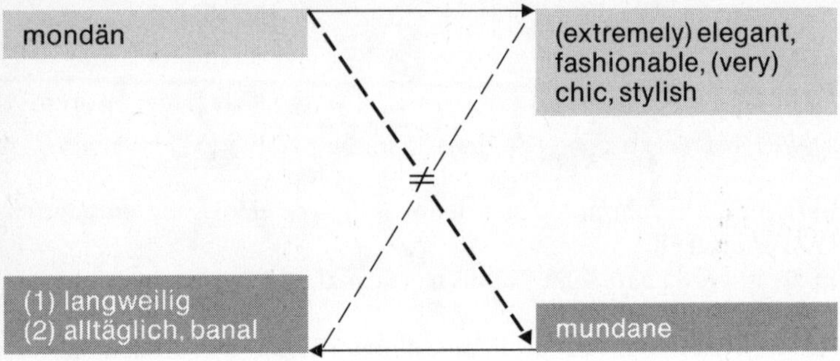

FALSE FRIENDS IN CONTEXT

Love-Sick

Society Correspondent: Tell me what did Roger Knight do after he met a certain blonde lady?
Informant: When Roger met the ________ (1) blonde from Brighton, he became love-sick. It was the beginning of his downfall.
Society Correspondent: Why?
Informant: It began with his birthday party in May when he chartered a helicopter to her home.
Society Correspondent: What happened after that?
Informant: Then Roger began buying her ________ (2) clothes and taking her to expensive restaurants in London.
Society Correspondent: Was that all?
Informant: Certainly not. Shortly after their trip to Paris he bought her a ________ (3) car. He lavished her with gifts.
Society Correspondent: Did he have the money for this kind of lifestyle?
Informant: No. He used to turn up here with his wallet full of credit cards. The couple even went on a world tour. 26-year-old Sandra was ________ (4) dressed when they flew to Moscow by Concorde to see the Bolshoi ballet.

Society Correspondent: Didn't his parents know about their love-sick son?
Informant: Whenever his parents tried to contact him, Roger put them off by saying, "I haven't got time to talk to you and discuss ________ (5) matters."
Society Correspondent: What happened in the end to the love-sick bachelor?
Informant: Roger has been jailed for six years. His former temptress has left England to join a ________ (6) club in the Bermudas.

SOLUTION

(1) elegant (2) fashionable (3) stylish (4) **fashionably** dressed
(5) **mundane** matters (6) **fashionable** club

ORDINÄR ≠ ordinary

ordinary [ˈɔːdɪŋrɪ] .... **ORDINÄR**

vulgar [ˈvʌlgə] **etc.** .... (unfein etc.)

ORDINÄR: (unfein etc.) vulgar, rude, common, coarse

Welcher mögliche Wert kann darin bestehen, Mülltonnen von Mitbewohnern umzuwerfen und dabei **ordinäre** Ausdrücke zu gebrauchen?
What possible merit can there be in kicking over fellow residents' dustbins, using **vulgar** language?
Aber ich werde mir seine **ordinären** Worte nicht gefallen lassen.
But I won't stand for his **rude** words.
"Wie der schon aussah. Ziemlich **ordinär**, um es vorsichtig auszudrücken", bemerkte sie.
"What a mess he looked. Rather **common**, to say the least," she remarked.
"Eine ziemlich **ordinäre** Frau mit einem Yorkshire-Akzent lachte auch noch über mich. Wirklich empörend, finde ich."
"A rather **coarse** woman with a Yorkshire accent even laughed at me. Really shocking, don't you think?"

ordinary: (1) normal, gewöhnlich
(2) '**Durchschnitts-**' (in combinations)

(1) "You should use re-cycled paper instead of **ordinary** paper," added my wife.
"Du solltest Recycling-Papier statt **normalem** Papier benutzen", fügte meine Frau hinzu.
"We are trying to form an **ordinary** family," Prince Charles stated clearly to the press.
"Wir versuchen, eine ganz **gewöhnliche** Familie zu sein", stellte Prinz Charles vor der Presse klar.
(2) Mrs. Joan Cherry wrote in a letter to the *Daily Mirror*: Fergie must seem the world's worst mother to **ordinary** folk.
Frau Joan Cherry schrieb in einem Brief an den *Daily Mirror*: Fergie muß dem **Durchschnitts**menschen (= dem Mann auf der Straße) als die schlimmste Mutter der Welt erscheinen.

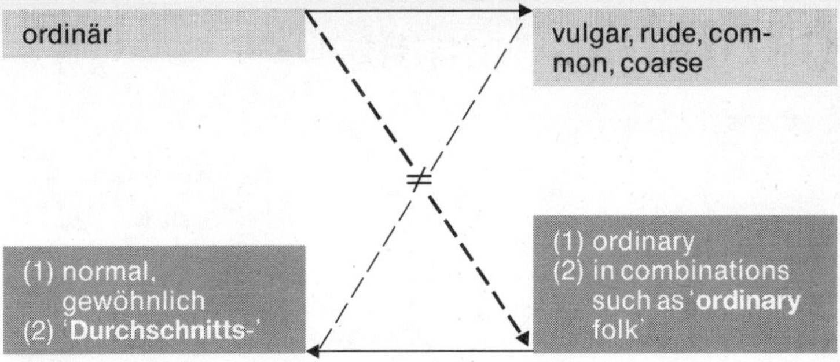

FALSE FRIENDS IN CONTEXT

Party Going

Toby (arriving at a party after the first few minutes): Isn't it great to be here? It would have been a great shame to have missed it. This is really the party atmosphere I like...
Toby (about an hour later at the same party talking to a woman sitting next to him): This is a very ________ (1) party, isn't it? Really! Quite an ________ (2) sit-down affair. No background music, no decent girls, no atmosphere! It's time I left this ________ (3) place. I'm going home.
Woman (sitting next to him): That's what a ________ (4) person like you should do. I'm your hostess, I don't like your behaviour, and there's the door.

SOLUTION

(1) **ordinary** party (2) **ordinary** sit-down affair (3) **ordinary** place
(4) **rude/common** person

PATHETISCH ≠ pathetic

pathetic [pə'θetɪk]

PATHETISCH
(= feierlich; salbungsvoll)

solemn ['sɒləm] **etc.**

PATHETISCH: (1) (feierlich, erhaben) solemn
(2) (salbungsvoll, übertrieben gefühlsvoll) (over-)emotional, passionate, impassioned

(1) Seine **pathetische** Ruhe verfehlte ihre Wirkung auf die Zuhörer nicht.
His **solemn** calm had its effect on the audience.
(2) Der Schlußteil von Harold Wilsons Rede klang mir zu **pathetisch**.
The final part of Harold Wilson's speech sounded too **emotional** for me.
Den **pathetischen** Aufruf des Gewerkschaftsführers, in dieser Situation mitzuhelfen, beantworteten die Arbeiter mit höhnischem Gelächter.
The workers answered with scornful laughter to the union leader's **passionate** appeal to cooperate in this situation.
Der Pfarrer wurde trotz eines **pathetisch** vorgetragenen Plädoyers seines Rechtsberaters vom Kirchengericht entlassen.
The vicar was dismissed by the church court despite an **impassioned** plea by his counsel.

Note: **pathetische** Parolen = emotionally worded slogans

pathetic: (1) bemitleidenswert, mitleiderregend
(2) traurig (machend), ergreifend, erschütternd
(3) 'unter aller Kanone' (koll.), lächerlich

Note: An adjective ***pathetical** does not exist in modern English.

(1) I was heart-broken to see the **pathetic** attempts of mother seals to protect their young.
Es brach mir das Herz, die **bemitleidenswerten** Versuche der Robbenmütter mit anzusehen, ihre Jungen zu schützen.
Winding up, the Queen's Counsel added, "This is above all a tragic and **pathetic** case."

In seinem Schlußwort fügte der Staatsanwalt hinzu: “Es handelt sich vor allem um einen tragischen, **mitleiderregenden** Fall.”
(2) “How **pathetic** that self-interest came into it,” Doris Day remarked afterwards.
“Wie **traurig**, daß Eigennutz sich damit verband”, bemerkte Doris Day hinterher.
“On the photo you can see the **pathetic** remnants of our town,” her son wrote in a **pathetic** letter from Namibia.
“Auf dem Foto kannst du die **traurigen** Überreste unserer Stadt erkennen”, schrieb ihr Sohn in einem **erschütternden** Brief aus Namibia.
(3) “Our team’s performance today was **pathetic**,” Everton’s manager commented. “The forwards didn’t work together and the defence was non-existent.”
“Die Vorstellung unserer Mannschaft war heute **unter aller Kanone**”, kommentierte Evertons Manager. “Die Stürmer spielten nicht zusammen, und die Verteidigung war nicht vorhanden.”
“The only word to describe the tackling of the problem of football hooliganism by police and politicians is **pathetic**,” he wrote.
“Das einzige Wort, das die Behandlung des Problems des Fußball-Rowdytums durch Polizei und Politiker beschreibt, ist **lächerlich**”, schrieb er.

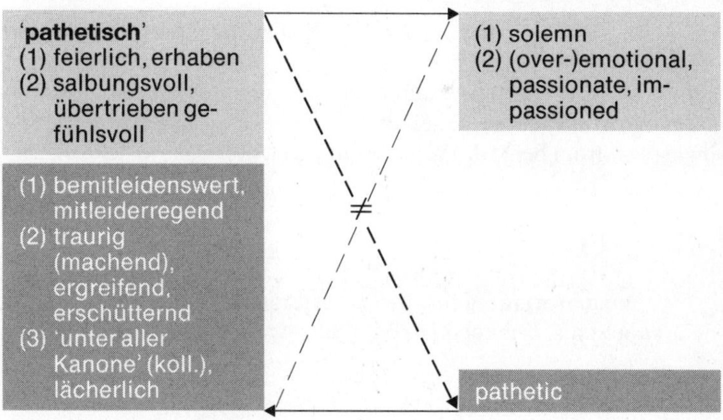

FALSE FRIENDS IN CONTEXT

Safari Law

Father (being interviewed at Nairobi Airport on his arrival from London): . . . I've not come here to make a ________ (1) statement to the press. I've come here to find out the truth about my daughter's death. And I've sworn to myself I *will* find out!
Press Reporter: You sound a bit too ________ (2) to me. Are there any doubts concerning the circumstances of your daughter's death?
Father: There are fundamental doubts. My ________ (3) appeal to the Kenyan police led to nothing. The question is whether my daughter was brutally murdered or killed by wild animals on her photographic safari.

* * *

Father (speaking from the witness box in Nairobi a year later): It was ________ (4) to learn the Kenyan police did not treat my daughter's death as murder. For them it was a ________ (5) accident caused by wild animals. But we started to search the game reserve at once. We found Sandy's ________ (6) remains seven miles away from the Mole River safari camp . . .
Judge: We've listened to your account of what you found out. Can you cite any further evidence?
Father: A post mortem examination by one of Britain's leading pathologists showed my daughter's head had been chopped off with a single blow from behind. I want her murderer brought to justice.

SOLUTION

(1) **pathetic** statement (2) sound too **emotional** (3) **passionate** appeal (4) pathetic (5) **pathetic** accident (6) **pathetic** remains

PRÄGNANT ≠ pregnant

pregnant [ˈpregnənt] ········ **PRÄGNANT**

pithy [ˈpɪθɪ] ········ (knapp, aber treffend)

PRÄGNANT: (knapp, aber treffend) pithy, succinct [səkˈsɪŋkt], concise

Von den Nachrufen für Greta Garbo stammt der **prägnanteste** von dem Schauspieler Anthony Quinn: “Mein Gott, war sie großartig.”
Among the tributes to Greta Garbo the **pithiest** came from Anthony Quinn, the actor, “My God, she was marvellous.”
Diese **prägnante** Entgegnung des Delegationschefs rettete die Friedensverhandlungen.
This **succinct** reply by the leader of the delegation saved the peace negotiations.
Sein **prägnanter** Stil beeindruckt nach wie vor viele seiner Leser.
His **concise** style still impresses many of his readers.
Der Streikführer formulierte es **prägnant**: “Die Zeit für Veränderungen ist gekommen.”
The strike leader put it **succinctly**, “The time has come for change.”

pregnant: (1) schwanger
(2) bedeutungsvoll, gewichtig (fig.)

(1) He couldn't believe his girlfriend was **pregnant** despite all the precautions they had taken.
Er konnte es nicht glauben, daß seine Freundin **schwanger** war, trotz aller Vorsichtsmaßnahmen, die sie getroffen hatten.
(2) When the chairman of the board of directors began to address the board members a **pregnant** silence came over them.
Als der Aufsichtsratsvorsitzende vor den Mitgliedern des Aufsichtsrats zu sprechen begann, breitete sich eine **bedeutungsvolle** Stille aus.
Two of the most **pregnant** phrases in political life are “Not as bad as we feared” and “could have been worse”.
Zwei der **gewichtigsten** Wendungen im politischen Leben lauten: “Nicht so schlimm, wie wir befürchteten” und “Hätte schlimmer sein können”.

Note: The noun is **pregnancy** (= Schwangerschaft).
Shortly after my **pregnancy** I put on a lot of weight.
but: be eight months **pregnant** = im achten Monat sein
Paula's eight months **pregnant** and she's taking no chances this time.

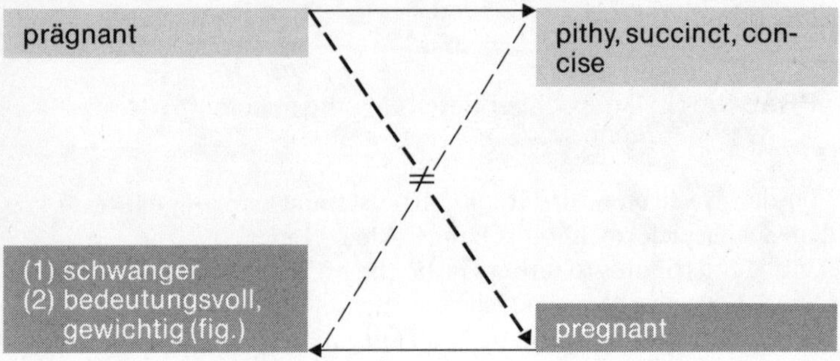

FALSE FRIENDS IN CONTEXT

A Wondering Smile

Mrs. Hackett meets her neighbour, Mrs. Cochrane, a gossipy woman not usually known for her ________ (1) remarks.
Mrs. Cochrane: Have you heard about Judy, your next-door neighbour's daughter?
Mrs. Hackett: No. What about her? She's such a good girl.
Mrs. Cochrane: I do wonder. Well, her mother took Judy to the schoolbus every morning and met her off it again in the afternoon...
She paused, adding with a wondering smile, "But she still doesn't know how Judy became ________ (2)."

SOLUTION

(1) **pithy** remarks (2) became **pregnant**

PROZESS ◑ process

process [ˈprəʊses]

PROZESS

trial etc.

PROZESS: (1) (Gerichts**prozeß**, allgemein) lawsuit, suit
(2) (zivilrechtlicher **Prozeß**) case
(3) (strafrechtlicher **Prozeß**) trial

(1) Für deinen Ruf ist es nicht gut, in zu viele **Prozesse** verwickelt zu sein.
It's not good for your reputation to be involved in too many **lawsuits**.
Der **Prozeß** dauerte fünf Jahre, und das Urteil endete mit Freispruch.
The **suit** took five years and ended with the verdict of not guilty.
(2) Hat Herr Fenwick seinen **Prozeß** gewonnen? – Nein, er hat den Scheidungs**prozeß** verloren.
Did Mr. Fenwick win his **case**? – No, he lost his divorce **case**.
(3) Der Mord**prozeß** dauerte insgesamt drei Jahre.
The murder **trial** lasted three years altogether.
Die beiden Komplicen wurden in dem **Prozeß** wegen Kindesentführung überführt.
The two accomplices were found guilty in the kidnapping **trial**.
Das Originalmanuskript von Franz Kafkas Roman *Der* **Prozeß** erzielte einen Rekordpreis von 1,1 Millionen Pfund auf einer Sotheby-Auktion.
The original manuscript of Franz Kafka's novel *The* **Trial** fetched a record price of £ 1.1 million at Sotheby's.

process: (1) Verfahren
(2) Vorgang, Verlauf

(1) This **process** is an important improvement on earlier methods in cancer research.
Dieses **Verfahren** ist eine bedeutende Verbesserung gegenüber den bisherigen Methoden in der Krebsforschung.
(2) The **process** of global warming will lead to dramatic changes in English weather.
Der **Vorgang** der globalen Erwärmung wird zu deutlichen Veränderungen des englischen Wetters führen.

The hunt for the kidnappers went on for a week, but they were caught in the **process** of a shoot-out on the Mexican border.
Die Jagd nach den Entführern dauerte eine Woche, aber sie wurden im **Verlauf** eines Schußwechsels an der mexikanischen Grenze gefangen.

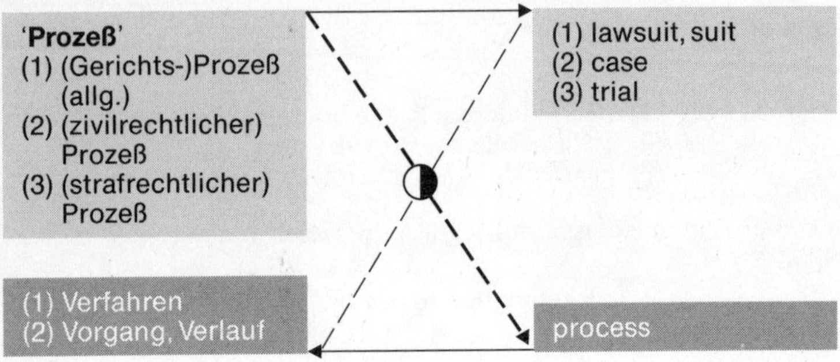

FALSE FRIENDS IN CONTEXT

New Ways of Applying Food Research

Two young doctors are exchanging their views:
Beate: Did you read about what is called the 'food revolution'?
Gabi: No. Is it a new type of food or a slimming technique?
Beate: It's more or less the opposite of what you'd expect. Scientists in New Zealand have developed a ________ (1) to remove cholesterol from meat and dairy food.
Gabi: That's interesting. Did they give any details?
Beate: Well, it seems the finished product is of a much better quality than the normal food that's on the market.
Gabi: That's really too bad. If we recommend the new food to our patients and the slimming results are bad, then we might be involved in ________ (2) for years, and I don't want to lose even one ________ (3) and pay thousands of pounds compensation.
Beate: But the food is on the market already and people are buying the products.
Gabi: Then let's buy some of the new food products and test them on ourselves.
Beate: So the food revolution is on...

SOLUTION

(1) process (2) lawsuits/suits (3) lawsuit/suit

FALSE FRIENDS TRAPS TEST 3

DIFFICULT FALSE FRIENDS

1.a. "You've got a choice of three ________ today," the landlady told her hotel guests (**Menü ≠ menu**).
1.b. Salmon will find its place on the ________ when it becomes cheaper than cod and haddock (**Menü ≠ menu**).
2.a. The strike leader's ________ reply shocked the shipyard owners (**prägnant ≠ pregnant**).
2.b. Flying when you are ________ is not advisable (**prägnant ≠ pregnant**).
3.a. The accused was released on ________ after having stayed in prison for three weeks (**Kaution ◑ caution**).
3.b. "I haven't done grown-up things like putting a ________ on a flat," the comedian told the audience (**Kaution ◑ caution**).
4.a. The Dutch have invented the modern ________ of the holiday village combined with a subtropical swimming paradise (**Konzept ◑ concept**).
4.b. "The final ________ of my budget speech isn't ready yet," the Chancellor of the Exchequer admitted (**Konzept ◑ concept**).
5.a. Scientists have developed a revolutionary ________ to remove cholesterol from meat and dairy food (**Prozeß ◑ process**).
5.b. "You'll lose the ________," warned his solicitor, "if you keep making rude remarks in court (**Prozeß ◑ process**)."
6. The ________ (**konsequent**) efforts of the Prime Minister led to an end of the transport strike.
7. These lorry drivers are such ________ (**ordinär**) people. One of them even tried to make love to Eve, our youngest daughter.
8. Many parents of all ________ (**Konfessionen**) will be pleased to know about the Christian atmosphere and academic record of St. George's School.
9. "________ (**kontrollieren**) in case the pilot light has gone out," she reminded her husband before they left the holiday apartment.
10. There's always ________ (**Konkurrenz**-) jealousy among high street banks. ________ (**Konkurrenz**) can be quite fierce at times.

ANSWER SHEET: TRUE FRIENDS TEST 3

DIFFICULT FALSE FRIENDS

1.a. "You've got a choice of three **set meals** today," the landlady told her hotel guests.
1.b. Salmon will find its place on the **menu** when it becomes cheaper than cod and haddock.
2.a. The strike leader's **pithy** reply shocked the shipyard owners.
2.b. Flying when you are **pregnant** is not advisable.
3.a. The accused was released on **bail** after having stayed in prison for three weeks.
3.b. "I haven't done grown-up things like putting a **deposit** on a flat," the comedian told the audience.
4.a. The Dutch have invented the modern **concept** of the holiday village combined with a subtropical swimming paradise.
4.b. "The final **draft** of my budget speech isn't ready yet," the Chancellor of the Exchequer admitted.
5.a. Scientists have developed a revolutionary **process** to remove cholesterol from meat and dairy food.
5.b. "You'll lose the **case**," warned his solicitor, "if you keep making rude remarks in court."
6. The **unremitting** efforts of the Prime Minister led to an end of the transport strike.
7. These lorry drivers are such **vulgar/common** people. One of them even tried to make love to Eve, our youngest daughter.
8. Many parents of all **denominations** will be pleased to know about the Christian atmosphere and academic record of St. George's School.
9. "**Check** in case the pilot light has gone out," she reminded her husband before they left the holiday apartment.
10. There's always **professional** jealousy among high street banks. **Competition** can be quite fierce at times.

RENTABEL ≠ rentable

rentable [ˈrentəbl]

RENTABEL

(= einträglich etc.)

profitable [ˈprɒfɪtəbl] **etc.**

RENTABEL: (einträglich, gewinnbringend etc.) profitable, paying, lucrative

Die Goldaktien erwiesen sich nach einem Jahr als äußerst **rentabel**.
The gold shares proved extremely **profitable** after a year.
"Ein **rentables** Unternehmen soll man nicht verkaufen", riet ihm der Bankier.
"You shouldn't sell a **paying** firm," the banker advised him.
"Ein solch **rentables** Angebot aus dem Ausland konnte ich nicht ausschlagen", bekannte mein Freund hinterher.
"I couldn't refuse such a **lucrative** offer from abroad," my friend confessed later.

Note: Die Post arbeitet nicht **rentabel** = The post office does not make a profit.

rentable: (1) mietbar, vermietbar
(2) pachtbar

(1) "I'm sorry, there is a severe shortage of **rentable** accomodation in this area," he explained.
"Es tut mir leid, aber in dieser Gegend sind **mietbare** Unterkünfte äußerst knapp", erklärte er.
"Have you any cars for rent at the next weekend?" – "Unfortunately not, none of them are **rentable** at the moment."
"Haben Sie am nächsten Wochenende Autos zu vermieten?" – "Unglücklicherweise nicht, keines davon ist im Augenblick **vermietbar**."
(2) "Is the farm **rentable**?" he asked the puzzled owner.
"Ist der Bauernhof **pachtbar**?" fragte er den verdutzten Besitzer.

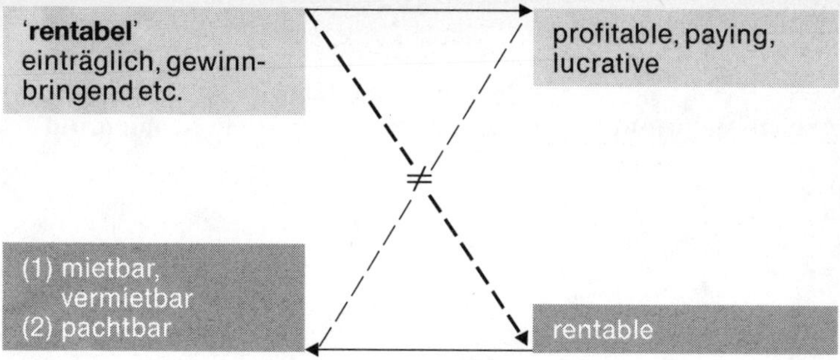

FALSE FRIENDS IN CONTEXT

A Snip for the Snobs

Auctioneer: I've just bought the lordships of nearly 40 English manors.
Partner: What for? It's a relic of the past and dead capital. Who wants to buy such titles nowadays?
Auctioneer: Well, a lordship represents a title of gentility. And by the way, it's a most ________ (1) business.
Partner: I don't believe it.
Auctioneer: I bought each title for £500, and they'll go on sale for three or four thousand each at our next auction.
Partner: Really?
Auctioneer: Many of our customers will regard these lordships as a ________ (2) proposal. We'll even get quite a few bids from abroad.
Partner: All this sounds a bit too risky, so I don't want any share in it.
Auctioneer: There'll even be four Aberdeenshire lairdships on offer expected to fetch more than £10,000 each. It'll turn out to be a more ________ (3) auction than any of our auctions in the past.
Partner: In that case, count me in. This one sounds a ________ (4) venture. I've just had an idea!
Auctioneer: Tell me about it.
Partner: I'll turn up for the auction in an old Bentley Continental convertible, provided it's ________ (5). And I'll make a bid for one of the Suffolk lordships myself.
Auctioneer: Good lord! A real snip for the snobs.

SOLUTION

(1) **profitable** business (2) **lucrative** proposal (3) **profitable** auction
(4) a **paying** venture (5) rentable

REZEPT ≠ receipt

receipt [rɪ'si:t] .... **REZEPT**

recipe ['resɪpɪ] **etc.** ——— (Koch-, Back**rezept** etc.)

REZEPT:	(1)	(Koch-, Back**rezept**) recipe
	(2)	(Arzt**rezept**) prescription
	(3)	(Rezept fig.) remedy, cure; way (of doing sth.)

(1) "Der Kuchen schmeckt aber gut. Könntest du mir dein **Rezept** geben?" bat ihre Nachbarin.
"Your cake is so tasty. Could you give me your **recipe**?" asked her neighbour.
"Natürlich, aber lies das **Rezept** sorgfältig durch", fügte sie hinzu.
"Of course, but read the **recipe** carefully," she added.
(2) "Ich kann Ihnen das Medikament nur auf **Rezept** geben," wiederholte die Apothekerin höflich.
"I can give you the medicine only on **prescription**," repeated the chemist politely.
Die neuen **Rezept**gebühren bedeuten für Patienten mit niedrigem Einkommen eine besondere Härte.
The new **prescription** charges place extra hardship on patients with low incomes.
(3) Ich habe ein gutes **Rezept** gegen aufdringliche Vertreter. Ich öffne nicht die Tür.
I've got a good **remedy** for pushy commercial travellers. I don't open my door.
Gegen Faulheit hat es noch immer ein **Rezept** gegeben.
There's always been a **cure** for laziness.
Die Welthungerhilfe hat noch kein **Rezept** gegen Hunger in Ländern der Dritten Welt gefunden.
The World Relief Fund hasn't found as yet a **way** of dealing with hunger in Third World countries.
Note: Patent**rezept** = ideal **way**, ideal **solution**
Most football clubs haven't found an **ideal way** of dealing with hooligans.
There is no ideal **solution** for marriage as yet.

receipt: Quittung; Kassenbeleg, Bon

(1) Could you issue a **receipt** for this sum, please? I need it for the tax return.
Bitte stellen Sie mir eine **Quittung** über diesen Betrag aus; ich benötige sie für die Steuererklärung.
Any item bought at B & Q can be exchanged or refunded – just keep your **receipt**.
Jeder bei B & Q gekaufte Artikel kann umgetauscht oder zurückerstattet werden – bewahren Sie einfach Ihren **Kassenbeleg** auf.
"This is a price tag, but not a **receipt**," answered the shop assistant.
"Das ist ein Preisschild, aber kein **Bon**", antwortete der Verkäufer.
(2) If you are handed money in an envelope in Japan and asked to sign for a **receipt** do not open to check the amount as this shows a lack of trust.
Wenn Sie in Japan Geld im Briefumschlag übergeben bekommen und gebeten werden, den **Erhalt** zu bestätigen, öffnen Sie ihn nicht, um die Summe zu überprüfen, da das Mangel an Vertrauen zeigt.

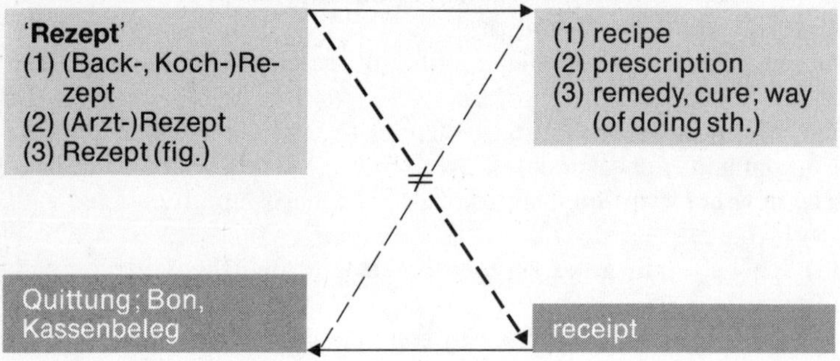

FALSE FRIENDS IN CONTEXT

At a Loss

Listen to this . . .
Mrs. Merrit: I thought I'd try out a new ________ (1) that Jane gave me. What do you think of the cake?
Mr. Merrit (after tasting a piece): There's something wrong with it. It tastes funny.

Mrs. Merrit: But I followed the ________ (2) in the cookery book exactly.
Mr. Merrit (unwilling to have his Sunday peace disturbed): Of course, I'm sure you did, but it should never have been in the book in the first place. Can't you see your doctor next week? Perhaps he can give you a ________ (3) for it!?
Mrs. Merrit: I'm sure he will!

SOLUTION

(1) recipe (2) recipe (3) prescription

. . . and to this
Mrs. Turley: In the 1979 election campaign Mrs. Thatcher said, "We have no intention of raising ________ (4) charges."
Mrs. Tower: That's right.
Mrs. Turley: The new cost of £3.05 is an increase of 1,425 per cent on every ________ (5) from the doctor.
Mrs. Tower: It's a tax on illness and a sick joke.

SOLUTION

(4) prescription (5) prescription

SENSIBEL ≠ sensible

sensible ['sensəbl]

SENSIBEL
(empfindsam etc.)

sensitive ['sensɪtɪv]

SENSIBEL: (1) (empfindsam; empfindlich) sensitive
(2) (gefährdet) sensitive
(3) (heikel, prekär) sensitive

(1) Maud ist **sensibel**. Lassen Sie sie daher bitte in Ruhe.
Maud is a **sensitive** person, so leave her alone, please.
Ein Computer-Virus, der Wal genannt, wurde geschaffen, um in **sensible** Computersysteme in Großbritannien einzubrechen.
A computer virus, called the Whale, has been created to destabilize **sensitive** computer systems in Britain.
(2) Die Flughafenbehörden haben die Sicherheitsmaßnahmen in besonders **sensiblen** Bereichen erhöht.
The airport authorities have stepped up security in particularly **sensitive** areas.
(3) Sie haben mit Ihrer Bemerkung einen **sensiblen** (= heiklen) Bereich der Außenpolitik angesprochen.
You've touched on a **sensitive** area of foreign policy with your remark.

Note: empfindlich sein gegen = be **sensitive** to
Linda is **sensitive to** heat.
but: aufschlußreiche Zahlen = **sensitive** figures

sensible: vernünftig

In this unfortunate position the decision of our relatives to emigrate to New Zealand was **sensible**.
In dieser fatalen Lage war die Entscheidung unserer Verwandten, nach Neuseeland auszuwandern, **vernünftig**.
Mr. Walker is the most **sensible** person I've ever met.
Herr Walker ist der **vernünftigste** Mensch, dem ich je begegnet bin.
"It would have been far more **sensible** to send a British citizen to Iraq rather than someone born in Iran," the editor commented.

"Es wäre viel **vernünftiger** gewesen, einen britischen Staatsangehörigen in den Irak zu schicken, als jemand, der im Iran geboren ist", kommentierte der Herausgeber.

Note: a reasonable price = ein **vernünftiger** (= reeller, fairer) Preis
a reasonable offer = ein **vernünftiges** (= reelles) Angebot
a reasonable article = ein preiswerter Artikel

but: This is not a very **sensible** price (= a price that may be too high or too low).

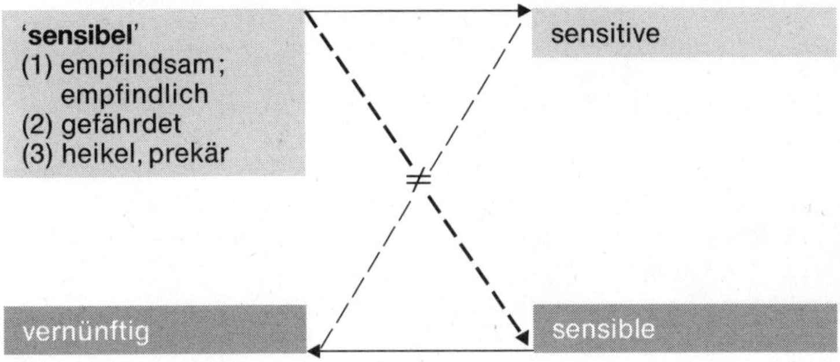

FALSE FRIENDS IN CONTEXT

A Tragic Farewell

"If I kill you," Mike said drawing a pistol from his pocket, "no other man will have to suffer from your behaviour as I have!"
"Please, Mike, be ________ (1)!" Elaine pleaded.
He was pointing the pistol straight at her, and she was ________ (2) enough to realize something tragic was going to happen.
"Put the pistol down," Elaine said quietly, "Let's talk about our relationship."
"There's nothing to talk about – nothing to say!" Mike shouted.
Suddenly there was a deafening noise, and he fell to the floor. Then Elaine fainted.

SOLUTION

(1) sensible (2) sensitive

SERIÖS ≠ serious

serious [ˈsɪərɪəs] → **SERIÖS**

reputable [ˈrepjʊtəbl] **etc.** ← (= angesehen; zuverlässig)

SERIÖS: (1) (angesehen, in gutem Ruf stehend) reputable, respectable, renowned [rɪˈnaʊnd]
(2) (zuverlässig, vertrauenswürdig) reliable, trustworthy
(3) (solide, reell) sound

(1) *Club Tenerife* ist ein **seriöses** britisches Touristik-Unternehmen mit Büros in Großbritannien, Spanien und den Kanarischen Inseln.
Club Tenerife is a **reputable** British tourist company with offices in Great Britain, Spain and the Canary Islands.
Bald darauf betrat ein **seriös** aussehender Herr die Bank.
A little later a **respectable** looking gentleman entered the bank.
Herr Jones, ein **seriöser** Rechtsanwalt, ist auf diesem Gebiet seit vielen Jahren tätig.
Mr. Jones, a **renowned** solicitor, has been working in the field for many years.
(2) In unserem Krankenhaus kommen nur **seriöse** Behandlungsmethoden zur Anwendung.
In our hospital only **reliable** methods of treatment are used.
Die algerische Delegation erwies sich als **seriöser** Verhandlungspartner.
The Algerian delegation proved a **trustworthy** partner in the negotiations.
(3) Der neue Trainer Graham Taylor verfügt über **seriöse** Management-Methoden und ist zweifellos der richtige Mann für die englische Nationalmannschaft.
The new coach, Graham Taylor, has **sound** management methods and there is no doubt he is the right man for the English national side.

serious: ernst, ernsthaft

"I'm not joking, I'm absolutely **serious**," my friend commented.
"Ich spaße nicht herum, ich meine es wirklich **ernst**", erläuterte mir mein Freund.

The Wiltshire Constabulary takes speeding very **seriously**. They are equipped with the latest technology in this field.
Die Polizei in Wiltshire nimmt Geschwindigkeitsüberschreitungen sehr **ernst**. Sie verfügt über die neueste Technologie auf diesem Gebiet.
Ayrton Senna considered the English driver Nigel Mansell as his only **serious** Formula One rival.
Ayrton Senna betrachtete den englischen Fahrer Nigel Mansell als seinen einzigen **ernsthaften** Konkurrenten in der Formel 1.

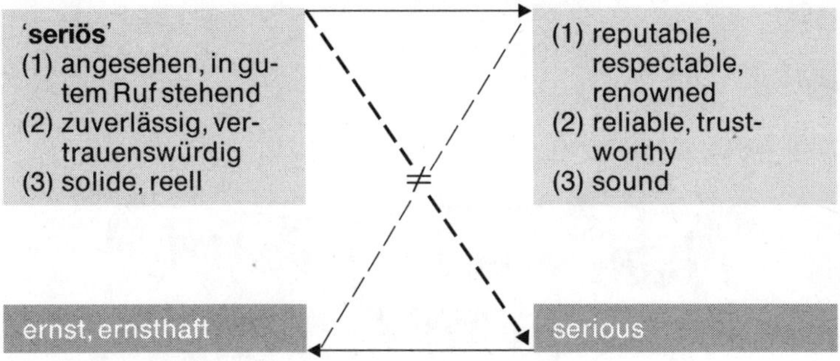

FALSE FRIENDS IN CONTEXT

The Rottweiler – A Devil Dog?

Baby Gordon's Mother: ... the devil dog leapt on my six-month-old boy as he slept in his cot and inflicted ________ (1) injuries on him.
Doctor in Casualty: So what exactly happened to the little boy?
Baby Gordon's Mother (still in a state of shock): It was a ________ (2) attack by our two-year-old Rottweiler dog, Pungo. Little Gordon was bitten on his spine down to his bottom and was lying in a pool of blood.
Family Doctor (after examining the baby carefully): Your boy will have to go into intensive care at Birmingham Children's Hospital. He's also got ________ (3) internal injuries.
Baby Gordon's Mother: I can't believe what happened.

* * *

NSPCC Representative (a few days later): . . . Rottweilers are potentially lethal and we are very concerned about them. Where did you buy it?
Baby Gordon's Father: I bought the dog from a ________ (4) dealer, who said it was used to being with children.
NSPCC Representative: A baby should never be left alone with *any* dog. Your little boy may have a ________ (5) spinal injury. I'm afraid your Rottweiler will have to be put down.
(NSPCC = *N*ational *S*ociety for the *P*revention of *C*ruelty to *Ch*ildren)

SOLUTION

(1) serious (2) serious (3) serious (4) reputable (5) serious

SPENDIEREN ≠ spend

spend

SPENDIEREN
(jdn. zu etwas einladen etc.)

stand s. o. sth. etc.

SPENDIEREN: (1) (jdn. zu etwas einladen) buy s. o. sth.; stand s. o. sth.
(2) (jdn. mit etwas verwöhnen) treat s. o. to sth.

(1) Mein Tennispartner **spendierte** uns einen Campari und duschte sich danach kalt.
My tennis partner **bought** us a Campari and then had a cold shower.
Als die Damenmannschaft des Heidelberger Tennisclubs die Deutsche Meisterschaft 1988 gewann, **spendierte** der Präsident ihnen mehrere Runden Champagner.
When the ladies' team of the Heidelberg Tennis Club won the German Championships in 1988, the club president **stood** them several rounds of champagne.
(2) Hast du schon das Neueste gehört? Unser Chef hat seiner neuen Sekretärin zum Geburtstag einen neuen Diamantring **spendiert**.
Have you heard? Our boss **treated** his new secretary **to** a new diamond ring on her birthday.

Note: sich etwas gönnen, sich etwas leisten = treat oneself to sth.
"**Treat yourself to** a test drive to find out what the new car is like," the car dealer suggested.

spend (on): (1) ausgeben (für)
(2) (Urlaub etc.) verbringen (**see** spenden ≠ spend)

(1) Gianni Agnelli **spent** over £ 25 million **on** new footballers, only to lose 5-1 to Napoli in the first league match of the new season.
Gianni Agnelli **gab** über 25 Millionen Pfund **für** neue Fußballer **aus** und verlor prompt 5:1 gegen Neapel im ersten Ligaspiel der neuen Saison.
(2) We **spent** our holidays in a small place near Eastbourne this year.
Wir **verbrachten** unsere Ferien in einem kleinen Ort bei Eastbourne in diesem Jahr.

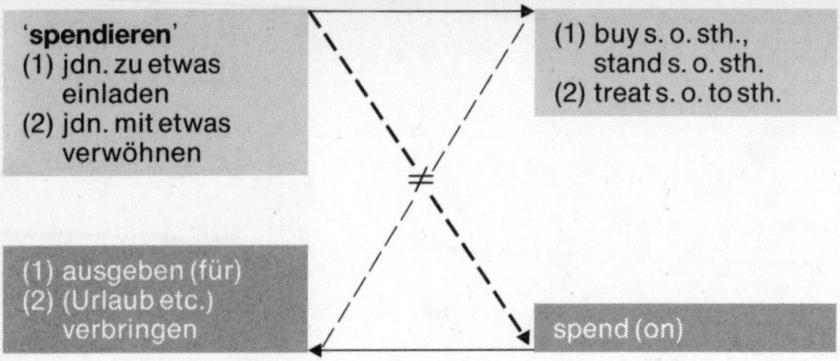

FALSE FRIENDS IN CONTEXT

The Wrong Diagnosis

Health Secretary: This country has ________ (1) its citizens to benefits in the *N*ational *H*ealth *S*ervice (= NHS) which people in other nations do not enjoy. Last year's reform of the Health Service brought improvements in many areas.
First Patient: I can't agree. I had to wait 65 weeks to see an eye surgeon at the out-patients' department.
Health Secretary: I'm sorry to hear that. In future we'll give the money to the individual hospitals and the doctors themselves. In fact, we'll be ________ (2) more money on the NHS.
Second Patient: I don't like my doctor ________ (3) me to a lot of fine medicines which do not help me in the least.
Health Secretary: That is true. Much depends on individual responsibility.
Third Patient: I don't see what you mean.
Health Secretary: Let me give you an example. Following the death of a man, nurses found three boxes containing more than 800 Mogadon tablets and no fewer than 4,000 Valium tablets. This is individual irresponsibility. What do you say now?
Fourth Patient: It just goes to show how doctors are ________ (4) their patients to NHS benefits on a large scale. A correct diagnosis must have a correct prescription. But how many prescriptions are based on a wrong diagnosis?

SOLUTION

(1) has **treated** its citizens **to** (2) spending (3) **treating** me **to** (4) treating . . . to

STIPENDIUM ≠ stipend

stipend [ˈstaɪpend]

STIPENDIUM

scholarship [ˈskɒləʃɪp] **etc.**

STIPENDIUM: (1) scholarship
(2) (Forschungs**stipendium**) fellowship
(3) (staatliche Studienförderung, in etwa Bafög) (state) grant
(4) (meist: Begabten**stipendium**, Ausbildungsbeihilfe) bursary

(1) John ging direkt von der Schule nach Oxford. Er unterzog sich einer Prüfung und erhielt ein **Stipendium**.
John went directly from school to Oxford. He sat an exam and won a **scholarship**.
(2) Unser neuer Dozent hat ein **Forschungsstipendium** in Cambridge bekommen. Da muß man schon sehr tüchtig sein.
Our new lecturer has won a **fellowship** at Cambridge. You've got to be pretty good.
(3) "Mein **Stipendium** (in etwa: Bafög) reicht nicht für das, was ich zum Leben benötige", betonte der Student.
"My **grant** doesn't cover what I need to spend," the student emphasized.
Die Studenten beklagen sich schon wieder über ihre **Stipendien**. Vielleicht könnten **Stipendien** in Form von Gutscheinen für Kleidung, Bücher, Miete gezahlt werden.
Students are complaining about their **grants** once again. Perhaps **grants** could be paid in coupons for clothes, books, rent.
(4) Als sein Vater plötzlich starb, wurde dem begabten Studenten ein **Stipendium** seines Colleges angeboten, so daß er sein Studium fortsetzen konnte.
When his father suddenly died the bright student was offered a college **bursary** so that he could continue his studies.
Dieser Junge aus einer Arbeiterfamilie erhielt eine **Ausbildungsbeihilfe**, um eine Privatschule besuchen zu können.
That boy from a working-class family received a **bursary** to go to a private school.

stipend: (1) Gehalt, Besoldung für Geistliche
(2) Aufwandsentschädigung; AE "Sportlergehalt" (für College-Studenten)

Note: 'Aufwandsentschädigung' in BE is normally **allowance**.

(1) "I'm doing the work of four vicars, and unless the **stipend** is raised there could be serious problems," the country vicar complained to his Oxford Diocese.
"Ich leiste die Arbeit von vier Pfarrern, und wenn das **Gehalt** nicht angehoben wird, könnten ernste Probleme entstehen", beschwerte sich der Landpfarrer bei seiner Oxforder Diözese.
Compared with the **stipend** for German clergymen that for British clergymen is low.
Die **Besoldung** britischer Geistlicher ist im Vergleich zu deutschen Geistlichen niedrig.
(2) "I'm not totally opposed to a **stipend** for college athletes, such as a $ 75 a month **stipend** for football players," the Nebraska football coach suggested.
"Ich bin nicht völlig gegen eine **Aufwandentschädigung** für College-Sportler, beispielsweise ein **Sportlergehalt** von monatlich 75 Dollar für Fußballspieler", schlug der Fußballtrainer von Nebraska vor.

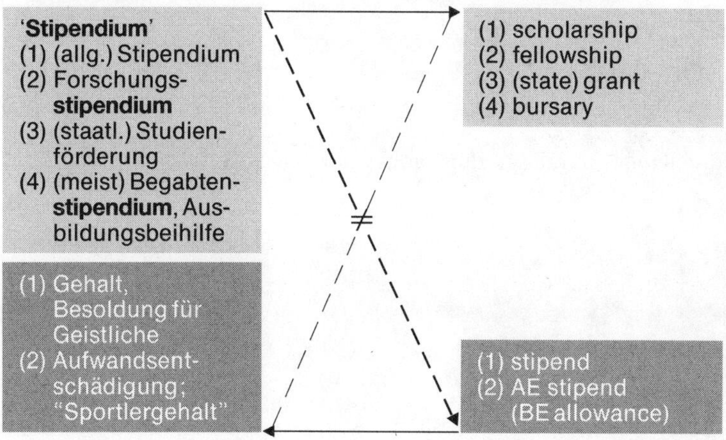

Smart Idea to Pocket the Difference

Robin (a pupil after looking briefly at a morning paper on the bus to school): I'm fed up reading about maintenance ________ (1) for students who have to work till the early hours.
Mrs. Saunders: But they do deserve our sympathy.
Robin: Do they really want our sympathy? They work on their projects while on a handsome ________ (2). Look at me. I'm 14 and almost every day I work until 1 a. m. to finish my homework without getting a ________ (3).
Mrs. Saunders: Come to think of it, even curates receive a nice ________ (4) for their sermons which are boring in many cases.
Robin: That's what I'm saying. I'd like...
Mrs. Saunders (interrupting him): Anyway. If you gave up watching East Enders or Brookside on TV, you could easily finish your homework by 8 p. m., do a paper round in the early morning and have some pocket money to look forward to. What about it, Robin?
Robin: Not a bad idea. But I'd prefer to have a ________ (5) for pupils in Britain. It would enable older pupils to be less reliant on their parents.

SOLUTION

(1) grants; scholarships (2) grant; scholarship (3) grant; scholarship
(4) stipend (5) grant

SYMPATHISCH ≠ sympathetic

sympathetic [ˌsɪmpəˈθetɪk]

pleasant; congenial [kənˈdʒɪ:njəl] **etc.**

SYMPATHISCH
(= angenehm, zusagend etc.)

SYMPATHISCH: (1) Adj. (bezogen auf Personen) pleasant, likeable, nice
(2) Adj. (bezogen auf Personen oder Umstände) congenial, agreeable
(3) Verb (sympathisch sein) take (to a person), like (a person)

(1) Für mich ist Tracy die **sympathischste** Person, der ich je begegnet bin.
For me Tracy is the **most likeable** person I've ever met.
Ihre **sympathische** Art hat mich einfach überwältigt.
Her **pleasant** manner simply overwhelmed me.
Lord Hume ist als ein außergewöhnlich **sympathischer** Mann beschrieben worden, weil er ein geborener Diplomat ist.
Lord Hume has been described as an exceptionally **nice** man because he is a born diplomat.
(2) Zwei Dinge kamen unserer Beziehung entgegen: die **sympathische** Umgebung von Grasmere und das **sympathische** Arbeitsklima.
Two things influenced our relationship favourably: the **congenial** surroundings of Grasmere and the **congenial** office atmosphere.
Nichts ist **sympathischer**, als sich in den Ferien der übrigen Familie anzuschließen.
Nothing is **more agreeable** than joining the rest of the family during the holidays.
(3) "Jim **war** mir vom ersten Augenblick an **sympathisch**", bestätigte Tracy später.
"I **took to** Jim from the first moment," Tracy confirmed later.
Jeremy **ist** mir sehr **sympathisch**.
I **like** Jeremy very much.

(be) sympathetic (to): (1) mitfühlend (sein gegenüber); anteilnehmend (sein gegenüber)
(2) wohlwollend (sein gegenüber), verständnisvoll (sein gegenüber)

(1) A mother whose screaming baby died after being given some sleeping powder was freed by a **sympathetic** judge.
Eine Mutter, deren schreiendes Kind nach Einnahme von etwas Schlafpulver starb, wurde von einem **mitfühlenden** Richter freigesprochen.
(2) My boss **was sympathetic to** my complaints.
Mein Chef stand meinen Beschwerden **wohlwollend** gegenüber.
The student found his new professor very **sympathetic** when he told him he had failed in the last exam.
Der Student fand seinen neuen Professor sehr **verständnisvoll**, als er ihm mitteilte, er wäre im letzten Examen durchgefallen.

'**sympathisch**'
(1) bezogen auf Personen
(2) bezogen auf Personen oder Umstände
(3) Verb: sympathisch sein

(1) adj.: pleasant, likeable, nice
(2) adj.: congenial, agreeable
(3) verb: take (to a person), like (a person)

(1) mitfühlend (sein gegenüber); anteilnehmend (sein gegenüber)
(2) wohlwollend (sein gegenüber); verständnisvoll (sein gegenüber)

(1) + (2) adj. (or verb): (be) sympathetic (to)

FALSE FRIENDS IN CONTEXT

Schooling – Mothers' Concern

Mrs. Jacket: Look at our schools today. Our present system is in pretty much of a mess.
Mrs. Young: That's why I'm still in favour of the old system of education.
Mrs. Jacket: Are you really?
Mrs. Young: In my view only our old grammar schools provide a ________ (1) atmosphere.

Mrs. Jacket: I don't go along with that. It is unfair to classify a child's intelligence at the age of eleven.
Mrs. Young: As I see it, our Americanised comprehensives are too large and impersonal, and what's more, every child does not have an equal chance.
Mrs. Jacket: I really don't know.
Mrs. Young: I think most of us are not truly ________ (2) to our children's needs.
Mrs. Jacket: I agree. Most of our children have not reached their natural intelligence peak at the age of eleven.
Mrs. Young: Look at John. He was such a ________ (3) boy. Now he's developed into a bully with very little education.

SOLUTION

(1) congenial (2) are . . . sympathetic to (3) likeable/nice

TEMPERAMENTVOLL ≠ temperamental

temperamental [ˌtempərəˈmentl] → **TEMPERAMENT-VOLL** (lebhaft, munter etc.) ← **vivacious** [vɪˈveɪʃəs] **etc.**

TEMPERAMENTVOLL: (lebhaft, munter) vivacious, lively

Beim Tanzen zeigte unsere italienische Nachbarin, was für eine **temperamentvolle** Frau sie wirklich ist.
During the dance our Italian neighbour showed what a **vivacious** woman she really was.
Die **temperamentvolle** Art des Conferenciers riß die Zuschauer förmlich mit.
The presenter's **lively** manner enthused the audience.

temperamental: (1) (vom Menschen) launisch, launenhaft
(2) (vom Auto etc.) nicht zuverlässig; 'im Stich gelassen'
(3) (vom Charakter) von der Veranlagung her

(1) The **temperamental** Californian student had been at the heart of the trouble at our students' hostel.
Der **launische** kalifornische Student war der Unruheherd in unserem Studentenheim gewesen.
(2) In contrast to my daughter's Peugeot, my Mercedes has never been **temperamental** after a cold winter's night.
Im Gegensatz zum Peugeot meiner Tochter hat mich mein Mercedes noch nie nach einer kalten Winternacht **im Stich gelassen**.
(3) Our cricket captain is **temperamentally** unsuited to cope with criticism.
Unser Kricket-Kapitän kann **von seiner Veranlagung her** keine Kritik ertragen.

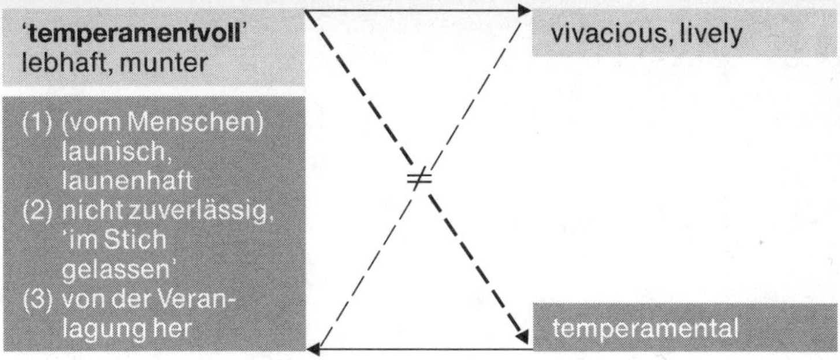

FALSE FRIENDS IN CONTEXT

Telling the Time

(one of Britain's memorable *Letters to the Editor*)
Sir, my ________ (1) neighbour shouts at her clock to make it go. Her manner is, I believe, a little too ________ (2).
Sir, my bedroom clock only goes if you lay it face down. This is what I call ________ (3).
Sir, my aunt's living-room clock only goes if you lay it on its back. That's ________ (4), too, isn't it?
Sir, I wonder why people say we humans are ________ (5), too.
(name and address supplied)

SOLUTION

(1) vivacious (2) lively (3) temperamental (4) temperamental (5) temperamental

TRAKT ≠ tract

tract

TRAKT

section (of a building) etc.

(= Gebäude**trakt** etc.)

TRAKT: (1) (Gebäude**trakt**) section (of a building etc.)
(2) (Seiten**trakt**) wing (of a building etc.)

(1) Das Forum im Hauptteil des Kirchen**trakts** schließt jetzt Gesellschaftsräume, Kunst- und Werkräume, Geschäfte und ein Hallenbad mit ein.
A forum in the main body of the church **section** now includes lounges, art and craft classes, shops and an indoor pool.
(2) Am 17. Oktober 1989 brachten zwei Sicherheitsbeamte Paul Hill, einen der vier Unschuldigen von Guildford, in einen anderen Gefängnis**trakt**, wo er zwei Tage später freigelassen wurde.
On October 17, 1989 security officers took Paul Hill, one of the innocent Guildford Four, to another **wing** of the prison to be freed two days later.
Der Besitzer des Schlosses bewohnt nur noch den Ost**trakt**.
The castle owner lives in its east **wing** only.

tract: (1) Traktat, kleine Flugschrift, Schrift
(2) Gebiet, (Land-)Strich

Note: The usual word for 'Flugschrift' is **pamphlet**.

(1) Some churchleaders had even published a **tract** on birth control in Britain.
Einige Kirchenführer hatten sogar eine **Schrift** zur Geburtenregelung in Großbritannien veröffentlicht.
The young Socialists were handing out **tracts** to workers leaving the car factory.
Die Jungsozialisten teilten **Traktate** an Arbeiter aus, die gerade die Autofabrik verließen.
(2) Like a mediaeval nobleman the former East German union boss would take over great **tracts** of countryside so that he and his friends could go hunting in peace.

Wie ein mittelalterlicher Edelmann pflegte der frühere ostdeutsche Gewerkschaftsführer große Land**gebiete** an sich zu bringen, damit er und seine Freunde in Ruhe jagen gehen konnten.
As far as he could remember his grandfather had bought the **tract** of land around the lake in the last century. Should he sell it?
Soweit er sich erinnern konnte, hatte sein Großvater den Land**strich** um den See im letzten Jahrhundert gekauft. Sollte er ihn verkaufen?

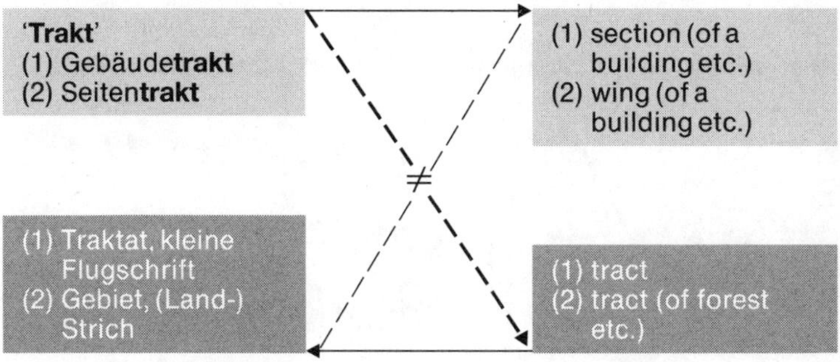

FALSE FRIENDS IN CONTEXT

In the Family Line

Artist: . . . It's true I'm a bit of an eccentric, but most artists are. Like Picasso who used to work in an old castle in Antibes.
Art Reporter: What are you working on just now?
Artist: I'm still covering the walls in the west ________ (1) of the castle with some giant murals. I've been working on those wall paintings for more than 15 years.
Art Reporter: And you get your inspiration for these murals from the estate?
Artist: Yes, I love the country around here and the ________ (2) of land our family inherited. In fact, it's been a family estate for 300 years.
Art Reporter: But what do you use the east ________ (3) of the old castle for?
Artist: That's where my family and other members of the household live.

Art Reporter: Apart from painting you recently published a _____ (4) on religious matters.
Artist: That's right. And I intend to continue writing on the main social and ecological issues of our country such as oil pollution and the conservation of our forests.

SOLUTION

(1) **wing/section** of the castle (2) tract of land (3) **wing/section** of the old castle (4) tract

TRANSPIRIEREN ≠ transpire

transpire [træn'spaɪə]

TRANSPIRIEREN
(gewählt für
'**schwitzen**')

perspire [pə'spaɪə]

TRANSPIRIEREN: (1) (gewählteres Wort für **schwitzen**) perspire
(2) (schwitzen) sweat [swet]

(1) "Ich habe die falschen Kleider angezogen. Ich **transpiriere** in der Hitze zu sehr, und ich bitte Sie, nochmals umzukehren", befahl Lady Ashley.
"I've put on the wrong clothes. I'm **perspiring** too much in this heat. Please let us go back," demanded Lady Ashley.
Die meisten Damen waren nicht auf die plötzliche Hitzewelle eingestellt und begannen zu **transpirieren**; Fächer erfreuten sich großer Nachfrage.
Most of the ladies were not prepared for the sudden heat wave and began to **perspire**; fans were in great demand.
(2) "Man **schwitzt** viel in der Wüstenhitze. Mein Hemd trieft so richtig", bemerkte einer der Männer.
"You **sweat** a lot in the desert heat. My shirt is soaking," remarked one of the men.

Note: warm werden, ins Schwitzen kommen = break sweat (sport)
The players had hardly broken **sweat** when Sharp drove his team mate's pass into the net.

transpire: (1) bekannt werden, sich herausstellen
(2) sich abspielen, vor sich gehen; passieren; sich anbahnen

(1) When the Spanish delegation left London, it **transpired** that no agreement had been reached on the Gibraltar problem.
Als die spanische Delegation London verließ, **stellte sich heraus**, daß keine Übereinkunft im Gibraltar-Problem erzielt worden war.
There were some American soldiers, it now **transpires**, who refused to kill in the My Lai massacre in Vietnam.

Es gab einige amerikanische Soldaten, die sich – wie erst jetzt **bekannt wurde** – weigerten, beim My-Lai-Massaker in Vietnam zu töten.
(2) What **transpired** recently should have made you aware not to make any decisive moves on the work front.
Was **sich** kürzlich **abspielte**, sollte Ihnen verdeutlicht haben, keine entscheidenden Veränderungen im Berufsleben vorzunehmen.
"What **transpires** during the next few weeks should make you realize that perhaps your future security can only be found in another country," the astrologer predicted.
"Was sich in den nächsten Wochen **anbahnt**, sollte Ihnen bewußtmachen, daß Ihre künftige Sicherheit möglicherweise nur in einem anderen Land gefunden werden kann", sagte der Astrologe voraus.

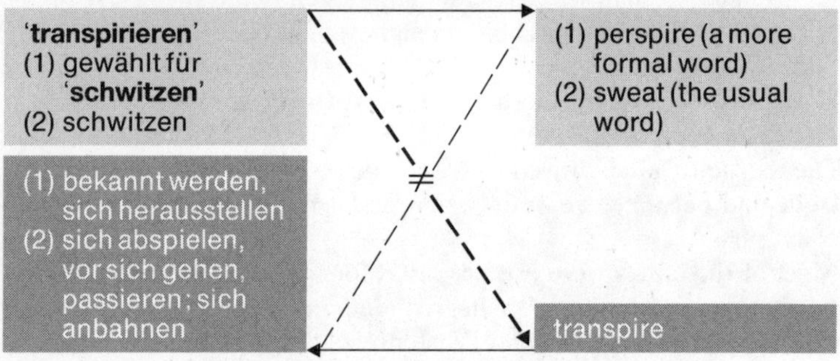

FALSE FRIENDS IN CONTEXT

The Time Ahead: Your Stars

First Starcall (on the phone-in horoscope line): I've got a few problems. Can you predict the weeks ahead for me? My star sign is Leo.
Astrologer: It's not easy, but I'll try. You rush around like a bull in a china shop early on, but what ________ (1) around the time of the New Moon will set the tone for weeks to come. Money gives cause for concern, at times you'll even ________ (2) when life does not go to plan. But understand that you need to relax and give your physical system a chance to recover. Bye (Presses button for the second phone-in).
Second Starcall: Hallo? Is that the horoscope line?
Astrologer: That's right. Can I help you?

Second Starcaller: My star sign is Virgo. Can you advise me on the month ahead?
Astrologer: Certainly. Your stars are on collision course. Business and legal matters must be handled with utmost caution. What ________ (3) during the next few weeks should raise your spirits. Friends and team mates can probably offer you more than close companions today. Expect the unexpected. Sudden surprises could unnerve you and make you ________ (4). Try not to make any snap decisions about your future. Bye (Presses button for the third phone-in).
Third Starcall: My personal star sign is . . .

SOLUTION

(1) transpires (2) sweat (3) transpires (4) sweat

UNSYMPATHISCH ≠ unsympathetic

unsympathetic
[ˌʌnˌsɪmpəˈθetɪk]

UNSYMPATHISCH

unpleasant etc.

UNSYMPATHISCH:	(1)	(adj.) unpleasant, disagreeable
	(2)	(unsympathisch sein) (verb) dislike, not like

(1) Meine Freundin konnte den Klang der **unsympathischen** Stimme der Schauspielerin nicht länger ertragen; deshalb verließ sie die Theatervorstellung.
My girlfriend couldn't stand the sound of the actress's **unpleasant** voice any longer; so she left the theatre.
Während des Vorstellungsgesprächs entpuppte sich der erste Bewerber als ein ganz **unsympathischer** Bursche.
During his interview the first applicant turned out to be an extremely **disagreeable** fellow.
(2) Der neue Kollege war mir gleich vom ersten Augenblick an **unsympathisch**.
I **disliked** my new colleague right from the start.
Es **ist** mir äußerst **unsympathisch**, Sie mitten in der Nacht anrufen zu müssen.
I really **don't like** having to ring you up in the middle of the night.

(be) unsympathetic (to):	(1)	(Adj.) teilnahmslos, gleichgültig
	(2)	(Adj.) gefühllos, herzlos
	(3)	(Verb) uninteressiert sein (an), desinteressiert sein (an)

(1) When the secret agent realized that I depended on his help, he listened to everything else in a thoroughly **unsympathetic** way.
Als der Geheimagent erkannte, daß ich auf seine Hilfe angewiesen war, hörte er sich alles andere völlig **teilnahmslos** an.
(2) Her **unsympathetic** treatment of the children was a disgrace.
Ihre **gefühllose** Behandlung der Kinder war eine Schande.
(3) The film producer **was** not **unsympathetic to** the millionaire's offer.
Der Filmproduzent **war an** dem Angebot des Millionärs nicht **uninteressiert**.

When Justine heard that her ex-husband had lost his job, she **was** utterly **unsympathetic**.
Als Justine hörte, daß ihr Exmann die Stellung verloren hatte, **war** sie völlig **desinteressiert**.

	≠	
(1) unsympathisch (2) unsympathisch sein		(1) (adj.) unpleasant, disagreeable (2) (verb) dislike, not like
(1) teilnahmslos, gleichgültig (2) gefühllos, herzlos (3) uninteressiert sein (an), desinteressiert sein (an)		(1) (adj.) unsympathetic (2) (verb) be unsympathetic (to)

FALSE FRIENDS IN CONTEXT

Caring Nurses, Uncaring Doctors?

Night Nurse: Your tone of voice sounds so ________ (1) when you start talking about the health service. Is there a reason?
First Patient: I've been undergoing surgery without proper anaesthetic, and now I've got a stiff leg which is going to be amputated. I ________ (2) (**unsympathisch sein**) the medical staff of this hospital from the very first moment.
Second Patient: After my operation I had to contend with the ________ (3) attitude of doctors here.
Night Nurse: I'm sorry to hear that.
Third Patient: It's the same as in animal experiments. I wonder how many dumb creatures have suffered the same way at the hands of ________ (4) doctors.
Night Nurse: But I do care for you, don't I?

SOLUTION

(1) unpleasant (2) disliked (3) **unsympathetic** attitude (4) **unsympathetic** doctors

FALSE FRIENDS TRAPS TEST 4

DIFFICULT FALSE FRIENDS

1.a. Just because I'm a traffic warden it is taken for granted that I'm not a ________ person (**sympathisch ≠ sympathetic**).
1.b. Most men would prefer a female secretary because she's likely to be more ________ to their moods (**sympathisch ≠ sympathetic**).
2.a. "I'm afraid I can't help you," said the chemist firmly. "You haven't got a ________ from your doctor (**Rezept ≠ receipt**)."
2.b. The new government hasn't found a ________ for unemployment (**Rezept ≠ receipt**).
3.a. "Shouldn't we have a ________ discussion about the problems in our company (**seriös ≠ serious**)? The situation is ________ and is worsening," the manager took the initiative (**seriös ≠ serious**).
3.b. "Don't buy from market stalls – go to ________ dealers and shops," the expert advised during the phone-in (**seriös ≠ serious**).
4.a. "I think the real reason is deeply embedded inside the 14-year-old's ________ mind," stated the psychologist calmly (**sensibel ≠ sensible**).
4.b. It seems ________ to close down the theatre now rather than wait for a crisis (**sensibel ≠ sensible**).
5.a. "Unless the ________ is raised there could be a growing dilemma for the Church of England," admitted the vicar reluctantly (**Stipendium ≠ stipend**).
5.b. She went to Bradenton in Florida after winning a $ 70,000 sporting ________ (**Stipendium ≠ stipend**).
6. Why don't you ________ (**spendieren**) me a drink? I won a Silver Medal at the Olympics last year.
7. "What a ________ (**unsympathisch**) person my boss is," the new secretary thought to herself and turned away abruptly.
8. It was April 1st when I heard on the news that Yugoslavia had annexed Albania. Later it ________ (**sich herausstellen**) it was a joke. Poor old BBC. Somehow they don't seem to get it right.
9. "The new ________ (**Trakt**) of the building can't be used yet," the headmaster told us after the summer vacation.
10. "It would be more ________ (**rentabel**) to stop production here and start production in East European countries," the manager suggested. "What about Hungary?"

ANSWER SHEET: TRUE FRIENDS TEST 4

DIFFICULT FALSE FRIENDS

1.a. Just because I'm a traffic warden it is taken for granted that I'm not a **likeable** person.
1.b. Most men would prefer a female secretary because she's likely to be more **sympathetic to** their moods.
2.a. "I'm afraid I can't help you," said the chemist firmly. "You haven't got a **prescription** from your doctor."
2.b. The new government hasn't found a **remedy/cure** for unemployment.
3.a. "Shouldn't we have a **serious** discussion about the problems in our company? The situation is **serious** and is worsening," the manager took the initiative.
3.b. "Don't buy from market stalls – go to **reputable** dealers and shops," the expert advised during the phone-in.
4.a. "I think the real reason is deeply embedded inside the 14-year-old's **sensitive** mind," stated the psychologist calmly.
4.b. It seems **sensible** to close down the theatre now rather than wait for a crisis.
5.a. "Unless the **stipend** is raised there could be a growing dilemma for the Church of England," admitted the vicar reluctantly.
5.b. She went to Bradenton in Florida after winning a $ 70,000 sporting **scholarship**.
6. Why don't you **stand** me a drink? I won a Silver Medal at the Olympics last year.
7. "What a **disagreeable**/an **unpleasant** person my boss is," the new secretary thought to herself and turned away abruptly.
8. It was April 1st when I heard on the news that Yugoslavia had annexed Albania. Later it **transpired** it was a joke. Poor old BBC. Somehow they don't seem to get it right.
9. "The new **wing/section** of the building can't be used yet," the headmaster told us after the summer vacation.
10. "It would be more **profitable** to stop production here and start production in East European countries," the manager suggested. "What about Hungary?"

TEIL II

PARTICULARLY DIFFICULT FALSE FRIENDS

TERRIBLE TWINS KURZ-EINFÜHRUNG

Was sind Terrible Twins?

Der Ausdruck bezeichnet im Englischen Wortpaare – in der Regel Adjektive oder Substantive –, die auf -**ic** oder -**ical** wie etwa **electric/electrical** enden und gleichzeitig verschiedene Bedeutung haben. Außerdem muß im Deutschen ein gleicher oder ähnlicher Begriff, hier **elektrisch**, vorhanden sein.
Der Ausdruck *Terrible Twin* stammt von Terry Hawkes, der diesen False Friends-Typ 1976 erstmals als besonders schwierig für Englischlernende in Peru erkannte. Das gilt auch für den deutschen Sprachbenutzer des Englischen.
Eine besondere Gruppe unter den Terrible Twins bilden Wortpaare vom Typ (*) **critic/critical** (Kritiker/kritisch), die dem Lernenden häufig Schwierigkeiten bereiten. Diese werden wegen der unterschiedlichen Wortart (Substantiv/Adjektiv) als *scheinbare* Terrible Twins bezeichnet.

ELEKTRISCH ◑ electric

electric ··········▸ **ELEKTRISCH**

electrical ——————▸ (allgemein auf Elektrizität bezogen)

ELEKTRISCH: (1) (allgemein auf Elektrizität bezogen) electrical
(2) (**Elektro-**') in combinations such as '**electrical** industry'

Note: **Electrical** is mainly used before 'general' terms.

(1) Ein Ampère ist eine **elektrische** Einheit.
An ampère is an **electrical** unit.
Unsere Abteilung hat schon seit Jahren an einer besseren Nutzung der **elektrischen** Energie gearbeitet.
Our department has been working towards a better use of **electrical** energy for years.
(2) Die Erfindung des Telefons durch A. G. Bell zog einen großen Bedarf an **Elektro**ingenieuren nach sich.
The invention of the telephone by A. G. Bell created a great need for **electrical** engineers.
Beim Gang durch das Warenhaus lief mir Helen in der **Elektro**abteilung über den Weg. Was für eine Überraschung!
As I was walking through the department store I bumped into Helen in the **electrical** department. What a surprise!

Note: **Elektro**technik = **electrical** engineering
Elektrogeschäft = **electrical** store
Elektroindustrie = **electrical** industry
Elektroinstallateure = **electrical** fitters

electric: (1) elektrisch (betrieben)
(2) '**Elektro-**' (in combinations)
(3) erregend, spannungsgeladen; elektrisierend (fig.)

Note: **Electric** is mainly used before the name of an apparatus.

(1) **Electric** current is needed to work any kind of **electric** clock or **electric** blanket.
Elektrischer Strom ist notwendig, damit **elektrische** Uhren oder **elektrische** Heizkissen funktionieren.
In this heat I can't manage without an **electric** fan.
In dieser Hitze kann ich ohne einen **elektrischen** Ventilator nicht auskommen.
An **electric** razor has an **electric** motor.
Ein **elektrischer** Rasierapparat hat einen **elektrischen** Motor.
(2) Trembling from the **electric** shock received from the wires, the Tube train driver averted another disaster at King's Cross.
Obwohl er noch von dem **Elektro**schock von den Leitungen zitterte, verhinderte der U-Bahn-Zugführer ein weiteres Unglück bei King's Cross.
(3) In an **electric** atmosphere at Flushing Meadow, Edberg again beat Lendl over five sets.
Edberg schlug Lendl wieder über fünf Sätze in einer **spannungsgeladenen** Atmosphäre in Flushing Meadow.
The new Prime Minister's speech had an **electric** effect on the delegates at the party conference.
Die Rede des neuen Premierministers hatte eine **elektrisierende** Wirkung auf die Delegierten beim Parteitag.

Note: **electric** light = **elektrisches** Licht
electric windows = **elektrische** Fenster(heber) (Auto)

Compare: The Terrible Twins **electric** and **electrical** are generally interchangeable in the following cases.
Electric equipment/**electrical** equipment as well as **electric** machine/**electrical** machine are both used without difference in meaning although **electrical** equipment (= **Elektro**geräte) and **electrical** machine (= **Elektro**maschine) is more generally used.

'elektrisch'
(1) elektrisch (allgemein auf Elektrizität bezogen)
(2) **'Elektro-'**

(1) electrical
(2) in compounds such as '**electrical** engineer'

(1) elektrisch (betrieben)
(2) **'Elektro-'**
(3) erregend, spannungsgeladen; elektrisierend (fig.)

(1) + (3) electric
(2) in compounds such as '**electric** generator'

FALSE FRIENDS IN CONTEXT

UFO Beam Riddle

A terrified family yesterday told a reporter of their encounter with a UFO. This is what Tony Silvestri, 36, and his frightened wife Gwendoline, 33, told him:
Tony: On the way home with my family a beam of brilliant green light, as if from an ________ (1) discharge, filled our car for several seconds. It was so bright I couldn't see through the windows. It was just like a scene from *Close Encounters.*
Reporter: Do you believe in UFOs or have you any explanation for what happened?
Tony: Until then we didn't believe in them. I left the car and couldn't see anything outside which might have caused it. But I'm not an ________ (2) engineer.
Reporter: What did you do next?
Gwendoline: My husband thought at first the car had an ________ (3) fault. But when he checked, there was nothing wrong.
Reporter: But didn't something like ________ (4) light come from outside?
Tony: It certainly wasn't a case of being dazzled by another car's lights. By the way, all this happened as we were driving through the village of Felinfach – that's here in West Wales.
Reporter: Thank you.

SOLUTION

(1) **electrical** discharge (2) **electrical** engineer (3) **electrical** fault
(4) **electric** light

HISTORISCH ◑ historic

historic ·········· → **HISTORISCH**

historical ―――――― → **HISTORISCH** (= geschichtlich bezeugt)

HISTORISCH: (1) (geschichtlich bezeugt, überliefert) historical
(2) (geschichtswissenschaftlich etc.) historical

Note: **Historical** either means concerned with or found in past events **or** based on history.

(1) Wie die meisten anderen Feste wurde Bonfire Night von seinem **historischen** Datum auf das nächstliegende Wochenende verschoben.
Like most other festivals, Bonfire Night has been shifted from its **historical** date to the nearest weekend.
Der *Gute-Burgen-Führer* führt 2000 Burgen auf und gibt eine Fünf-Sterne-Bewertung auf der Grundlage des **historischen** Interesses.
The *Good Castle Guide* lists 2,000 castles and gives five star ratings for **historical** interest.
Impington hatte zu keiner Zeit eine **historische** Bedeutung.
At no time did Impington have any **historical** significance.
(2) "Du wirst nie lernen, **historisch** zu denken", kritisierte ihn sein Geschichtslehrer.
"You'll never learn to think in **historical** terms," his history teacher criticized him.
Es ist wenig bekannt, daß A. C. Doyle, der Schöpfer von Sherlock Holmes, auch einen **historischen** Roman, *Sir Nigel*, schrieb.
It is little known that A. C. Doyle, the creator of Sherlock Holmes, also wrote a **historical** novel, *Sir Nigel*.

historic: (1) historisch bedeutend, geschichtlich bedeutsam
(2) geschichtsträchtig

Note: **Historic** either means important or memorable in history **or** having a long history.

(1) Prince Charles surpassed himself by making an excellent speech on this **historic** occasion.
Prinz Charles übertraf sich, als er bei diesem **historisch bedeutenden** Anlaß eine famose Rede hielt.
1990 is revealing itself as one of those **historic** years, like 1789, 1815 or 1848, when everything changed.
1990 offenbart sich als eines jener **geschichtlich bedeutsamen** Jahre, wie 1789, 1815 oder 1848, als sich alles änderte.
(2) This coin commemorates an **historic** event, the Tercentenary of the Bill of Rights.
Diese Münze gedenkt eines **geschichtsträchtigen** Ereignisses, der dreihundertjährigen Wiederkehr der Bill of Rights.

Note: Bei diesem False Friend kann es sich auch um einen fachsprachlichen Terrible Twin aus dem Bereich der Steuer-Terminologie handeln.
"In accounting, however, **historic cost** is established as a variant of **historical cost**, meaning the original cost of an asset as opposed to the current cost of replacing it" (*see* Greenbaum/Whitcut, p. 340).
In der Steuer-Terminologie unterscheidet man zwei Arten von Kosten:
historic cost = **historische** Anschaffungs- oder Herstellungskosten eines Wirtschaftsguts
historical cost = **aktuelle** Wiederbeschaffungskosten eines Wirtschaftsguts.

Compare: The Battle of Hastings was an **historic** event which was to change England's course of development. **Historic** here means it was decisive and memorable or a turning point in the course of English history.
The site of the **historical** battle of Hastings is in fact a place called Battle. **Historical** in this case refers simply to the course or sequence of events.

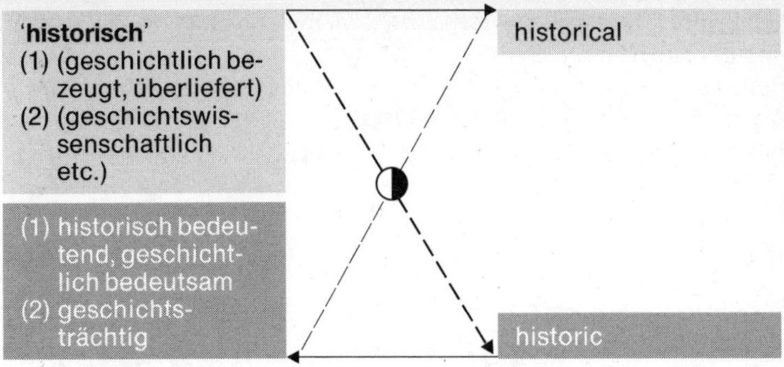

FALSE FRIENDS IN CONTEXT

A Church Row

Dean (of Salisbury Cathedral): This ________ (1) building urgently needs a new toilet block.
Secretary of the RFAC (= *R*oyal *F*ine *A*rt *C*ommission): Why? There **are** lavatories in the cathedral.
Dean: Perhaps you haven't noticed but there's an all-pervading smell in the ________ (2) cathedral which churchgoers can no longer ignore.
Secretary of the RFAC: In ________ (3) terms, Salisbury is a beautiful example of an early English cathedral. Building new lavatories south of the ________ (4) chapter house inside the cathedral would be quite wrong. In addition, it is a building with listed status, according to a ________ (5) ruling.
Dean: Apart from being a place of worship Salisbury Cathedral remains a place of ________ (6) interest for today's tourist. We are also concerned with the practical running of the Cathedral every day of the year.
Secretary of the RFAC: Well, the row over a new toilet block for tourists in the ________ (7) Salisbury Cathedral has certainly split Church and State.

SOLUTION

(1) **historic** building (2) **historic** cathedral (3) in **historical** terms (4) **historic** chapter house (5) **historic** ruling (6) **historical** interest (7) **historic** Salisbury Cathedral

KLASSISCH ◑ classic

classic

KLASSISCH
(= traditionell in Form oder Stil etc.)

classical

KLASSISCH: (1) (traditionell in Form oder Stil) classical
(2) (Musik: ernst) classical
(3) (Sprachen: tot) classical

Note: **Classical** usually applies to the (Roman, Greek, Hebrew etc.) classics such as '**classical** Greek tragedy' or to classicism as in 'the **classical** revival of Regency style'.
'**Classical** music' is serious or traditional as opposed to light or popular music.

(1) Noch heute ist eine **klassische** Bildung eine gute Grundlage.
Even today a **classical** education is a good grounding.
Das **klassische** Ballett wird auch als romantisches Ballett bezeichnet; hierfür ist *Der Nußknacker* ein typisches Beispiel.
Classical ballet has also been called romantic ballet; *The Nutcracker* is a typical example of it.
(2) Die **klassische** Musik kommt für mich vor jeder Art moderner Musik.
I prefer **classical** music to any kind of modern music.
Sandras 6000 Platten umfassende Sammlung **klassischer** Musik war auf wundersame Weise gegen Alben harter Rockmusik ausgetauscht worden.
Sandra's 6,000-strong **classical** record collection was mysteriously replaced with hard rock albums.
(3) Ich kann überhaupt kein Griechisch; ich kann noch nicht einmal das **klassische** griechische Alphabet lesen.
I don't know any Greek. I can't even read the **classical** Greek alphabet.
Nicht viele Menschen wissen, daß die folgenden drei Sprachen zu den ältesten der Welt gehören: das **klassische** Arabisch, das **klassische** Sanskrit und das **klassische** Hebräisch.
Not many people know that the following three languages are among

the oldest in the world: the **classical** Arabic language, the **classical** Sanskrit language and the **classical** Hebrew language.

classic: (1) klassisch, (arche-)typisch
(2) großartig; zeitlos
(3) '**Modell**-' (in combinations)
(4) (ein) Klassiker (Sport)
(5) die Klassiker (Lit.)

Note: **Classic** may mean – 'of the highest class' suggesting or establishing a standard as 'the **classic** English lawn'
– 'archetypal' as in 'a **classic** error'
– 'elegant, expensive' such as 'a **classic** blazer'.
Classic may also be a noun such as 'a cycling **classic**'.

(1) His behaviour is an almost **classic** example for the majority of the population.
Sein Verhalten ist ein fast **klassisches** Beispiel für die Mehrheit der Bevölkerung.
The final statement is a **classic** illustration of the philosophy of the age.
Die Schlußaussage ist als **typische** Veranschaulichung der Auffassungen des Zeitalters einzustufen.
The Tour de France is a **classic** cycling race.
Die Frankreich-Rundfahrt ist ein **klassisches** Rennen im Radsport.
(2) Sir Laurence Olivier gave a **classic** performance in Shakespeare's history play *Richard III.*
Sir Laurence Olivier bot eine **großartige** Vorstellung in Shakespeares Geschichtsdrama *Richard III.*
(3) "This was a **classic** case of mistaken identity," the judge noted in his summing-up.
"Dies war ein **Modell**fall für eine Verwechslung", führte der Richter in seiner Begründung aus.
(4) The Derby, which is held at Epsom every year, is a horse racing **classic**.
Das (englische) Derby, das jedes Jahr in Epsom ausgetragen wird, ist ein **Klassiker** des Pferderennsports.
(5) Shakespeare and Milton are among the **classics** in English literature.
Shakespeare und Milton gehören zu den **Klassikern** der englischen Literatur.

Note: **Classic** and **classical** are only partly interchangeable in meaning. "Shakespeare's *Julius Caesar* is **classic** as to its literary status and **classical** as to its subject matter" (*see* Greenbaum/Whitcut, p. 137).

Compare: **Classic** and **classical** overlap in the sense of *refined* as in 'She's a **classic** beauty' meaning an exceptionally good-looking woman *and* 'the **classical** beauty of Greek sculpture' referring to Greek culture.

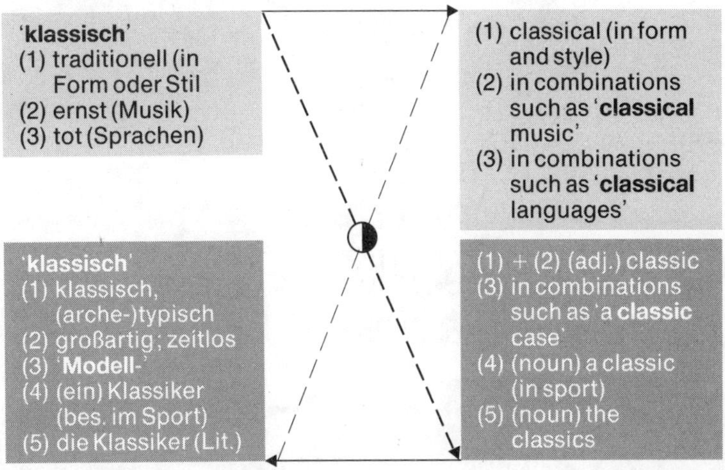

FALSE FRIENDS IN CONTEXT

Driving down the Aisle

Female Labour M. P.: I've nothing against advertising in principle even if married life is involved. But the new car ad is a ________ (1) example of the cheapening of marriage.
Marriage Guidance Expert: I still don't quite understand what you mean. If I'm correctly informed the ad is based on the ________ (2) film *The Graduate*. What's wrong with it?
Female Labour M. P.: The ad shows a bride-to-be being snatched from the altar by a Yuppie with ________ (3) music in the background – in a Rover 2000 saloon.
Marriage Guidance Expert: And what's wrong with that?

Female Labour M. P.: The ad quite clearly trivializes the wedding ceremony, the ________ (4) Latin of the priest and is generally condescending towards women.
Marriage Guidance Expert: I would have expected a more responsible attitude from the advertising manager.
Female Labour M. P.: It's a disgrace. The ad also promotes the 1967 ________ (5) *The Graduate* at the cinema next week. Many female voters were upset and told me to do something about it.

SOLUTION

(1) **classic** example (2) **classic** film (3) **classical** music (4) **classical** Latin (5) classic

KOMISCH ◑ comic

comic

KOMISCH
(= unbeabsichtigt komisch)

comical etc.

KOMISCH: (1) (unbeabsichtigte, ungewollte Komik) comical, funny
(2) (merkwürdig) strange, weird, odd

Note: **Comical** always has a humorous result; it is something that makes you laugh whether it was intended or not intended. It describes.

(1) Es war stets etwas **komisch** an Charlie Chaplin, besonders an seinem Gang.
There was always something **comical** about Charlie Chaplin, especially in his walk.
Wenn ich an dieses Ereignis denke, bekomme ich noch heute ein ganz **komisches** Gefühl im Magen.
When I think of that incident, I have a very **funny** feeling in my stomach even today.
(2) Hast du den Mann eben gesehen? Das war aber ein **komischer** Heiliger.
Did you see that man just now? He really was a **strange** fellow.
Ihr Bruder hatte den Film gesehen und mochte die Handlung, fand aber die Musik **komisch**.
Her brother had seen the film and liked the storyline, but found the music **weird**.
Im Zusammenhang mit dieser Debatte klang die Feststellung des Ministers **komisch**.
In the context of that debate the minister's statement sounded **odd**.

comic: (beabsichtigte, gewollte Komik) komisch

Note: The adjective **comic** is intended to make you laugh because it has the characteristics of comedy; it classifies.

In one of the **comic** operas by W. S. Gilbert the singer took the part of the **comic** character.
In einer der **komischen** Opern von W. S. Gilbert übernahm der Sänger die Rolle des **komischen** Charakters.
Gilbert wrote many **comic** songs for the Savoy Operas; several became **comic** masterpieces.
Gilbert schrieb viele **komische** Songs für die Savoy-Opern; mehrere wurden **komische** Meisterstücke.
The function of the porter scene in Shakespeare's *Macbeth* is to create **comic** relief.
Der Zweck der Pförtner-Szene in Shakespeares *Macbeth* besteht darin, **komische** Entspannung zu schaffen.

Note: The term **comic** may also be used as a noun.
comic = Komiker
Mike is a well-known **comic** who often appears on TV shows.
comic = Comic-Heft (AE comic book)
When the maths teacher found me reading a **comic** in his lesson, he was very angry.

Compare: There is often not much difference between the Terrible Twins **comic** and **comical**.
– He wore a **comic** expression on his face and I just couldn't help laughing. **Comic** here is used to make others laugh.
– He wore a **comical** expression on his face and I wondered whether he was only half serious. **Comical** in this case could be used when someone has told a dubious joke.
– 'A **comic** figure' (e. g. a clown) is intended to make the spectator laugh, whereas 'cut a **comical** figure' (e. g. Charlie Chaplin) always strikes the spectator as humorous; the humour may be accidental or planned.

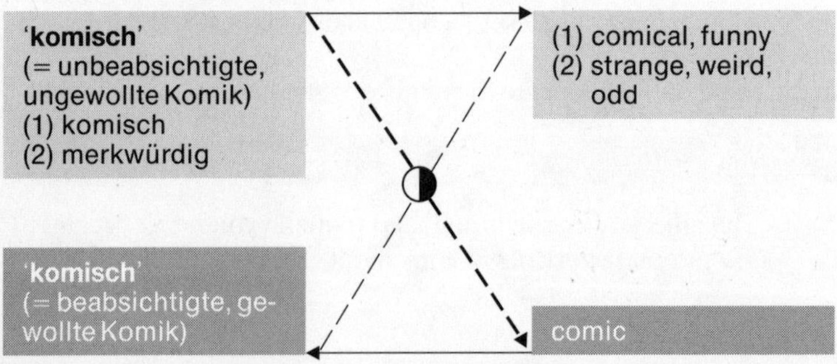

FALSE FRIENDS IN CONTEXT

It's Red Nose Day

1. Red Nose Day '89
Nearly five million people in Britain supported the nation-wide campaign "________ (1) Relief '89". All of them wore ________ (2) red noses. The aim was to raise £ 20,000,000 for charity organisations.

2. The TV Charity Gala Show '90
"Welcome to this year's Red Nose Day charity gala. As you see we're all wearing ________ (3) hooters. I hope you are doing the same at home. It's great you've joined our ________ (4) relief TV show," the presenter began.
"My life can be summed up in two sentences," said the comedian Rowan Atkinson, introducing his first gag. "My parents called me Griffith up-Rhys-Davies and promptly moved from Sussex to Cardiff. So I've had to spend my time getting to know something about rugby and singing in men's choirs," he said, pointing to his red nose with a ________ (5) expression on his face. "I'll never go to that plastic surgeon again," he added. "And the rest, as they say, is history."

SOLUTION

(1) **Comic** Relief (2) **comic** red noses (3) **comic hooters** (4) **comic** relief TV show (5) **comical** expression

KRITIK ≠ critic

critic ['krɪtɪk] → **KRITIK**

criticism ['krɪtɪsɪzəm] **etc.** ← **KRITIK**

KRITIK: (1) (Kritik, allg.) criticism
(2) (Buch-, Theater**kritik** etc.) review
(3) (wissenschaftlich fundierte Kritik) critique [krɪ'ti:k]

(1) Nach dem Tod von mehr als sechzig Zuschauern war die **Kritik** an der Luftfahrtschau in Ramstein berechtigt.
After the deaths of more than sixty spectators the **criticism** of the Air Show at Ramstein was justified.
(2) Sein Buch erhielt in der Presse sehr günstige **Kritiken** und verkaufte sich daher gut.
His book received very favourable **reviews** in the press and consequently sold well.
Das Musical *Aspekte der Liebe*, das in London mäßige **Kritiken** erhielt, brachte im Vorverkauf am Broadway 7,5 Millionen Pfund ein.
The musical *Aspects of Love*, which received mixed **reviews** in London, has earned £ 7.5 million in advance bookings on Broadway.
(3) Die **Kritik** an der Darwinschen Theorie durch den Nobelpreisträger sollte das Denken der Gegenwart revolutionieren.
The Nobel Prize winner's **critique** of Darwin's theory was to revolutionize current thinking.
Der Philosoph Kant veröffentlichte die **Kritik** *der Praktischen Vernunft* im Jahre 1788.
Kant, the philosopher, published his **Critique** *of Practical Reason* in 1788.

Note: The German word **Kritik** (in the singular) is often **criticisms** (in the plural) in English.
He had been a club member for 35 years and agreed with the **criticisms** of the club management.

critic: (1) Kritiker(in)
(2) '-**kritiker(in)**' (in combinations)

(1) Don't you hate the way some **critics** falsify the facts in order to make a point?
Haßt du nicht auch die Art, wie manche **Kritiker** die Tatsachen verfälschen, um ein Argument anzubringen?
(2) The editor of this paper is looking for a literary **critic** to start work on September 1st.
Der Herausgeber dieser Zeitung sucht einen Literatur**kritiker** zum 1. September.
Don't you know Clive James is an author and art **critic** himself?
Weißt du nicht, daß Clive James selbst Autor und Kunst**kritiker** ist?

Note: reviewer = **Kritiker**, Rezensent
Desmond MacCarthy was the principal **reviewer** at the *Sunday Times* for nearly 25 years.

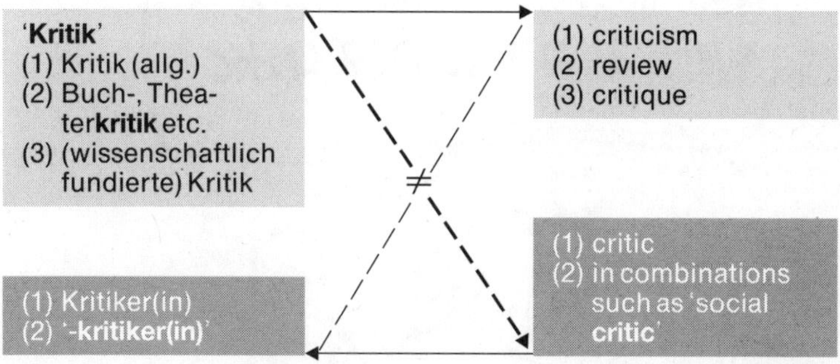

FALSE FRIENDS IN CONTEXT

A First Night

They had turned up for the first night of a new play by a young playwright. A well-known theatre ________ (1) had come up from London to see it.
Very soon it became obvious that the production was going to be a flop. The acting was poor. The stage properties were somehow inadequate. The subject matter was not to the liking of the theatre-goers. Bad ________ (2) were certainly inevitable.
The audience's reaction was more dramatic than the play itself.
Several theatre-goers left after the first act. Most of those remaining

began to leave the theatre after the second act. At this point the London theatre ________ (3) jumped to his feet from his front row seat and raised his hand for attention.
"Don't panic," he announced, "women and children first."

SOLUTION

(1) theatre **critic** (2) reviews (3) London theatre **critic**

KRITISCH ≠ (*) critic

(*) **critic** ['krɪtɪk]

KRITISCH

critical ['krɪtɪkl] **etc.**

KRITISCH: (1) critical
(2) disapproving
(3) (verb) (be) critical (of)

(1) Mein Großvater hat jetzt ein besonders **kritisches** Alter erreicht.
My grandfather has now reached a particularly **critical** age.
"Was soll denn deine **kritische** Bemerkung?" fragte er zurück.
"What is your **critical** remark supposed to mean?" he asked back.
Die Gespräche der Minister sind in ein **kritisches** Stadium eingetreten.
The ministers' talks have entered a **critical** stage.
(2) Die Filmschauspielerin warf den Kameraleuten einen **kritischen** Blick zu.
The film-star cast a **disapproving** glance at the cameramen.
(3) Er ist gegen den Kommunismus und gleichzeitig **kritisch gegenüber** dem Westen.
He is opposed to Communism and, at the same time, **critical of** the West. (*see* Kritik ≠ critic)

critic: (1) Kritiker(in)
(2) '-**kritiker(in)**' (in combinations)

Note: There is no adjective * **critic** in English; it is always a noun.

(1) The **critic** was at a loss to explain his views.
Der **Kritiker** wußte nicht mehr weiter, als er seine Ansichten erklären sollte.
The result has done much to silence the **critics**.
Das Ergebnis hat viel dazu beigetragen, die **Kritiker** zum Schweigen zu bringen.
(2) For the first time in his life the art **critic** was lost for words as to what to write for the next edition of the art magazine.
Zum erstenmal in seinem Leben wußte der Kunst**kritiker** nicht, was er in der nächsten Ausgabe der Kunstzeitschrift schreiben sollte.

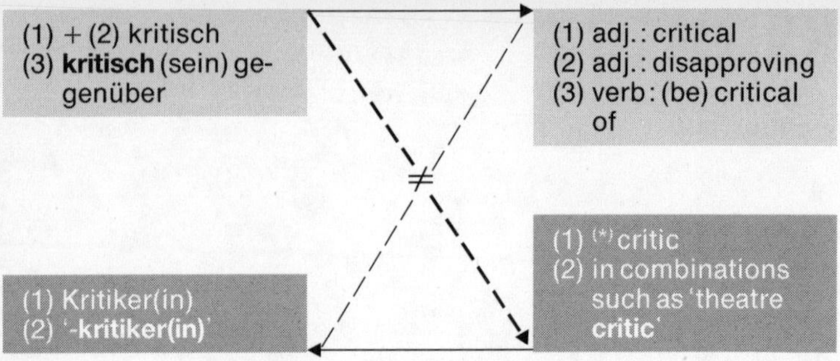

FALSE FRIENDS IN CONTEXT

Undercover Action

Steve: Mind you, nothing ________ (1) was happening, the business was taking off.
June: When there's no ________ (2), success is just around the corner. And the money begins to flow.
Steve: I've heard that before. You've got to be ________ (3) nowadays. I've come to know quite a few self-employed and small businessmen who enjoyed initial success. Then they became ill or some other disaster struck them.
June: That's right. These businessmen are often hardest hit. Look at John. People like him rely on their business rather than employee schemes. And what's your solution?
Steve: I'm always very ________ (4) in case of long-term illness. What would happen to you and me if we became disabled? As a ______ (5) of our system the answer is undercover action in the form of Priorities.
June: Priorities? What's that?
Steve: Priorities, the insurance company. It provides a lump sum in case of a ________ (6) illness or a regular income in case of disability. It's best to have cover against such an eventuality.
June casting him a ________ (7) glance, but smiling all of a sudden: Really, Steve. Very clever of you.

SOLUTION

(1) nothing **critical** (2) critic (3) to be critical (4) critical (5) critic
(6) a **critical** illness (7) a **critical** glance

MAGISCH ◑ magic

magic

MAGISCH
(= zauberhaft; erstaunlich)

magical

MAGISCH: (1) (zauberhaft, bezaubernd) magical
(2) (märchenhaft; erstaunlich) magical

Note: In the case of the adjective **magical** the change is fascinating or surprising, but not supernatural (as in 'a **magical** attraction'). A holiday may be described as **magical** as to its memorable experience.

(1) Ihre Begegnung mit der Königin war ein **magisches** Erlebnis.
Her encounter with the Queen was a **magical** experience.
"Ich kann nicht glauben, daß der neue Jaguar wirklich mir gehört", bekannte der Preisgewinner dem Showmaster. "Dies ist ein **magischer** Tag für mich!"
"I can't believe the new Jaguar is really mine," the prize winner confessed to the compère. "This is a **magical** day for me!"
(2) Tiere haben eine **magische** Anziehungskraft auf viele Kinder.
Animals have a **magical** attraction for many children.
"Die Medizin hatte auf unsere Patienten eine **magische** Wirkung", erzählte der Arzt seiner Frau zu Hause.
"That medicine had a **magical** effect on our patients," the doctor told his wife at home.

magic: (1) magisch (= die Magie betreffend)
(2) '**Zauber-**' (in combinations)
(3) Zauberei, Magie
(4) Zauber (fig.)

Note: In the case of the adjective **magic** the change is supernatural, but not necessarily surprising (as in '**magic** art'). **Magic** may also be used as a noun.

(1) He had devoted himself to **magic** art, because he felt he had received **magic** powers.

Er hatte sich der **magischen** Kunst verschrieben, weil er meinte, **magische** Kräfte empfangen zu haben.
Do you know why seven is one of the **magic** numbers?
Weißt du, warum Sieben eine der **magischen** Zahlen ist?
(2) His audience was surprised. While he was saying his **magic** formula, he first showed his **magic** ring, then touched each top hat with his **magic** wand – and out came three white rabbits.
Das Publikum war überrascht. Während er seine **Zauber**formel hersagte, zeigte er zunächst seinen **Zauber**ring, berührte dann jeden Zylinder mit seinem **Zauber**stab – und heraus kamen drei weiße Kaninchen.
While he was reading Thomas Mann's *The* **Magic** *Mountain*, Mozart's *The* **Magic** *Flute* was playing in the background.
Während er Thomas Manns '*Der* **Zauber***berg*' las, spielte Mozarts '**Zauber***flöte*' im Hintergrund.
(3) The language of **magic** can be found throughout the world.
Die Sprache der **Magie** ist überall in der Welt anzutreffen.
"Pure **magic**," was all the commentator could say when the diver performed his final dive from the high board.
"Das grenzt fast an **Zauberei**", war alles, was der Kommentator hervorbringen konnte, als der (Kunst-)Springer seinen Schlußsprung vom Zehnmeterturm ausgeführt hatte.
(4) It was the **magic** of Christmas that had touched the old man's heart.
Es war der **Zauber** von Weihnachten, der das Herz des alten Mannes angerührt hatte.

Note: **magic** carpet = fliegender Teppich
magic lantern = Laterna **magica**
magic square = Zahlenquadrat, **magisches** Quadrat
magic eye = Lichtschranke (Toilette, Lift etc.); **magisches** Auge
"Don't pull the towel. Place your finger over the **magic** eye," the instruction ran.

Compare: In some cases there is not much difference between the Confusibles **magical** and **magic**.
A magician's performance may be **magic** as to its supernatural origin, but **magical** as to its fascinating quality.

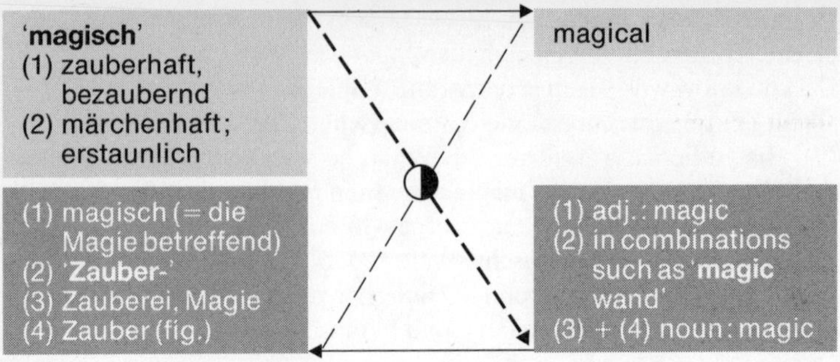

FALSE FRIENDS IN CONTEXT

Having One's Tooth Out

Mother: Did you see the dentist?
Laurie: I've had my wisdom tooth out. It wasn't painful at all.
Mother: But it must have been...
Laurie: It was ________ (1)! The new dentist at Didcot has found a new method. He confronts the patient with ________ (2) art before he does anything.
Mother: What's that got to do with your teeth?
Laurie: It's a new way of relaxing patients. His performing conjuring tricks made me forget about my pains and relax.
Mother: I still don't understand.
Laurie: Oh, Mum, I've told you already. The dentist's performance had a ________ (3) effect on me, that is before the treatment started. Having the wisdom tooth out was just a matter of course. It wasn't painful at all. I tell you, the new dentist's method was simply ________ (4).
Mother: How do you feel now?
Laurie: Good, but I can't eat anything for the next few hours, and I'll have to eat soft food for the next three days.
Mother: You've got to be careful. At one side of your face you look like a hamster. Still, I don't believe in ________ (5) treatment, and I think it's a lot of nonsense.

SOLUTION

(1) magical (2) **magic** art (3) **magical** effect (4) magical (5) **magic** treatment

ÖKONOMISCH ◑ economic

economic

ÖKONOMISCH
(= sparsam, kostengünstig)

economical

ÖKONOMISCH: (1) (sparsam, kostengünstig) economical
(2) (im Sport: kraftsparend) economical

(1) Dein Plan für den Umbau ist **ökonomischer**.
Your plan for the alterations is more **economical**.
Denk bloß an den Energieverlust im alten Haus. Im neuen Haus benötigen wir ein **ökonomisches** Heizungssystem. Dadurch sparen wir eine Menge Geld.
Just think of the loss of energy in the old house. We need an **economical** heating system in the new house. It'll save us a lot of money.
Mein neues Auto fährt sehr **ökonomisch**; es verbraucht auf 80 Kilometer etwa eine Gallone (= BE 4,55 Liter).
My new car is very **economical**; it does fifty miles to the gallon.
(2) Schau dir die Marathonläufer an. Die meisten von ihnen haben einen **ökonomischen** Laufstil.
Look at the marathon runners. Most of them have an **economical** style of running.

economic: (1) wirtschaftlich
(2) '**Wirtschafts-**' (in combinations)
(3) konjunkturell
(4) '**Konjunktur-**' (in combinations)

(1) At the meeting the **economic** development of the former East Germany was on the agenda.
Bei dem Treffen stand die **wirtschaftliche** Entwicklung der neuen Bundesländer auf der Tagesordnung.
The **economic** policy of the present government does not consider the **economic** arguments of the last report.
Die Wirtschaftspolitik der neuen Regierung läßt die **wirtschaftlichen** Faktoren des letzten Gutachtens unberücksichtigt.
(2) At the end of the negotiations a new **economic** agreement was signed between the two countries.

Am Ende der Verhandlungen wurde ein neues **Wirtschafts**abkommen zwischen den beiden Ländern unterzeichnet.
The late Chancellor Erhard has often been described as the Father of the German **economic** miracle in the Fifties.
Der verstorbene Kanzler Erhard ist oft als Vater des deutschen **Wirtschafts**wunders beschrieben worden.
(3) England's **economic** situation has considerably improved in the last six months.
Die **konjunkturelle** Lage Englands hat sich in den letzten sechs Monaten deutlich verbessert.
(4) During the whole period there was only a slight **economic** decline. Generally the German **economic** cycle indicates a bright **economic** outlook.
In dem gesamten Zeitraum gab es nur einen unbedeutenden **Konjunktur**rückgang. Allgemein zeigt der deutsche **Konjunktur**verlauf gute **Konjunktur**aussichten.

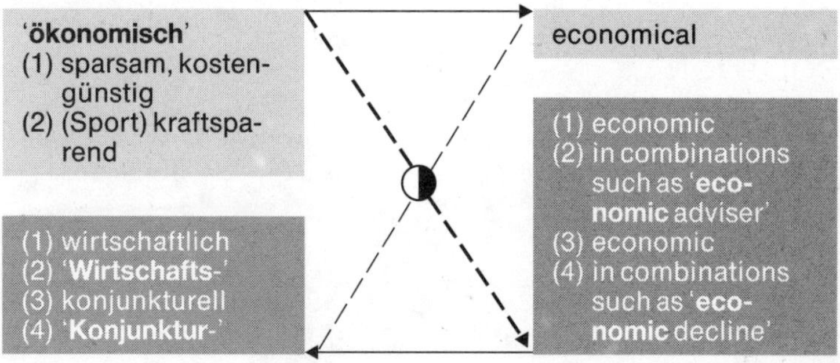

FALSE FRIENDS IN CONTEXT

A Special Offer

Husband (on Sunday afternoon, reading to his wife from the *Sunday Times*): "The new ________ (1) policy of the Single Market has created a new ________ (2) situation. After 1992 Britain can compete on all markets in EEC member states."
Wife: So we can, for example, buy products from Germany in the future without import tax.
Husband: Well, I suppose that is what it'll mean in practice.

* * *

Wife doing some shopping in a department store in London's West End on Monday: (listening) "... Look at this new aluminium steamer from Germany!"
Product Demonstrator: It's practical and extremely ________ (3). All vegetables and other food such as fish, fruit and some puddings really taste better and healthier. For those who need to cut down on fat this ________ (4) steamer is essential.
Wife: Tell me, what's so practical about this steamer?
Product Demonstrator: It's in three tiers, the bottom one to hold water, the other two with perforations to hold the food. And it's ________ (5), too. You can cook the whole meal from just one heat source.
Wife: What about the price?
Product Demonstrator: Well, the price for the steamer helps you to be ________ (6), too. It's a special offer for just £ 19.95.
Wife: I'll have one, but only if there's a guarantee with it.

SOLUTION

(1) **economic** policy (2) **economic** situation (3) economical (4) **economical** steamer (5) economical (6) economical

POLITISCH ≠ politic

politic [ˈpɒlətɪk]

POLITISCH

political [pəˈlɪtɪkl]

POLITISCH: political

Note: There is no such **noun** as 'a *political' (= Politiker) in BE or AE. The correct English word for 'Politiker' is **politician** [ˌpɒlɪˈtɪʃn].

In dieser Woche baten viele Vietnamesen um **politisches** Asyl.
Many Vietnamese asked for **political** asylum this week.
In Ungarn hängt die künftige **politische** Unabhängigkeit von der wirtschaftlichen Entwicklung ab.
In Hungary, future **political** autonomy depends on economic development.

Note: im **politischen** Leben stehen = (be) in politics
You can't do that. You are in **politics**.
Außerdem werden sich die Leute fragen, wo du **politisch** stehst.
What is more, people will ask themselves what your **politics** are.

politic: (1) diplomatisch, (taktisch) klug
(2) ratsam

Note: The word **politic** can never be used as a noun in English; the noun is **politics**.

(1) It wouldn't be **politic** at this stage to change our strategy.
Es wäre nicht **diplomatisch**, in diesem Stadium unsere Strategie zu ändern.
Had he been more **politic** than outspoken he would be a wealthier man today.
Hätte er sich **taktisch klüger** verhalten und nicht so offen, wäre er heute ein wohlhabenderer Mann.

(2) John had won the case against his landlord. But he didn't think it would be **politic** to ask for a new contract at present.
John hatte den Prozeß gegen seinen Hauswirt gewonnen. Aber er glaubte nicht, daß es **ratsam** sei, gegenwärtig wegen eines neuen Mietvertrags vorstellig zu werden.

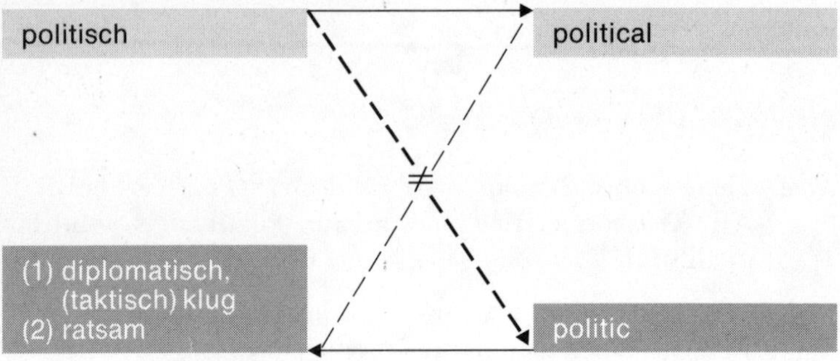

FALSE FRIENDS IN CONTEXT

Double Trouble

Chairman of the EC (= *E*nvironment *C*ommittee): No ________ (1) party wants to keep the current system of taxation. The SLD and the Greens favour local income tax which, for ________ (2) reasons, is unfair.
Back-Bencher: Labour wants to replace one tax by two: a rate based on the value of a person's home whether they own it or not *and* a local income tax. We on the other hand want a double tax which would be more ________ (3).
Chairman of the EC: These Labour proposals are unfair. Millions of people, including those on low incomes, would have to pay far more.
Back-Bencher: From a ________ (4) point of view the public has, of course, a right to know how much the double tax will cost them.
Chairman of the EC: As it is a vital issue it wouldn't be ________ (5) to make a decision without consulting the voters. Otherwise you'll be faced with double trouble.

SOLUTION

(1) **political** party (2) **political** reasons (3) more politic (4) **political** point of view (5) politic

ZYNISCH ≠ (*) cynic

(*) cynic ['sɪnɪk]

ZYNISCH
(= verletzend-spöttisch)

cynical ['sɪnɪkl]

ZYNISCH: (verletzend-spöttisch etc.) cynical

Es war für den Diskussionsleiter schwierig, in dieser Situation nicht **zynisch** zu werden.
It was difficult for the chairman of the panel not to become **cynical** in this situation.
Die hohen Betonhotels auf Mallorca werden heute **zynisch** als 'Bettenburgen' bezeichnet.
The high-rise concrete hotels of Majorca are now **cynically** referred to as 'bed factories'.
"Vergessen wir meine **zynische** Bemerkung", entschuldigte er sich am Ende.
"Let's forget my **cynical** remark," he apologized at the end.

cynic: Zyniker

Note: There is no adjective (*) **cynic** in BE and AE; it is always a noun.

A **cynic** is someone who knows the price of everything and the value of nothing.
Ein **Zyniker** ist jemand, der den Preis von allem kennt und den Wert von nichts.
His new wife, who at 36, was young enough, as **cynics** observed, to be his daughter.
Seine neue Frau war mit 36 jung genug – wie **Zyniker** bemerkten –, um seine Tochter sein zu können.

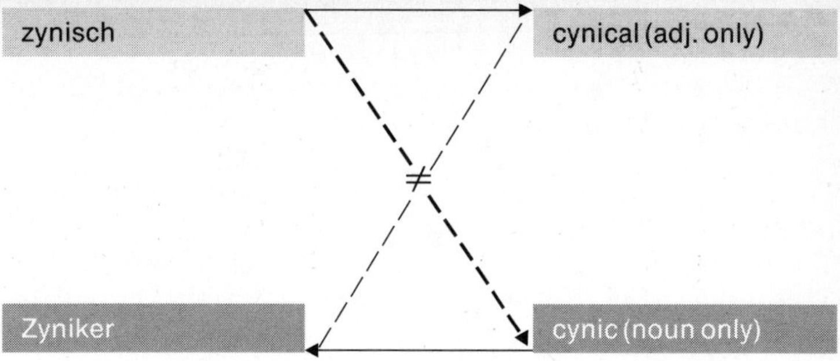

FALSE FRIENDS IN CONTEXT

Defining the Impossible

Fred: ... And what I don't understand is why our form tutor is always so ________ (1) when someone's late for school.
Head Teacher: Hm. I don't know either.

* * *

Head Teacher (in class): Fred, can you tell me what a ________ (2) is?
Fred: Of course I can. A ________ (3) is a boy who goes to school with a smile on his face when he's late.

SOLUTION

(1) cynical (2) cynic (3) cynic

FALSE FRIENDS TRAPS TEST 5

TERRIBLE TWINS

1.a. "In ________ engineering these problems do not exist," the expert told me (**elektrisch ◑ electric**).
1.b. "I prefer steam trains to ________ trains (**elektrisch ◑ electric**). They remind me of great inventions", answered the train enthusiast.
2.a. The youths' behaviour was a ________ example of soccer hooliganism (**klassisch ◑ classic**).
2.b. "Our daughter has been taking a close interest in ________ music," her mother told me afterwards (**klassisch ◑ classic**).
3.a. This car is ________ to run, comfortable, and even after ten years has no sign of rust (**ökonomisch ◑ economic**).
3.b. "Tory ________ policy is leading us all to ruin," one of the men shouted (**ökonomisch ◑ economic**).
4.a. "After all, there has always been a ________ link between the Church and the pub," said the speaker finishing his talk (**historisch ◑ historic**).
4.b. The Loch Ness Centre includes all the ________ evidence of Nessie's existence (**historisch ◑ historic**).
5.a. You and your partner can stay in the same hotel on the ________ Greek island of Mykonos (**magisch ◑ magic**).
5.b. "This man has ________ powers," the presenter announced (**magisch ◑ magic**). "All he needs is a ________ (**magisch ◑ magic**) ring and a ________ formula," he added (**magisch ◑ magic**).
6. Currys is Britain's favourite ________ (**Elektro-**) store.
7. The new filmstar is a ________ (**klassisch**) case of someone taking life easy.
8. Nine-tenths of the ________ (**historisch**) literature about marriage concerns property.
9. "Stop being ________ (**kritisch**) of our company's policy," the manager remarked. "It is unjust ________ (**Kritik**) levelled against me."
10. "Don't be so ________ (**zynisch**)," the Prime Minister continued. "Future ________ (**politisch**) independence depends on future ________ (**wirtschaftlich**) independence."

ANSWER SHEET: TRUE FRIENDS TEST 5

TERRIBLE TWINS

1.a. "In **electrical** engineering these problems do not exist," the expert told me.
1.b. "I prefer steam trains to **electric** trains. They remind me of great inventions," answered the train enthusiast.
2.a. The youths' behaviour was a **classic** example of soccer hooliganism.
2.b. "Our daughter has been taking a close interest in **classical** music," her mother told me afterwards.
3.a. This car is **economical** to run, comfortable, and even after ten years has no sign of rust.
3.b. "Tory **economic** policy is leading us all to ruin," one of the men shouted.
4.a. "After all, there has always been a **historic** link between the Church and the pub," said the speaker finishing his talk.
4.b. The Loch Ness Centre includes all the **historical** evidence of Nessie's existence.
5.a. You and your partner can stay in the same hotel on the **magical** Greek island of Mykonos.
5.b. "This man has **magic** powers," the presenter announced. "All he needs is a **magic** ring and a **magic** formula," he added.
6. Currys is Britain's favourite **electrical** store.
7. The new filmstar is a **classic** case of someone taking life easy.
8. Nine-tenths of the **historical** literature about marriage concerns property.
9. "Stop being **critical of** our company's policy," the manager remarked. "It is unjust **criticism** levelled against me."
10. "Don't be so **cynical**," the Prime Minister continued. "Future **political** independence depends on future **economic** independence."

TRICKY OVER- / UNDER-COMPOUNDS KURZ-EINFÜHRUNG

Was sind Over- / Under-Compounds?

Unter **Over- / Under-Compounds** versteht man Wortkombinationen, die sich aus der Vorsilbe **over-** bzw. **under-** und in der Regel einem Substantiv oder Verb zusammensetzen. Durch trügerische Analogiewirkung entstehen False Friends-Paare wie **übernehmen ≠ overtake**, **überschlafen ≠ oversleep**, **Unternehmer ≠ undertaker** oder **unterschreiben ≠ underwrite**. Bei einem kleineren Teil von **Over- / Under-Compounds** kommen False Friends durch fälschliche Ähnlichkeitswirkung zustande wie bei **überhören ≠ overhear** oder **Unterarm ≠ underarm**.
Ausdrücklich sei davor gewarnt, alle **Over- / Under-Compounds** als False Friends anzusehen. Wortkombinationen wie **overdress** (sich herausputzen) oder **understate** (untertreiben) sind keine False Friends, da der ähnliche bzw. analoge Begriff im Deutschen fehlt.

ÜBERBLICKEN ◑ overlook

overlook [ˌəʊvəˈlʊk]

ÜBERBLICKEN

survey [səˈveɪ];
assess [əˈses] **etc.**

ÜBERBLICKEN: (1) (Landschaft etc. überblicken) survey; assess (also fig.)
(2) (kritisch überblicken) have a clear view of, grasp sth.

(1) Vom Swimmingpool auf der Terrasse kann man die kahlen Ebenen des amerikanischen Westens **überblicken**.
From the swimming pool on the terrace one can **survey** the bare plains of the American West.
Die politische Lage in China ist im Augenblick schwer zu **überblikken**; daher ist es besser, nicht dorthin zu reisen.
It is difficult to **assess** the political situation in China at the moment, so we'd better not travel there.
(2) Solange wir die wirtschaftliche Entwicklung nicht **überblicken** können, werden wir nichts investieren.
As long as we do not **have a clear view of** the economic development, we'll not invest anything.
"Wir konnten die Folgen einer solchen Entscheidung nicht **überblikken**", stellte der Gewerkschaftsführer fest. "Deshalb bliesen wir den Streik ab."
"We couldn't **grasp** the consequences of such a decision," stated the union leader, "so we called off the strike."

overlook: (1) (Fehler etc.) übersehen, vergessen
(2) Aussicht haben auf, einen Blick bieten auf

(1) The link between natural radon gas and certain forms of cancer has been **overlooked** by scientists in the past.
Der Zusammenhang zwischen natürlichem Radongas und bestimmten Krebsarten ist von Wissenschaftlern in der Vergangenheit **übersehen** worden.
When it comes to improvements, from the glove box to the petrol cap, we've made sure nothing has been **overlooked**.

Bei den Verbesserungen vom Handschuhfach bis zum Tankdeckel haben wir darauf geachtet, daß nichts **vergessen** wurde.
(2) In the afternoon we went up to a mountain restaurant **overlooking** the valley.
Am Nachmittag gingen wir zum Bergrestaurant hinauf, von wo wir **Aussicht auf** das Tal **hatten**.
The narrow streets wound their way up to the medieval castle **overlooking** the Atlantic.
Die engen Straßen schlängelten sich den Weg hinauf zur mittelalterlichen Burg, die **einen Blick auf** den Atlantik **bot**.

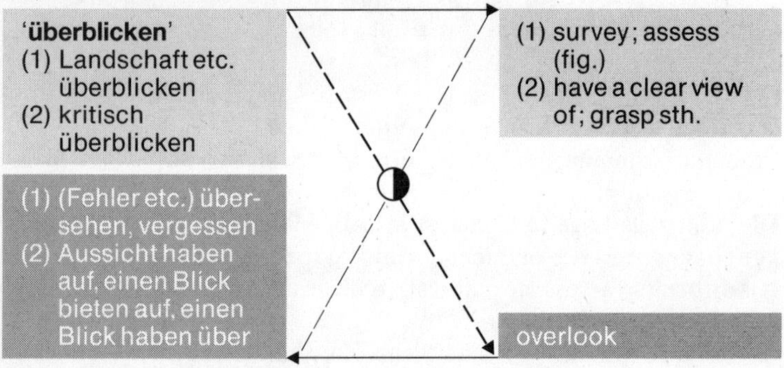

FALSE FRIENDS IN CONTEXT

A Reunion of 'False' Friends

Former RAF Pilot: During the last war, I was flying a Walrus flying boat ________ (1) the Mediterranean when I spotted a damaged submarine flying a white flag, with the German crew on deck.
War Correspondent: What did you do?
Former RAF Pilot: I immediately flew back to the nearest British warship to report and was ordered to ________ (2) the situation once again.
War Correspondent: So what exactly happened?
Former RAF Pilot: ________ (3) the scene again I found an American plane machine-gunning the German submarine. Its crew had jumped into the water.
War Correspondent: That was a crucial situation. What did you decide to do?

Former RAF Pilot: After trying to ________ (4) the odds for a few seconds, I landed our flying boat and eventually managed to pick up sixteen Germans including the captain.
War Correspondent: And what's so special about the story after so many years?
Former RAF Pilot: About a month ago I was invited to Germany as a guest of honour at a reunion of the former U-boat crew. They hadn't ________ (5) their former rescuer. I'm looking forward to being presented with a plaque commemorating their rescue.

* * *

P. S. Dr. Roy Blatchley, the former pilot of the flying boat, died a week after his return from Germany…

SOLUTION

(1) overlooking (2) assess (3) overlooking (4) assess (5) overlooked

'ÜBERFLUSS' ≠ overflow

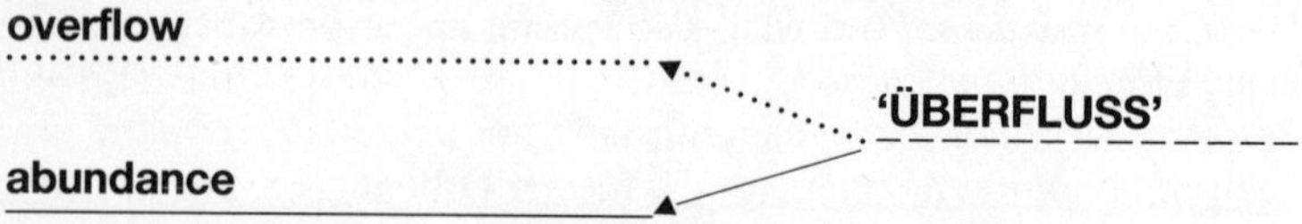

'ÜBERFLUSS': (1) (Überfülle) abundance, profusion
(2) (Reichtum, Wohlstand) affluence, (Üppigkeit, Prunk) opulence, (Luxus, Komfort) luxury

(1) Wir haben zwar nicht Geld im **Überfluß**, aber wir können gut leben.
We don't have, it is true, money in **abundance**, but we can afford to live well.
Wohin die neuen Besitzer auch schauten, überall gab es Obst im **Überfluß**.
Wherever the new owners looked, there was fruit in **profusion**.
(2) Die Flüchtlinge aus Polen waren es nicht gewohnt, im **Überfluß** zu leben.
The refugees from Poland were not used to living in **affluence**.
Als die Pilger den St. Petersdom betraten, konnten sie den unermeßlichen **Überfluß** an Formen und Farben nicht fassen.
When the pilgrims entered St. Peter's, they were unable to grasp the immense **opulence** of the forms and colours.
Das junge Paar hatte schon lange den Wunsch, nur eine Woche in völligem **Überfluß** zu leben.
The young couple had wished for a long time that they could live for just a week in complete **luxury**.

Note: **Überfluß**-Gesellschaft = affluent society

overflow: (1) Überflutung, Überschwemmung
(2) ausströmendes Wasser; Überfließen
(3) (fig.) Überschuß, Überbestand; Andrang, Ansturm
(4) (tech.) Überlauf, '**Überlauf**-' (in combinations)
(5) '**Neben**-', '**Parallel**-' (in combinations)

(1) In spring the **overflow** of the Ganges fertilizes the surrounding valleys.

Im Frühjahr befruchtet die Ganges-**Überflutung** die umgebenden Täler.
The burst pipe caused an **overflow** in the bathroom.
Der Rohrbruch verursachte eine **Überschwemmung** im Badezimmer.
(2) The **overflow** from the mains left the village with ankle-deep mud.
Das aus der Hauptleitung **ausströmende Wasser** ließ das Dorf in knöcheltiefem Schlamm versinken.
(3) There was an **overflow** of applicants for the diplomatic service.
Es bestand ein **Überschuß** an Bewerbern für den diplomatischen Dienst.
The **overflow** of library books was stored in another building.
Der **Überbestand** an Bibliotheksbüchern wurde in einem anderen Gebäude gelagert.
The charter airline had more passengers than expected. So they had to bring in more planes to cope with the **overflow**.
Die Charter-Fluglinie hatte mehr Passagiere als erwartet. Daher mußte man mehr Flugzeuge bereitstellen, um den **Ansturm** zu bewältigen.
(4) The **overflow** from the washbasin was blocked, so he called a plumber.
Der **Überlauf** des Waschbeckens war verstopft, daher bestellte er einen Installateur.
It had been raining for hours. Suddenly water began to issue from the **overflow** pipes.
Es hatte schon seit Stunden geregnet. Plötzlich begann Wasser aus den **Überlauf**rohren auszutreten.
(5) Many had to listen to the service through loudspeakers in an **overflow** room.
Viele mußten den Gottesdienst über Lautsprecher in einem **Nebensaal** anhören.

Note: catch the **overflow** = das Regenwasser auffangen
In Britain, many people still use tubs to **catch the overflow**.
Compare: filled to **overflowing** = bis auf den letzten Platz gefüllt; zum Bersten voll sein

The chapel at Barham Crematorium in Kent was filled to **overflowing**, and many people had to wait outside.
overflow with = angefüllt mit, überquellen vor

She's a slut. Her bedroom is carpeted with dirty underwear and the kitchen sink **overflowing with** mouldy dishes.
From the Duddon Bridge he passed two villages with as many tubs **overflowing with** pink petunias as there were 'For Sale' signs.

'Überfluß' (1) Überfülle (2) Reichtum, Wohlstand; Üppigkeit, Prunk; Luxus, Komfort	(1) abundance, profusion (2) affluence; opulence; luxury
(1) Überflutung, Überschwemmung (2) ausströmendes Wasser; Überfließen (3) (fig.) Überschuß, Überbestand; Andrang, Ansturm (4) (tech.) Überlauf, '**Überlauf-**' (5) '**Neben-**', '**Parallel-**'	(1) –(3) overflow (4) in combinations such as '**overflow** pipes' (5) in combinations such as '**overflow** meeting'

FALSE FRIENDS IN CONTEXT

A Computer Freak

Former Patient: Dr. Fraser has always lived in ________ (1). I can't believe what the papers write about him.
Neighbour: Neither can I. He was such a conscientious doctor. But somehow he seems to have developed a real obsession for computers.
Former Patient: Things went wrong when he gave up his practice and went to work for Shell as a computer specialist.
Neighbour: This gave him the chance to live in even greater ________ (2) than before. He earned money in ________ (3) and bought holiday homes in the Bahamas and in the Virgin Islands.
Former Patient: He took computer equipment worth more than

£ 60,000 from his office, so he was able to work in the evening and over the weekends on computer problems. Eventually he had so much hardware and software, he had to put the ________ (4) in his garage.
Neighbour: How did they find out?
Former Patient: He set off an alarm at 6 a. m. at his office.
Neighbour: His wife says he's been obsessed by computers since the age of 12.
Former Patient: Really, a married man and a computer freak!

SOLUTION

(1) affluence (2) luxury (3) abundance (4) overflow

ÜBERHÖREN ≠ overhear

overhear [ˌəʊvəˈhɪə]

ignore (I) — **ÜBERˈHÖREN (I)**
hear enough of (II) — **ˈÜBERHÖREN (II)**

ÜBERˈ**HÖREN** (I): (1) (absichtlich oder bewußt überhören) ignore
(2) (unabsichtlich überhören) miss hearing sth.
(3) (akustisch nicht verstehen) fail to hear, not hear

(1) Der schottische Nationalist hat bewußt den Einwand des Parlamentsabgeordneten **überhört**.
The Scottish nationalist deliberately **ignored** the M. P.'s objection.
(2) Am Ende seines Vortrags habe ich wohl **überhört**, daß wir uns noch in dem Café treffen wollten.
At the end of his talk I must have **missed hearing** him say that we should meet in the café.
(3) Ich hörte gerade Musik. Daher habe ich **überhört** (akustisch nicht verstanden), was du gesagt hast.
I was listening to the music, so I **didn't hear** what you were saying.
Jenny war gerade im anderen Teil des Hauses; aus diesem Grunde hat sie das Klingeln des Telefons **überhört**.
Jenny was in the other part of the building just then; so she **failed to hear** the telephone ring.

Note: Das möchte ich aber **überhört** haben = I didn't hear that.

ˈ**ÜBER**HÖREN (II): (sich etwas ˈüberhören) hear enough of

(4) Bitte sei nicht beleidigt, wenn ich heute abend mit dir nicht ins Konzert gehe. Ich **habe mich** an Henry Purcells Musik im Augenblick **übergehört**.
Please don't be upset if I don't go with you to the concert tonight. I've **heard enough of** Henry Purcell's music for the time being.

OVERHEAR: (1) (zufällig) etwas mit anhören; (unabsichtlich) mitbekommen
(2) (absichtlich) belauschen

(1) Hugh **overheard** his parents talking about his birthday present since he had come home earlier from the youth club.
Hugh **bekam zufällig mit**, als seine Eltern über sein Geburtstagsgeschenk sprachen; er war etwas früher vom Jugendklub nach Hause gekommen.
(2) One of the five dealers **was overheard** by an attentive cleaner from the women's toilet.
Einer der fünf Rauschgifthändler **wurde** von einer aufmerksamen Aufwartefrau von der Frauentoilette aus **belauscht**.

Note: bug = abhören; Wanzen einbauen, Abhörgeräte installieren
Our secret meeting at the café had been **bugged**.
Security agents had **bugged** the new embassy building.

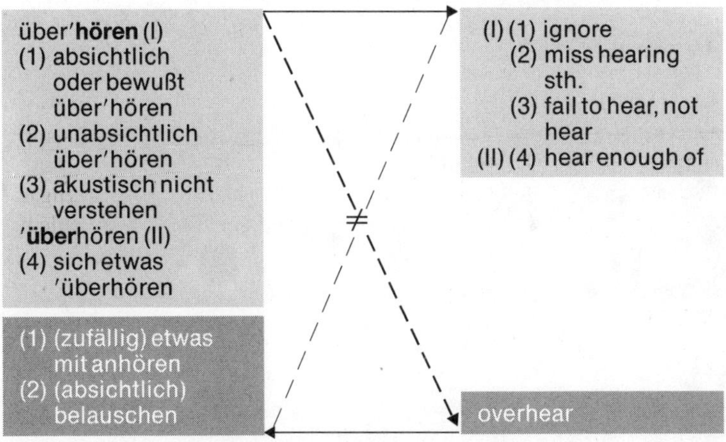

FALSE FRIENDS IN CONTEXT

Eavesdroppings

By the way, eavesdropping means ________ (1) a remark. Here are three of my eavesdroppings: As I was walking into a slimming club the other day, I couldn't help ________ (2) the following remark at the weigh-in: "It's raining and I'm soaked through. So I'm bound to weigh more."

* * *

This is the beginning of a conversation I ________ (3) in the bus shelter: "He has another woman now. He didn't really need one, as I never refused him maple syrup."

* * *

Walking slowly down the street I approached a man and a woman who stopped kissing each other when they saw me. As I went past them, I picked up this piece of conversation:
Lover: Can I see you tomorrow?
Girl: Well, I'm getting married in the morning, but I'll meet you here at five in the afternoon, darling.
Unfortunately I ________ (4) the rest of their conversation.

SOLUTION

(1) overhearing (2) overhearing (3) overheard (4) did not hear / missed hearing

ÜBERNEHMEN ≠ overtake

overtake [ˌəʊvəˈteɪk]

ÜBERNEHMEN

take over etc.

(etwas übernehmen)

ÜBERNEHMEN: (1) (etwas übernehmen) take sth. on, take sth. over; take (a call)
(2) undertake (**see** unternehmen ≠ undertake)
(3) adopt (an idea, a plan etc.)

(1) Unser neuer Chef wollte nicht die Verantwortung **übernehmen** und entließ 200 Arbeiter.
Our new boss didn't want to **take on/take over** the responsibility and made 200 workers redundant.
Die streikenden Sanitäter weigerten sich, Notrufe zu **übernehmen**.
Striking ambulancemen refused to **take** 999 calls.
"Prinz Charles wird im nächsten Jahr den Thron **übernehmen** und nur drei Jahre regieren", sagte die Astrologin voraus.
"Prince Charles will **take over** the throne next year and will reign for only three years," the astrologer predicted.
(2) Unsere New Yorker Zentrale hat es **übernommen**, Sie von den Wahlergebnissen zu informieren.
Our New York headquarters have **undertaken** to inform you about the election results.
(3) Später **übernahm** sie seine Arbeitsweise mit Erfolg.
Later on she **adopted** his way of working with success.

Note: **sich** (finanziell oder beruflich) **übernehmen** = take on too much
The firm's manager has had a nervous breakdown. He had **taken on too much**.

overtake: (1) (im Verkehr etc.) überholen
(2) überraschen (fig.); hereinbrechen (über)

(1) "You cannot **overtake** on the left," the London policeman pointed out to me when he stopped my car.

"Sie können nicht links **überholen**", wies mich der Londoner Polizist zurecht, als er meinen Wagen anhielt.
On their way down from the summit of K2, the mountaineers were **overtaken** by an avalanche.
Beim Abstieg vom Gipfel des K2 wurden die Bergsteiger von einer Lawine **überrascht**.
Profoundly shaken, the British rescue team continued their search for survivors until darkness **overtook** them.
Sichtlich erschüttert setzte die britische Rettungsmannschaft die Suche nach Überlebenden fort, bis die Dunkelheit **über** sie **hereinbrach**.

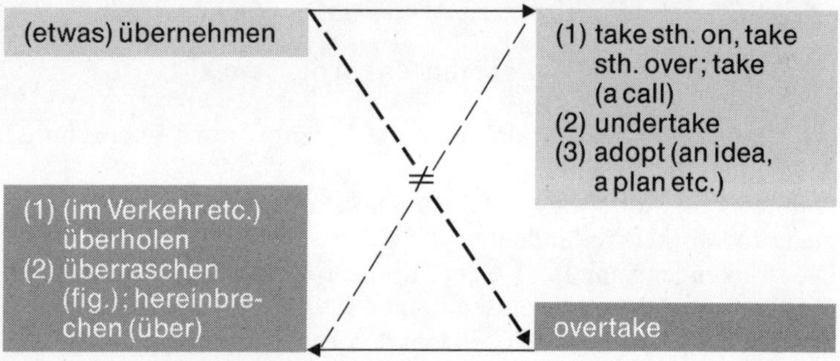

FALSE FRIENDS IN CONTEXT

Who is Running the Show?

Stage Manager: The new stage show of *Treasure Island* doesn't appeal to me in its present form.
Producer: I think we'd better ________ (1) the old plan.
Stage Manager: Putting a real parrot with Long John Silver on stage is quite an outstanding feature.
Producer: Ok. I'll ________ (2) to advertise for a possible 'candidate' in the local paper.

* * *

Stage Manager: Sorry, I'm late. I just couldn't ________ (3) any cars on the way here. The streets were blocked with them. They are even outside the theatre.
Producer: Don't you remember? We're auditioning for a parrot today.

Stage Manager: I'll ________ (4) now and choose the right 'candidate' for the show.

* * *

Stage Manager (two hours later): Ok. Your parrot is just right for the role. What's his name?
Owner: Humbert.

* * *

Producer: We have been trying to work with Humbert for ten days now, but that parrot is impossible.
Stage Manager: Why?
Producer: Humbert continually turns his back to the audience and won't stop squawking when the others speak. Then he bit Long John Silver so hard that he drew blood. But worst of all, Humbert covered Long John Silver from head to foot during rehearsals.
Stage Manager: The last thing we want is the show to be ________ (5) by a parrot. Go ahead and sack him.

SOLUTION

(1) adopt (2) undertake (3) overtake (4) take over (5) be taken over

ÜBERREICHEN ≠ overreach

overreach [ˌəʊvəˈriːtʃ]

ÜBERREICHEN

(= übergeben)

hand over etc.

ÜBERREICHEN: (1) (übergeben) hand over (to), present s. o. with
(2) (formell übergeben) present sth. (to)

(1) Sir Harold **überreichte** seinem Nachfolger alle Schlüssel und Unterlagen und verließ danach sofort das Rathaus.
Sir Harold **handed over** all the keys and documents **to** his successor and left the town hall at once.
Der Vereinsvorsitzende **überreichte** jedem Mitglied der siegreichen Tennismannschaft eine Goldmedaille und einen Scheck von 500 Dollar.
The club president **presented** each member of the winning tennis team **with** a gold medal and a 500 dollar cheque.
(2) Der neue italienische Botschafter **überreichte** der Königin sein Beglaubigungsschreiben.
The new Italian ambassador **presented** his credential **to** the Queen.

overreach (o. s.): (1) sich übernehmen
(2) zu weit gehen, über das Ziel hinausschießen
(3) jdn. übervorteilen, überlisten

(1) "The last job was too much for him. Henry simply **overreached** himself," his wife sobbed.
"Die letzte Arbeit war zuviel für ihn. Henry hat sich einfach **übernommen**", schluchzte seine Frau.
(2) In introducing the Poll Tax Margaret Thatcher **overreached herself** and as a consequence fell from power.
Mit der Einführung der Kopfsteuer **ging** Margaret Thatcher **zu weit** und verlor als Folge die Macht.
(3) In the last phase of the campaign, the candidate tried to **overreach** his opponent, but failed.
In der letzten Phase seiner Aktion versuchte er seinen Gegner zu **überlisten**, aber es mißlang.

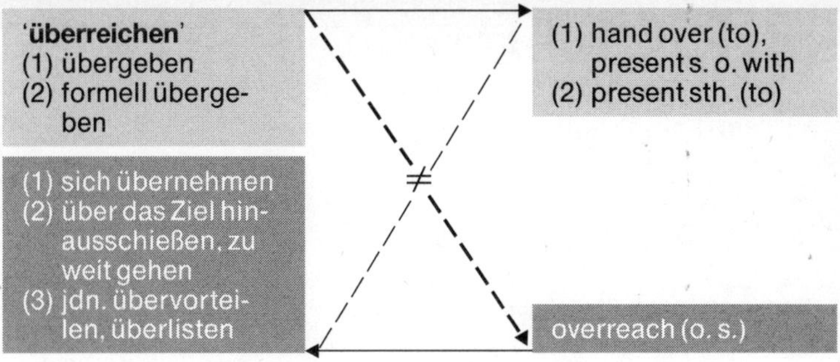

FALSE FRIENDS IN CONTEXT

A Child's View

Six-year-old Carol ________ (1) her drawing to me and watched me expectantly. I could see it was an aeroplane.
"And what is it?" I asked.
"Oh," she replied, "it's the flight into Egypt." And ________ (2) herself, she added pointing to the man in the cockpit, "That's Pontius the Pilate, of course."
"The what?" I insisted.
"Can't you see, the pilot," she repeated.

SOLUTION

(1) handed over (2) overreaching

ÜBERSCHLAFEN ≠ oversleep

oversleep [ˌəʊvəˈsliːp] → **ÜBERSCHLAFEN**

sleep on sth. ← (= in Ruhe überdenken)

ÜBERSCHLAFEN: (etwas in Ruhe überdenken) sleep on sth.

"Ihr Telefonanruf kommt völlig überraschend. Ich muß das Ganze erst **überschlafen**, ehe ich endgültig entscheide, ob ich die Stelle annehme."
"Your telephone call comes as a complete surprise. I'll **have to sleep on it** before finally deciding whether to take the job or not."
"Es tut mir leid", wiederholte er, "aber ich muß das Ganze erst einmal **überschlafen**."
"I'm sorry," he repeated, "but I'll have to **sleep on it** first."

oversleep: (sich) verschlafen; die Zeit verschlafen

Tom was late for work again; he had **overslept** and had to think of an excuse to satisfy his personnel manager.
Tom war schon wieder zur Arbeit zu spät gekommen; er hatte **(sich) verschlafen** und mußte für den Personalchef eine Ausrede finden.
The Kenyan runner had been practising for the last four years and had got through to the Olympic final. He had rested a little in one of the rooms of the stadium, then **overslept** and missed the final.
Der Läufer aus Kenia hatte die letzten vier Jahre trainiert und war ins olympische Finale gekommen. Er hatte sich ein wenig in einem der Räume des Stadions ausgeruht, dann **die Zeit verschlafen** und den Endlauf verpaßt.

Note: (be) unaware of sth.; (be) out of touch with sth. = **etwas verschlafen (fig.)**

Our firm **has** simply **been unaware** of the latest developments in computer technology.
Many people in Albania **were** at one time completely **out of touch with** modern life.

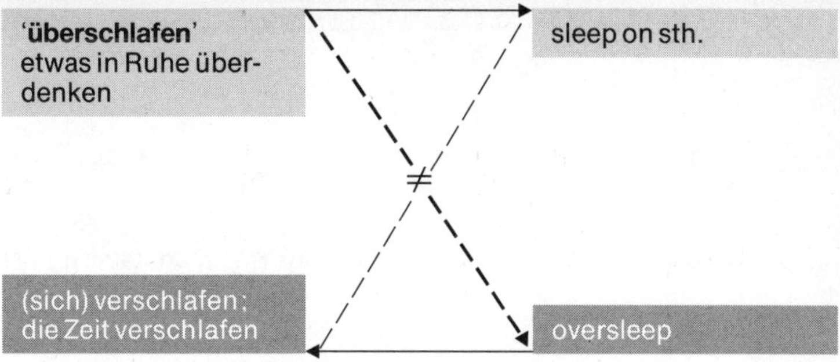

FALSE FRIENDS IN CONTEXT

The Tide Trap

Artist's Wife (62): I don't really want to go down the coastroad to Lepe today, but I'll ________ (1) on it and tell you in the morning.
Elderly Artist (81): Why have you always got to ________ (2) on things?

* * *

Elderly Artist: This is a nice spot. It's level with the sea. So we can sit peacefully in the car.
Artist's Wife: It was a good idea to come here. The sea's so calm and the air's so pleasant (after a while both start to nod off).

* * *

Artist's Wife (suddenly waking up in surprise): Look, there's water all around us. We've ________ (3).
Elderly Artist (still somewhat sleepy): What? I'll start the engine.
Artist's Wife: You can't. We're trapped by the tide. This comes from ________ (4). What shall we do?
Elderly Artist: Look over there. Some windsurfers are sailing towards us. They'll help us.

* * *

Artist's Wife (an hour later talking to her neighbour): The surfers were wonderful. They not only took us to the shore, but drove us back to Dibden Purlieu in their car. We were lucky to have survived the tide trap.

Elderly Artist: I've always said, "The best place to ________ (5) is at home."

SOLUTION

(1) I'll **sleep on it** (2) **sleep on things** (3) we've overslept (4) over-sleeping (5) oversleep

ÜBERSEHEN ≠ oversee

oversee [ˌəʊvəˈsiː] ·················· ÜBER'SEHEN (I)

overlook (I)
be tired of sth. (II) —————— 'ÜBERSEHEN (II)

ÜBER'**SEHEN** (I): (1) (unabsichtlich) overlook, miss, fail to see
(2) (absichtlich) ignore, turn a blind eye to
(3) (die Folgen etc. über**sehen**) foresee, assess (fig.)

(1) Ich hatte Glück, daß mein Lehrer den Fehler **übersehen** hat.
I was lucky my teacher **overlooked** the mistake.
"Sie haben das Stoppschild **übersehen**", sagte mir der Polizist, als ich angehalten hatte.
"You **missed** the halt sign," the policeman told me, after I had stopped.
Mein Kollege **übersah** völlig, welche Bedeutung die Bemerkung des Chefs für seine berufliche Zukunft hatte.
My colleague completely **failed to see** how important our boss's remark was for his professional future.
(2) Keith **übersah** seine frühere Frau geflissentlich auf der Geburtstagsfeier.
Keith deliberately **ignored** his former wife at the birthday party.
"Sie können als zuständiger Minister nicht einfach die Lage der Bauern länger **übersehen**", warnte ein Vertreter der Bauern.
"As responsible minister you simply can't **turn a blind eye to** the farmers' situation any longer," a farmers' representative warned.
(3) Können Sie schon **übersehen**, wann die Produktion in dem Stahlwerk eingestellt wird?
Can you **foresee** when production will stop at the steel works?
"Die schrecklichen Folgen der Luftverschmutzung durch verbleites Benzin für Großbritannien lassen sich noch nicht **übersehen**", betonte ein Sprecher des Umweltministeriums.
"The terrible consequences for Britain of air pollution from leaded petrol cannot be **assessed**," a spokesman for the Department of the Environment emphasized.

'ÜBERSEHEN (II): (4) (sich etwas '**über**sehen) be tired of sth., be fed up with
(5) (sich nicht '**über**sehen können an) (not) get enough of

(4) After a week our Japanese visitor **was tired of** looking at the paintings in the National Gallery.
Unser japanischer Besucher **hatte sich** die Gemälde in der Nationalgalerie nach einer Woche **übergesehen**.
"People are **fed up with** American films and do not go to the cinema as much as in the past," a cinema-owner remarked critically.
"Die Leute **haben sich** die amerikanischen Filme **übergesehen** und kommen nicht mehr ins Kino wie früher", merkte ein Kinobesitzer kritisch an.
(5) At first the West German tourists **couldn't get enough of** Russian art, but soon they discovered the Russian theatre.
Zunächst **konnten sich** die westdeutschen Touristen **nicht an** russischer Kunst **übersehen**, aber bald entdeckten sie das russische Theater.

oversee: überwachen, beaufsichtigen

After the King's Cross disaster Sir Keith Bright stayed on at London Regional Transport to **oversee** the introduction of new safety measures.
Nach der King's Cross-Katastrophe blieb Sir Keith Bright weiter bei London Regional Transport, um die Einführung neuer Sicherheitsmaßnahmen zu **überwachen**.
That foreman has the job of **overseeing** the work of road construction.
Dieser Vorarbeiter hat die Aufgabe, die Straßenbauarbeiten zu **beaufsichtigen**.

über'**sehen** (I) (1) unabsichtlich über**sehen** (2) absichtlich über**sehen** (3) die Folgen etc. über**sehen** '**über**sehen (II) (4) sich etwas '**über**sehen (5) sich nicht '**über**sehen können an	≠	(I) (1) overlook, miss, fail to see (2) ignore, turn a blind eye to (3) foresee, assess (fig.) (II) (4) be tired of sth., be fed up with sth. (5) (not) get enough of
beaufsichtigen, überwachen		oversee

FALSE FRIENDS IN CONTEXT

Hot Gossip, Hot Kisses

Bank Raider (rushing into a Nat West Bank branch in South London): This is a bank raid. No funny business... I won't ________ (1) any nonsense (threatening the bank clerks and cashiers with his gun and his knife).
Female Bank Cashier (Muriel Budge, 22, addressing him calmly): We won't ________ (2) your demands. I can assure you there'll be no nonsense from us.
Bank Raider (Jeremy McClaire, 29, as identified later): Right, everyone keep perfectly quiet, turn to the wall and put your hands behind your backs.

* * *

Female Bank Cashier (two hours later): Armed police have surrounded the bank. Why not surrender now while you can still ________ (3) the situation?
Bank Raider: Ok. I can't ________ (4) your sweet-talk any longer. Listen, the rest of you, you've got to thank this young lady for your release, but there's one condition. She's got to kiss me first (He pulls up his mask, walks up to her and gets a kiss on both cheeks).
Ok. I'll untie your hands now and you walk out through the main entrance.

Female Bank Cashier (after her last colleague has left): I think you'd better give up now, don't you? I'll put in a good word for you with the police outside.
Bank Raider: Listen, my young lady. I'll release you after a final cigarette, but give me two good kisses first. Now turn your back to the entrance to cover me (He walks up to her and she kisses the raider twice).
Female Bank Cashier: All right.
Bank Raider: All right. I've ________ (5) the consequences. You walk outside, but don't be frightened when I throw my gun and knife out after you (She gives him a swift farewell kiss and walks out).

SOLUTION

(1) turn a blind eye to (2) ignore (3) assess/weigh up (4) ignore
(5) assessed/weighed up

ÜBERSICHT ≠ oversight

oversight ['əʊvəsaɪt]

ÜBERSICHT

survey ['sɜ:veɪ], **summary etc.**

ÜBERSICHT: (1) (zusammenfassende Übersicht) survey, summary, synopsis, abstract, outline
(2) (tabellarische Übersicht) list, table
(3) (Übersicht, allgemein) (overall) view (of), (general) idea (of)
(4) (verbal: die **Übersicht** verlieren) lose track of

(1) Der Band vermittelt eine reich illustrierte **Übersicht** der privilegierten Welt des Bankwesens.
The new volume contains a richly illustrated **survey** of the privileged world of banking.
In ihrer **Übersicht** enthüllen die amerikanischen Forscher die geläufigsten amerikanischen Kosenamen: Honey, dicht gefolgt von Baby, Sweetheart, Dear.
In their **summary** American researchers disclosed the most common American expressions of endearment: Honey, closely followed by Baby, Sweetheart, Dear.
Die knappe **Übersicht** am Ende des Buchs vermittelt Ihnen eine erste thematische Orientierung.
A short **synopsis** at the end of the book provides you with some basic information on the subject.
Außerdem habe ich für Sie eine fotokopierte **Übersicht** mitgebracht, die aus den Buch stammt.
In addition, I've brought with me a photocopied **abstract** taken from the book.
Wer sich noch etwas weiter mit dem Thema beschäftigen will, dem steht eine allgemeine **Übersicht** dieses Zeitalters zur Verfügung.
For those of you intending to go into the subject in greater detail, there is a general **outline** of that historical period.
(2) Können Sie mir eine **Übersicht** der einzelnen Chöre mit ihren Dirigenten erstellen?
Could you make up a **list** for me of the individual choirs with their conductors?

"Hier ist eine Ergebnis-**Übersicht** der ersten und zweiten Bundesliga", sagte der Sportkommentator am Ende der Sendung.
"Here's a **table** with the results from the first and second divisions," announced the sports commentator at the end of the programme.
(3) Wie bekomme ich am schnellsten eine **Übersicht über** die Lage der Schwarzen in Südafrika?
Which is the quickest way for me to get an **overall view of** the situation of the black population in South Africa?
In diesem Stadium hatte meine Tante die **Übersicht über** die Dinge verloren.
At this stage my aunt had no **idea of** what was going on.
(4) Seit ihrer Scheidung scheint Jane jede **Übersicht verloren** zu haben.
Since her divorce Jane seems to have **lost track of** what is going on.

oversight: Versäumnis, Versehen

The delay in posting the letter was caused by an **oversight** on my brother's part.
Die Verzögerung bei der Absendung des Briefs entstand durch ein **Versäumnis** meines Bruders.
It is true the cheque was made out incorrectly, but this was an **oversight** on my part.
Es ist richtig, daß der Scheck falsch ausgeschrieben ist, aber das kam nur durch ein **Versehen** meinerseits zustande.

'Übersicht'
(1) zusammenfassende Übersicht
(2) tabellarische Übersicht
(3) Übersicht (allgemein (über)
(4) verbal: die **Übersicht** verlieren

(1) survey, summary, synopsis, abstract, outline
(2) list, table
(3) (overall) view (**of**), (general) idea (**of**)
(4) lose track of

≠

Versäumnis, Versehen

oversight

FALSE FRIENDS IN CONTEXT

The Kitchen Revolution

Young TV Housewife: Nowadays housewives are starting to lose ________ (1) of the kitchen business. Do you agree?
Middle-Aged Lady: I think the modern kitchen is different from the English kitchen before the war. Even if I don't have an ________ (2) of the latest developments, progress has certainly been made in the modern kitchen. Take frozen food and the freezer, for example.
Young TV Housewife: A ________ (3) of the modern kitchen should include other items such as modern kitchen furniture. But weren't we taught about modern kitchen techniques at school?
Middle-Aged Lady: You're quite right. In the 1930s I taught housecraft to girls only, in the 1960s I started to teach domestic science to boys and girls, and in the 1970s teaching home economics to both sexes seemed quite normal. A ________ (4) on the kitchen revolution would not be complete without mentioning changes of this nature.
Young TV Housewife: Yes, that's a common ________ (5) in many discussions on the subject. But the most revolutionary advance in the kitchen of today is the microwave oven.
Middle-Aged Lady: Certainly. Like many young mini-chefs, I use a microwave oven myself. And what's so revolutionary is that I have no saucepan to wash up.

SOLUTION

(1) lose track of (2) overall view of (3) survey (4) survey (5) oversight

ÜBERWINDEN ≠ overwind

overwind [ˌəʊvəˈwaɪnd]

ÜBERWINDEN

overcome [ˌəʊvəˈkʌm] **etc.**

ÜBERWINDEN: (1) (Probleme, Schwierigkeiten etc.) overcome, conquer
(2) (Schock, Erlebnisse etc.) get over, recover from, get the better of
(3) (sich nicht überwinden können [im Deutschen stets negativ konstruiert]) bring o. s. to, be reluctant to

(1) "Wir können die Probleme mit den Fußball-Rowdies nur **überwinden**, wenn der Sportminister persönlich eingreift", merkte der Fußball-Manager an.
"We can only **overcome** the problems with soccer hooligans by the personal intervention of the Sports Minister," the football manager remarked.
Die Saudis versuchen gerade, die Gefahren der Umweltverschmutzung im Persischen Golf zu **überwinden**.
The Saudis are now trying to **conquer** the dangers of pollution in the Arabian Gulf.
(2) "Vorurteile dieser Art können ohne große Schwierigkeiten **überwunden** werden, wenn man mit den Betroffenen redet", behauptete der Psychologe.
"Prejudices of this kind can be **got over** without much difficulty if you talk to those affected," maintained the psychologist.
Jane brauchte lange Zeit, um den Schock zu **überwinden**, ihren Verlobten im Golfkrieg verloren zu haben.
Jane took a long time to **recover from** the shock of losing her fiancé in the Gulf War.
Mutter Teresas Liebe **überwand** alle Klassenschranken, und sie gewann die Herzen der Armen.
Mother Teresa's love **got the better of** all the class barriers, winning the hearts of the poor.
(3) Sie konnte sich nicht **überwinden**, ihrem Vater die Wahrheit zu sagen.

She couldn't **bring herself to** tell her father the truth.
Als es soweit war, **konnte sich** mein Freund **nicht überwinden**, mit dem Fallschirm abzuspringen.
When it came to it, my friend **was reluctant to** do the parachute jump.

overwind: (eine Uhr) zu weit aufziehen; (ein Uhrwerk) überdrehen

"I've got that watch from my grandfather. Take care not to **overwind** it," my father advised me.
"Ich habe die Uhr von meinem Großvater geerbt. Achte darauf, sie nicht **zu weit aufzuziehen**", riet mir mein Vater.

'**überwinden**' (1) (Probleme, Schwierigkeiten etc.) überwinden (2) (Schock, Erlebnisse etc.) überwinden (3) (sich) nicht überwinden (können)	→	(1) overcome, conquer (2) get over, recover from, get the better of (3) bring o. s. to, be reluctant to
(eine Uhr) zu weit aufziehen; (ein Uhrwerk) überdrehen	←	overwind

FALSE FRIENDS IN CONTEXT

A Change of Attitudes

Does Christmas ________ (1) people's negative attitudes? I don't believe in miracles, but I think little things do happen now and then.
It was snowing last Xmas Eve when, after some last-minute shopping, I saw two cars bump into each other in the car park. As expected, one of them jumped out of his car in anger, then ________ (2) from his initial shock, got a grip on himself and walked over to the other car.
Slowly the other driver climbed out of his car and I wondered how he was going to ________ (3) his initial anger.
The men looked at each other for a few seconds, exchanged the usual details as on any other day of the year. But then they shook hands, got

into one car and drove off together. Later on I met them in a nearby pub drinking each other's health.
Reflecting on it a year later I'm sure many people would never have ________ (4) to change their initial attitudes. "This comes from ________ (5) your watch," as my grandfather often used to say in such cases.

SOLUTION

(1) overcome (2) **recovered from** his initial shock (3) get the better of (4) would never have brought themselves to (5) **overwinding** your watch

UNTERARM ≠ underarm

underarm [ˈʌndərɑ:m]

UNTERARM

forearm [ˈfɔ:rɑ:m]

UNTERARM: forearm

Bei dem Unfall brach der linke **Unterarm** des Fahrers an zwei Stellen.
In the accident, the driver's left **forearm** was broken in two places.
In einer internationalen Begegnung mit den Westindischen Inseln wurde der englische Kricketspieler Small vom Ball am **Unterarm** getroffen, der dann im Tor einschlug.
In a Test Match against the West Indies the English cricketer, Small, was hit on the **forearm** by the ball, which then hit the wicket.

underarm: (1) (unter der) Achsel; Achsel(höhlen)bereich
(2) '**Achsel**-' (in combinations)
(3) (im Sport, besonders im Kricket und Tennis) (den Ball) **von unten** werfen; **von unten** aufschlagen etc.

(1) Before Pamela went on the tennis court she quickly put on an **underarm** spray.
Bevor Pamela auf den Tennisplatz ging, nahm sie schnell noch einen Spray für die **Achselhöhle**.
(2) **Underarm** odours are thought to be used in communicating sexual and social messages.
Man glaubt, daß **Achsel**gerüche dazu dienen, sexuelle und zwischenmenschliche Botschaften mitzuteilen.
(3) "If you throw the ball, don't throw **underarm**," the PT teacher told his pupils.
"Wenn ihr den Ball werft, werft ihn nicht **von unten** (= im Schockwurf)", sagte der Sportlehrer zu den Schülern.
In the early days of cricket the bowler could bowl **underarm** or overarm; nowadays all bowling is overarm.
In der Frühzeit des Kricketspiels konnte der Werfer **von unten** oder von oben werfen; heutzutage wird nur von oben geworfen.

To John McEnroe's utter surprise his opponent served the ball **under-arm**.
Zu John McEnroes nicht geringem Erstaunen schlug sein Gegner den Ball **von unten** auf.

Unterarm	≠	forearm
(1) (unter der) Achsel; Achsel(höhlen)bereich (2) '**Achsel-**' (3) (den Ball) **von unten** werfen; **von unten** aufschlagen etc.		(1) + (2) in combinations such as '**underarm** odour' (3) throw, bowl or serve **underarm**

FALSE FRIENDS IN CONTEXT

Shame of a Top Trainer

SCENE 1 (at Button Sheriff's stables watched by stable hands)
Grand National Trainer: (shouting) ... You didn't gallop that horse and you didn't obey my orders. I'll teach you a lesson (hurls a stick at Ian, a stable boy).
Stable Boy, in pain as the stick hits his ________ (1): Look what you've done. You've injured my ________ (2) ... That's a lame horse!
Grand National Trainer (now in a fit of rage): That horse isn't lame at all. You're a liar and now you're sacked [hits Ian again on the ________ (3), this time with his trainer's whip].
Stable Boy (runs away with blood trickling from his hand): You'll be sorry for this.

* * *

SCENE 2
Doctor examining Ian's ________ (4): Your ________ (5) doesn't look good. I'm afraid you'll have to forget about playing cricket.
Ian: I normally bowl. Can't I even do any harmless ________ (6) bowling?
Doctor: No, you can't.

* * *

SCENE 3 (at the Crown Court in York)

Judge (to Grand National Trainer): Do you plead guilty?

Grand National Trainer: No. I threw the branch because the horse was going to lash out with its hind legs.

Judge: You've been found guilty on the evidence given. You have to pay £420 prosecution costs, and in addition, £1.400 for unfair dismissal and £3.500 for causing bodily harm to the former stable boy's ________ (7).

Grand National Trainer: Your Honour, do you realize the Jockey Club Association will also be investigating?

Judge: That doesn't concern our court decision.

SOLUTION

(1) forearm (2) forearm (3) forearm (4) forearm (5) forearm (6) **underarm** bowling (7) forearm

UNTERGEHEN ≠ undergo

undergo [ˌʌndəˈgəʊ]

UNTERGEHEN

sink etc.

UNTERGEHEN: (1) (sinken, untergehen) sink, go under (also fig.), go down
(2) (umkommen, vergehen) perish (also fig.)
(3) (zusammenbrechen) collapse
(4) (von Himmelskörpern: versinken) set (sun etc.)

(1) Joe Kay, ein Überlebender des Fährenunglücks bei Zeebrugge, befand sich in seinem Lastwagen, als das Schiff **unterging**.
Joe Kay, a survivor of the Zeebrugge ferry disaster, was in his lorry when the ship **sank**.
Während der Weltwirtschaftskrise **gingen** im Schiffsbau viele Firmen **unter**.
During the Depression many shipbuilding firms **went under**.
Der Kapitän wurde von einem Hubschrauber gerettet, kurz bevor das Schiff **unterging**.
The captain was saved by a helicopter, shortly before the ship **went down**.
(2) Millionen **gingen** im Golfkrieg in den Flammen des Fanatismus **unter**.
Millions **perished** in the flames of fanaticism during the Gulf War.
(3) Mit dem Fall Konstantinopels **ging** das Römische Reich endgültig **unter**.
With the fall of Constantinople the Roman Empire finally **collapsed**.
(4) Es war Zeit nach Hause zu gehen, da die Sonne langsam hinter den Hügeln **unterging**.
It was time to go home as the sun slowly **set** behind the hills.

Note: Selbst wenn ich durchs Examen falle, **geht** davon die Welt **nicht unter** = Even if I fail in the exam, it'll **not be the end** of the world.
Ihre Hilferufe **gingen** im Lärm **unter** = Her cries for help **were drowned** by the noise.

undergo: (1) sich unterziehen
(2) durchstehen
(3) durchlaufen, durchmachen

(1) He **underwent** special training to become an interpreter at the United Nations.
Er **unterzog sich** einer Spezialausbildung, um Dolmetscher bei den Vereinten Nationen zu werden.
The 'dead' businessman had **undergone** plastic surgery and was living under a new name.
Der 'tote' Geschäftsmann hatte sich einer Gesichtsoperation **unterzogen** und lebte unter einem neuen Namen.
(2) Neil, 12, has **undergone** chemotherapy in the last few weeks.
Der zwölfjährige Neil **hat** in den letzten Wochen eine Chemotherapie **durchgestanden**.
(3) The new spray is currently **undergoing** tests and could go on sale next year.
Der neue Spray **durchläuft** zur Zeit Tests und kann nächstes Jahr zum Verkauf kommen.
Nicky has **undergone** a complete transformation since he became a Christian.
Nicky hat eine völlige Wandlung **durchgemacht**, seit er Christ wurde.

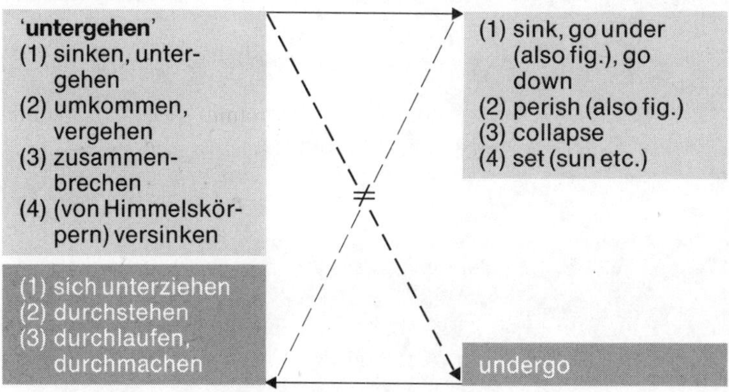

FALSE FRIENDS IN CONTEXT

The Sickest Joke

Veteran Actor: The *Marchioness* ________ (1) within a few minutes after it had collided with another boat on the Thames. Everyone's talking about the tragic victims who ________ (2) in the pleasure boat disaster.
Veteran Actress: But who speaks for those who escaped death now suffering from depression and other physical diseases?
Veteran Actor: Nothing has been done for the people who were rescued. Look at Burt for example. He had to ________ (3) several operations, aftercare and then had to have his left leg amputated. Now his family is planning to sue the shipowners for compensation.
Veteran Actress: That's right. Only the relatives of the dead victims have received some compensation. The persons who were rescued didn't get a penny. It's just the sickest joke imaginable!

SOLUTION

(1) sank/went down (2) went down; perished (3) undergo

UNTERLIEGEN ≠ underlie

underlie [ˌʌndəˈlaɪ]

UNTERLIEGEN

be defeated etc.

UNTERLIEGEN: (1) (im Kampf etc.) be defeated, lose
(2) (Sport) go down (to), lose (to)
(3) (erliegen fig.) yield to, succumb [səˈkʌm] to
(4) (den Bestimmungen, dem Wandel etc.) be subject to; come within, fall within
(5) (der Besteuerung, den Zollbestimmungen) be liable to

(1) Es ist eine Tragödie, daß die armenischen Kurden am Ende im Kampf um größere Autonomie **unterlagen**.
It's a tragedy the Armenian Kurds **were** finally **defeated** in their battle for greater autonomy.
Die Banken müssen die Zinsen senken, sonst **unterliegen** wir im Kampf gegen die Inflation.
The banks have to lower their interest rates, otherwise we'll **lose** the fight for inflation.
(2) In einem Pokalspiel **unterlag** Aston Villa den Bristol Rovers 3:2.
Aston Villa **went down to** Bristol Rovers 3–2 in a cup tie match.
Der Mittelgewichtler Mark Duran **unterlag gegen** Leonard nach dramatischem Kampf nach Punkten.
The middleweight Mark Duran **lost** on points **to** Leonard after a dramatic fight.
(3) Viele osteuropäische kommunistische Führer **unterlagen** der Korruption.
Many East European Communist leaders **yielded to** corruption.
Wie manche vor ihm **unterlag** der amerikanische Milliardär schließlich der Versuchung des Geldes.
As many others before him, the American billionaire eventually **succumbed to** the temptation of money.
(4) Kein Arzt **unterliegt** öffentlicher Kritik, wenn er sich weigert, ärztliche Sterbehilfe zu leisten.
No doctor **is subject to** censure for refusing to give medical help to die.

Machtpolitik wird stets dem Wandel der Zeit **unterliegen**.
Power politics will always **come within** the changes of time.
Leider **unterliegt** der Fall nicht dem internationalen Recht.
Unfortunately that case does not **fall within** international law.
(5) Selbst wenn du in Monaco wohnst, **unterliegt** dein Einkommen der Besteuerung.
Even if you live in Monaco, your income will **be liable to** taxation.
Auf jeden Fall **unterliegen** die aus Kolumbien eingeführten Waren den Zollbestimmungen.
The goods imported from Colombia **are liable to** duty anyway.

underlie: (1) zugrunde liegen
(2) liegen unter (geol. etc.)

(1) What **underlies** that question? – Social and ethnic problems.
Was **liegt** dieser Frage **zugrunde**? – Soziale und ethnische Probleme.
Unfortunately the judge didn't see the intention **underlying** her action.
Leider erkannte der Richter nicht die Absicht, die ihrem Handeln **zugrunde lag**.
(2) The new Scottish oilfields **underlie** the North Sea and will make Scotland Britain's fastest growing region.
Die neuen schottischen Ölfelder **liegen unter** der Nordsee und werden Schottland zur wirtschaftlich am schnellsten wachsenden Region Großbritanniens machen.

Note: underlying = zugrundeliegend
Her **underlying** assumption had been different; it had been wrong from the start.

'unterliegen' (1) im Kampf etc. unterliegen (2) (im Sport) unterliegen (3) erliegen (fig.) (4) den Bestimmungen, dem Wandel etc. unterliegen (5) der Besteuerung, den Zollbestimmungen unterliegen	(1) be defeated, lose (2) go down (to), lose (to) (3) yield to, succumb to (fig.) (4) be subject to; come within; fall within (5) be liable to
(1) zugrunde liegen (2) liegen unter (geol. etc.)	underlie

≠

FALSE FRIENDS IN CONTEXT

The Right Track with a Twist

Church Leader: It's a human tragedy. The Colombian Indians were first exploited and then most tribes ________ (1) in their battle for survival.

Influential Politician: I refuse to comment on that, but our government now recognizes the Indians' legal right to their land. This will be ________ (2) changes in Colombia.

Church Leader: I'm glad to hear that, but it comes as a surprise to me.

Influential Politician: Not to me. The Colombian Amazon can't exist without the Indians. They alone have the knowledge and experience to manage the rain forests. The white man is ________ (3) the fight to protect the rain forests. The earth's climatic stability is at stake.

Church Leader: I must warn you not to ________ (4) the temptation of mixing up the drugs issue with the Amazon Indians.

Influential Politician: Certainly not. They are the only people who can 'save' the rain forests in the Amazon. For the Colombian Amazon it is therefore this rather than the drugs issue that ________ (5) the government's future policy. Some people should be put on a boat down the Amazon and never allowed to return.

SOLUTION

(1) were defeated (2) will be **subject to** changes (3) is losing (4) **yield to** the temptation (5) underlies

UNTERNEHMEN ◑ undertake

undertake [ˌʌndəˈteɪk] ····· **UNTERNEHMEN** (= Verb)

do sth., do nothing etc. ← **UNTERNEHMEN** (= Verb)

UNTERNEHMEN: (1) (etwas, nichts etc. unternehmen) do sth., do nothing etc.
(2) (Reise; Versuch unternehmen) take (a trip); make (an attempt)
(3) (juristisch etwas unternehmen) take action (against)

(1) "Wir müssen **etwas unternehmen**, um die Entwicklung aufzuhalten", schrie der Oppositionsführer plötzlich.
"We've got to **do something** to stop this development," shouted the leader of the opposition suddenly.
Laß uns heute abend **etwas** gemeinsam **unternehmen**.
Let's **do something** together this evening.
In dieser Situation können wir **nichts unternehmen**.
We can **do nothing** in this situation.
(2) Letzte Woche **unternahmen** wir einen Ausflug an die Küste, aber es regnete die meiste Zeit.
Last week we **took** a trip to the seaside, but it rained most of the time.
Gestern **unternahmen** einige Häftlinge den Versuch, zu fliehen.
Yesterday some prisoners **made** an attempt to escape.
(3) Unser Mandant erwägt, **etwas gegen** seine Firma zu **unternehmen**.
Our client is considering **taking action against** his company.

undertake: (1) übernehmen, anpacken
(2) wahrnehmen, auf sich nehmen
(3) sich verbürgen, sich verpflichten
(4) (Vertrag etc.) eingehen

(1) The millionaire paid for a specialist security company to **undertake** these duties.
Der Millionär hatte ein Spezial-Sicherheitsunternehmen beauftragt, diese Aufgaben zu **übernehmen**.
My friend **undertook** this mammoth task without complaint.

Mein Freund **packte** diese Mammutaufgabe ohne Klagen **an**.
(2) Her Royal Highness **undertook** official engagements in Leicestershire.
Ihre Königliche Hoheit **nahm** offizielle Verpflichtungen in Leicestershire **wahr**.
(3) Amnesty International **undertake** that human rights will be kept in West European countries.
Amnesty International **verbürgt sich**, daß die Menschenrechte in westeuropäischen Ländern eingehalten werden.
The princess **undertook** to love, honour and obey her husband.
Die Prinzessin **verpflichtete sich**, ihren Mann zu lieben, zu ehren und ihm zu gehorchen.
(4) Claire Gooding always ensures that one clause is included in any new contract she **undertakes** – stabling and food for her horse, Chloe.
Claire Gooding stellt stets sicher, daß eine Klausel in jedem Vertrag enthalten ist, den sie **eingeht** – Stallung und Futter für ihr Pferd Chloe.

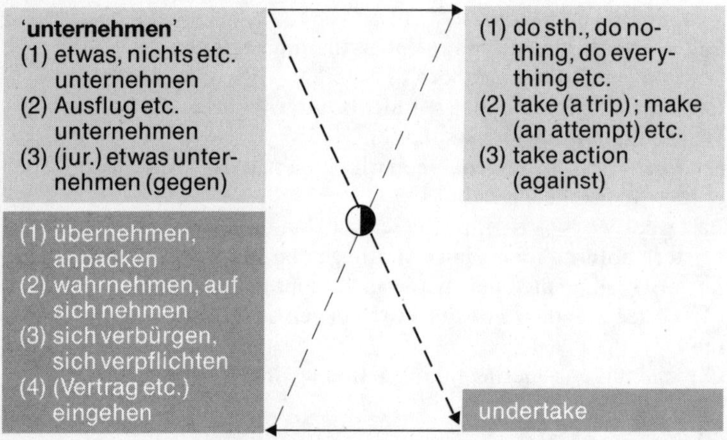

FALSE FRIENDS IN CONTEXT

Girlfriend Trouble

Being the new sales assistant in the Christmas card department soon brought me some problems, and I realized I should have to ______ (1) something about it.
The other day a young lady asked me for a special card for a husband and his girlfriend. On another occasion a girl walked in demanding a card for dad and his girlfriend.
Fortunately, I managed to get round it by suggesting a card which said, *To Both of you at Christmas*.
Unfortunately, some of my customers ________ (2) to explain their situation in this way, "I don't speak to the girlfriend" and left the shop.
After a series of 'tests' ________ (3) by myself I developed a new card meeting the demand, *For Daddy and Girlfriend*...
All went well until a girl walked into the shop wanting a card *For my Uncle and his Girlfriend*...
I was in trouble again, and I began to hate the girlfriend trouble.

SOLUTION

(1) do something about it (2) undertook (3) undertaken

UNTERNEHMEN ◑ undertaking

undertaking [ˌʌndəˈteɪkɪŋ] → **(das) UNTERNEHMEN** (in Industrie, Wirtschaft etc.)

business etc. ← **(das) UNTERNEHMEN** (in Industrie, Wirtschaft etc.)

(das) UNTERNEHMEN (in Industrie, Handel, Wirtschaft etc.):
(1) (**Unternehmen** je nach Größe und Rechtsform): business, company, concern, firm; enterprise etc.
(2) (Vertrags**unternehmen** wie Bau**unternehmen**, Reinigungs**unternehmen** etc.): building **contractor,** cleaning **contractor,** heating **contractor** etc.
(3) (spezielle Dienstleistungs**unternehmen**): (Beförderungs-, Transport-, Speditions**unternehmen** etc.) (by air) carrier(s), firm of carriers; (by road) haulier(s), firm of hauliers

(1) Haben Sie jemals daran gedacht, ein eigenes, unabhängiges **Unternehmen** zu gründen?
Have you ever thought about starting your own independent **business**?
Das **Unternehmen** ist an Entwicklung und Verkauf von Qualitätsimmobilien beteiligt.
The **company** is involved in the development and sale of quality properties.
Es wird schwierig sein, die in Konkurs geratene MCEG, eine Filmgesellschaft aus Los Angeles, als bestehendes **Unternehmen** zu veräußern.
It will be difficult to sell the bankrupt MCEG (= *M*anagement *C*ompany *E*ntertainment *G*roup), a Los Angeles film company, as a going **concern**.
Mittlere **Unternehmen** mit guten Computersystemen werden auf Kosten der Kleinen profitieren.
Medium-sized **firms** with good computer systems will benefit at the expense of small ones.
(2) Die meisten Geschäftsleute erhoben Einwände, Reinigungs**unternehmen** eine Reinigungsmaschine auf Bürgersteigen nachts benutzen zu lassen.

Most businessmen objected to cleaning **contractors** using a pavement washer at night.
Der Lastwagen des Bau**unternehmens** versperrte die enge Straße von 8 Uhr morgens bis zum frühen Abend.
The building **contractor**'s lorry blocked the narrow road from 8 a. m. to early evening.
(3) British Airways ist das größte Luftverkehrs**unternehmen** in Europa, das einst Interesse an Interflug, der ostdeutschen Fluggesellschaft, hatte.
British Airways is the largest **carrier** in Europe which once had an interest in Interflug, the East German airline.
Mehrere westdeutsche Transport**unternehmen** schickten Lastwagen mit Kleidung, Medikamenten und Nahrungsmitteln nach Rumänien, ohne etwas dafür zu verlangen.
Several West German **hauliers** sent lorries with clothes, medical supplies and food to Romania without charging anything.

undertaking: (1) Unternehmung; Unternehmen (= Durchführung) (einer Reise etc.)
(2) (formell, auch jur.) Verpflichtung, Versprechen

(1) My friend didn't want to build another factory, an **undertaking**, which could take several years.
Mein Freund wollte keine weitere Fabrik bauen, eine **Unternehmung**, die mehrere Jahre in Anspruch nehmen würde.
The tourist company's **undertaking** was called off for lack of interest.
Das **Unternehmen** der Touristikfirma wurde aus Mangel an Interesse abgeblasen.
(2) In 1991 a Zimbabwe golfer gave a written **undertaking** not to play in South Africa until all apartheid laws were lifted.
Im Jahre 1991 unterzeichnete ein Golfspieler aus Zimbabwe eine schriftliche **Verpflichtung**, nicht in Südafrika zu spielen, bis alle Apartheid-Gesetze aufgehoben würden.
The former manager admitted to violating a court order as well as an **undertaking** not to transfer money to a tax haven.
Der frühere Manager gab zu, eine gerichtliche Verfügung und ein **Versprechen** verletzt zu haben, nicht Geld in Steuerparadiese zu transferieren.

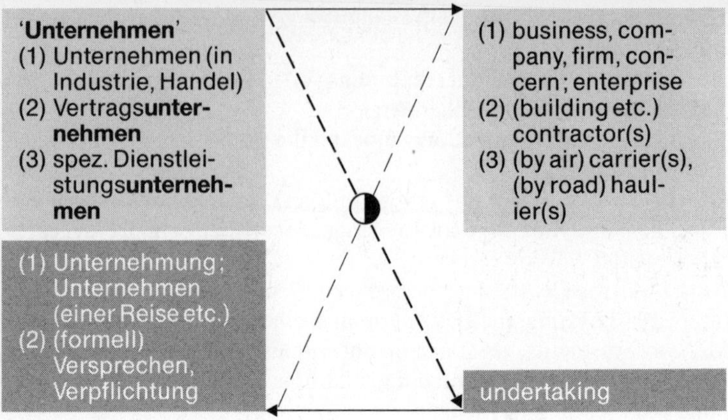

FALSE FRIENDS IN CONTEXT

Your Own Business

Dave: I'm down on my luck after wanting to start two small ______ (1), but it all came to nothing.
Helen: Why don't you give it a try a third time?
Dave: I've just made a decision. We're going to run a family ______ (2) where we're all involved.
Helen: And how's it going to work out?
Dave: We'll hire out jetskis during the holiday season.
Helen (surprised): Down at the lake?
Dave: No, on the Welsh coast at the New Quay Beach near Cardigan Bay.
Helen: Wonderful! Have you got a contract? And what about the jetskis?
Dave: Everything will be provided by a big holiday ______ (3). I don't even have to invest in the jetskis.
Helen: Wait a minute, Dave. What about the family of dolphins in Cardigan Bay?
Dave: They won't be affected. It's a promising ______ (4). Anyway, the profit is right and the time is right.

SOLUTION

(1) businesses (2) family **business** (3) holiday **contractor** (4) undertaking

UNTERNEHMER ≠ undertaker

undertaker [ˈʌndəˌteɪkə]

entrepreneur
[ˌɒntrəprəˈnɜː] **etc.**

UNTERNEHMER
(in Wirtschaft, Handel etc.)

UNTERNEHMER(IN):
(1) (woman) entrepreneur
(2) (Bau**unternehmer**) (building) contractor
(3) (Industrieller) industrialist
(4) (Transport**unternehmer**) haulier (by road), haulage contractor; AE hauler; carrier (by air)
(5) (Geschäftsmann/-frau) businessman, businesswoman
(6) (die **Unternehmer**) the bosses, the employers

(1) In den letzten Jahren hat sich die Zahl der **Unternehmerinnen** verdoppelt; die Zahl der selbständig tätigen Männer ist in Großbritannien nur um 50% gestiegen.
In the last few years the number of **women entrepreneurs** has doubled; the number of self-employed men has risen by only 50 per cent in Britain.
Gegenwärtig ist Victor Kiam einer der erfolgreichsten und populärsten amerikanischen **Unternehmer**.
At present, Victor Kiam is one of the most successful and popular American **entrepreneurs**.
(2) "**Subunternehmer** haben im letzten Sommer viel Geld verdient, aber in den Wintermonaten fast nichts. Das ist die Situation im Baugewerbe", erklärte der **Bauunternehmer** kurz nach Weihnachten.
"**Subcontractors** earned a lot of money last summer, but almost nothing during the winter months. That's the way it is in the building trade," the **contractor** explained shortly after Christmas.
(3) "Ähnlich ist es in der Stahlindustrie. Wenn wir keine Aufträge in den nächsten 14 Tagen bekommen, müssen wir die ersten 200 Arbeiter entlassen", betonte der **Unternehmer** aus der Industrie.
"It's similar in the steel industry. If we don't get any contracts in the next fortnight, we'll have to lay off the first two hundred workers," the **industrialist** emphasized.

(4) Fraser, einem Londoner Transport**unternehmer**, wurden in einer Nacht zwei Lastwagen im Werte von 55000 Pfund gestohlen.
Fraser, a London **haulier**, has had two lorries worth £55,000 stolen in one night.
Wie erwartet, war die Lufthansa der Transport**unternehmer** für die Waren in die Vereinigten Staaten.
As expected the **carrier** for the goods to the United States was Lufthansa.
(5) "Als unabhängiger **Unternehmer** bin ich nicht dem Aufsichtsrat verantwortlich", antwortete der Geschäftsführer zum Schluß.
"As an independent **businessman** I'm not responsible to the board of directors," answered the manager at the end.
(6) "Wir müssen zusammenhalten", sagte einer der Streikposten. "Dann werden die **Unternehmer** unseren Forderungen nachkommen."
"We've got to stick together," said one of the pickets. "Then the **bosses** will meet our demands."
"Aber ich bestehe darauf, daß unsere Bedingungen zwischen den **Unternehmern** und unserer Gewerkschaft ausgehandelt werden", rief ein Arbeiter.
"But I insist on our terms being negotiated between the **employers** and our union," shouted one of the workers.

Note: unternehmerisch = entrepreneurial
He had never met anyone with such **entrepreneurial** skills.
British girls are beginning to flaunt their **entrepreneurial** qualities in growing numbers.
Er ist **Unternehmer** = He has a business of his own.

undertaker: (1) Leichenbestatter (AE mortician); Bestattungs**unternehmer**; auch: funeral director; AE funeral(-home) man
(2) Bestattungsinstitut (undertaker's, undertaker's office; AE funeral home, AE funeral parlor, AE auch undertaking parlor); Bestattungs**unternehmen** (undertakers, firm of undertakers)

(1) An **undertaker** at Blois, France, was about to nail down the lid of a coffin ... when the corpse started to move.
Ein **Leichenbestatter** in Blois, Frankreich, war gerade dabei, den Sargdeckel zuzunageln ... als sich der Leichnam zu bewegen begann.

Undertakers prefer to keep a low profile. People like them to be anonymous men in dark suits.
Bestattungsunternehmer ziehen es vor, sich diskret im Hintergrund zu halten. Die Leute sehen sie gerne als anonyme Männer in dunklen Anzügen.
(2) Several **firms of undertakers** were involved in Churchill's state funeral.
Mehrere **Bestattungsinstitute** waren an Churchills Staatsbegräbnis beteiligt.

Note: mortuary or morgue = Leichenhalle

'Unternehmer'	≠
(1) Unternehmer(in) (allg.) (2) (meist) (Bau-) Unternehmer (3) Industrie-Unternehmer (4) Transportunternehmer (5) Geschäftsmann/-frau (6) (Pl.) **die** Unternehmer	(1) (woman) entrepreneur (2) (building) contractor (3) industrialist (4) haulier (by road), haulage contractor; carrier (by air) (5) businessman, businesswoman (6) the bosses, the employers
(1) Leichenbestatter, Bestattungs**unternehmer** (2) Bestattungsinstitut, Bestattungs**unternehmen**	(1) undertaker (BE); mortician (AE) etc. (2) (firm of) undertakers (BE), funeral parlor (AE); also undertaking parlor (AE) etc.

FALSE FRIENDS IN CONTEXT

Making Sure

Her father-in-law had been a millionaire and like most successful American ________ (1) had been actively involved in business and industry all his life. He died finally at the age of 92.

Mrs. Hardcastle had gone to meet an ________ (2) to arrange the funeral.
"Would you like him buried, cremated or embalmed?" asked the ________ (3) courteously.
"All three," Mrs. Hardcastle replied without thinking twice. "We're taking no chances."

SOLUTION

(1) entrepreneurs (2) undertaker (3) undertaker

The Blind Leading the Blind

Rory Brookman: I'm blind myself, and I want to help other blind ________ (4).
Radio Reporter: But how can you help them if you are blind yourself?
Rory Brookman: I'm going on a sponsored parachute jump near Swansea during an air-show. The proceeds from the charity jump will go to a fund for blind ________ (5) and ________ (6) (**Bauunternehmer**).
Radio Reporter: I wish you all the best for a successful first jump.

SOLUTION

(4) entrepreneurs (5) entrepreneurs (6) (building) contractors

UNTERSCHREIBEN ≠ underwrite

underwrite [ˈʌndəraɪt]

UNTERSCHREIBEN

sign etc.

UNTERSCHREIBEN: (1) sign, put one's name (to)
(2) (gutheißen) subscribe to (fig.)

(1) "Bitte **unterschreiben** Sie hier", sagte der Standesbeamte zur Braut.
"Please **put your name** here," the registrar said to the bride.
"Aber ich kann den Vertrag in dieser Form nicht **unterschreiben**", entgegnete mein Geschäftspartner.
"I'm sorry I can't **sign** the contract in this form," replied my business partner.
Wir können das nicht akzeptieren; Sie müssen eigenhändig **unterschreiben**.
We can't accept that, you've got to **sign** personally.
(2) "Ich weiß nicht, ob ich diese Äußerung so **unterschreiben** würde", warf ein Diskussionsteilnehmer ein.
"I don't know whether I'd **subscribe to** that statement," one of the participants in the discussion objected.

Note: ein auf der Rückseite **unterschriebener** Scheck = an endorsed cheque

underwrite: (1) (Projekt, Verlust etc.) finanziell (mit)tragen, finanziell garantieren; bürgen (für)
(2) (ein Wagnis etc.) versichern (gegen)
(3) (Versicherungen, Verträge etc.) abschließen; sich versichern lassen
(4) (Sport: eine Leistung etc.) eindrucksvoll untermauern; den Nachweis liefern (für)

(1) Rich art lovers **underwrote** the cost of an exhibition of French paintings in the United States.
Reiche Kunstliebhaber **trugen** die Kosten für eine Ausstellung französischer Gemälde in den Vereinigten Staaten **finanziell mit**.

Several Stock Exchange companies **underwrote** the privatization of British Gas.
Mehrere an der Börse vertretene Gesellschaften **bürgten für** die Privatisierung von British Gas.
(2) "We are agreeing to **underwrite** any losses or damages that may occur during the trip," Lloyd's confirmed in a letter.
"Wir stimmen zu, alle Verluste oder Schäden zu **versichern**, die während der Reise eintreten", bestätigte Lloyd's in einem Brief.
(3) James Gulliver, a Scottish millionaire, was the first to **underwrite** a cost cutting policy at Lloyd's.
James Gulliver, ein schottischer Millionär, war der erste, der eine kostensenkende Versicherungspolice bei Lloyd's **abschloß**.
The rich and famous **underwrite** at Lloyd's of London.
Die Reichen und die Berühmtheiten **lassen sich** bei Lloyd's in London **versichern**.
(4) In the final set Boris Becker hit winners on the run to **underwrite** his passage into the third round in Wimbledon.
Im letzten Satz schlug Boris Becker Gewinnbälle am laufenden Band und **untermauerte eindrucksvoll** sein Weiterkommen in die dritte Runde in Wimbledon.

Note: an (insurance) underwriter = ein Versicherer, ein Versicherungsgeber
In the short term, Lloyd's **underwriters** have profited from the airlift of American troops into Saudi Arabia.
underwriting loss = Versicherungsverlust
Britain's largest household insurer Sun Alliance's **underwriting loss** was £ 100.3 million in the UK in 1987.

'**unterschreiben**' (1) unterzeichnen (2) gutheißen (fig.)	(1) sign, put one's name (to) (2) subscribe to (fig.)
(1) (Projekt etc.) finanziell (mit)tragen; bürgen für (2) (Wagnis etc.) versichern (gegen) (3) (Versicherungen etc.) abschließen; sich versichern lassen (4) (Sport: Leistung etc.) eindrucksvoll untermauern; den Nachweis liefern (für)	underwrite

≠

FALSE FRIENDS IN CONTEXT

Mr. Fixit of Athletics

Treasurer of BAA (= *B*ritish *A*mateur *A*thletics): Several banks ________ (1) the cost of the international athletics meeting at Crystal Palace. I'll write you a cheque.
Mr. Fixit: Athletes from Russia or Africa won't accept cheques. I need £ 28,000 appearance money in cash.
Treasurer of BAA: Ok., but get every athlete to ________ (2) a receipt for the cash.

* * *

Mr. Fixit (complaining to the hotel manager): ... Thieves broke into my bedroom and stole my bag containing the cash for the athletics meeting tonight.
Hotel Manager: How much money?
Mr. Fixit: About £ 28,000.
Hotel Manager: You should have put the money into the hotel safe! Did you call the police?
Mr. Fixit: Yes. Fortunately the insurance company agreed to ________ (3) any losses.

Hotel Manager: Hm. Thank God!
Mr. Fixit: So there's no loss for BAA. But keep quiet about it.

* * *

Police Inspector: I'm here to investigate. Why did you carry so much in cash?
Mr. Fixit: It's normal practice for me to carry so much money around because payments to top athletes are always in cash.
Police Inspector: I don't ________ (4) to your statement.

SOLUTION

(1) underwrote/have underwritten/are underwriting (2) sign (3) underwrite (4) subscribe to

FALSE FRIENDS TRAPS TEST 6

TRICKY OVER-/UNDER-COMPOUNDS

1.a. To survive, blind people have to ________ rigorous mobility training (**untergehen ≠ undergo**).
1.b. The captain and crew were rescued by helicopter, shortly before the oil tanker ________ (**untergehen ≠ undergo**).
2.a. When I ________ my teacher's remark on purpose, everything went wrong at school during the next few days (**überhören ≠ overhear**).
2.b. A new theory is that the police might have ________ a terrorist radio transmission and stumbled upon one of their operations (**überhören ≠ overhear**).
3.a. Lorry drivers often frighten motorists out of their way as they pull out to ________ (**übernehmen ≠ overtake**).
3.b. Why should our company ________ to construct nuclear power stations? (**übernehmen ≠ overtake**)
4.a. Prince Charles and Princess Diana ________ an official visit to Hong Kong, but they refused to meet any Boat People (**unternehmen ◑ undertake**).
4.b. "Why don't the soccer clubs in this country ________ something to stop violence before and after matches?" asked the M. P. for Romford (**unternehmen ◑ undertake**).
5.a. Brian couldn't ________ to tell his father he had failed the exam for a second time (**überwinden ≠ overwind**). So he went on a trip to Canada.
5.b. Unfortunately she had ________ her great-grandfather's gold watch (**überwinden ≠ overwind**) and had to send it away as there was no one in the town to repair it.
6. "May I see your driving licence? You seem to have ________ (**übersehen**) that no-entry sign over there," remarked the policeman.
7. "Before I came to Las Vegas I was an honest man, but then I ________ (**unterliegen**) to the temptation of money," the old man admitted.
8. "What else could I do? I had to ________ (etwas juristisch **unternehmen**) against the investment firm," he stated. "I had lost everything."
9. "We can't ________ (**übersehen**) the damage caused by the hurricane as yet," Harry told his insurance company in the letter.

10. Every small-company ________ (**Unternehmer**) has to take certain risks. This also applies to many building ________ (Bau**unternehmer**).

ANSWER SHEET: TRUE FRIENDS TEST 6

TRICKY OVER-/UNDER-COMPOUNDS

1.a. To survive, blind people have to **undergo** rigorous mobility training.
1.b. The captain and crew were rescued by helicopter, shortly before the oil tanker **went down (sank)**.
2.a. When I **ignored** my teacher's remark on purpose, everything went wrong at school during the next few days.
2.b. A new theory is that the police might have **overheard** a terrorist radio transmission and stumbled upon one of their operations.
3.a. Lorry drivers often frighten motorists out of their way as they pull out to **overtake**.
3.b. Why should our company **undertake** to construct nucelar power stations?
4.a. Prince Charles and Princess Diana **undertook** an official visit to Hong Kong, but they refused to meet any Boat People.
4.b. "Why don't the soccer clubs in this country **do something** to stop violence before and after matches?" asked the M. P. for Romford.
5.a. Brian couldn't **bring himself to** tell his father he had failed the exam for a second time. So he went on a trip to Canada.
5.b. Unfortunately she had **overwound** her great-grandfather's gold watch and had to send it away as there was no one in the town to repair it.
6. "May I see your driving licence? You seem to have **overlooked** that no-entry sign over there," remarked the policeman.
7. "Before I came to Las Vegas I was an honest man, but then I **succumbed to** the temptation of money," the old man admitted.
8. "What else could I do? I had to **take action against** the investment firm," he stated. "I had lost all my properties."
9. "We can't **assess** the damage caused by the hurricane as yet," Harry told his insurance company in the letter.
10. Every small-company **entrepreneur** has to take certain risks. This also applies to many building **contractors**.

CONFUSIBLES KURZ-EINFÜHRUNG

Was sind Confusibles?

Englische Wortpaare wie **elementary/elemental** oder **sensual/sensuous**, die gleich oder ähnlich aussehende deutsche Entsprechungen haben (hier **elementar** bzw. **sinnlich**), werden als *Confusibles* bezeichnet; teilweise wird der Begriff auch *Confusables* geschrieben. Es handelt sich um einen wichtigen Sondertyp aus dem False Friends-Bereich, der in bestimmten Fällen selbst dem *native speaker* Schwierigkeiten bereiten kann.
Nicht alle *Confusibles* sind gleichzeitig False Friends. Die Adjektivpaare **forceful/forcible** oder **populated/populous** gehören zweifellos zu den *Confusibles*, können aber nicht beanspruchen, False Friends zu sein; denn es fehlt ein entsprechender gleicher oder ähnlicher Begriff im Deutschen. Daher scheiden hier alle *Confusibles* aus, die nicht gleichzeitig den Bedingungen für False Friends genügen.

BARBARISCH ◑ barbaric

barbaric [bɑː'bærɪk]

BARBARISCH

barbarous ['bɑːbərəs]

BARBARISCH: barbarous

Note: Its sense is strongly pejorative; it especially has the meaning of 'ugly or harsh in sound' (*see* Tennant, p. 12).

Das Verhalten der Fußball-Rowdies von Liverpool war **barbarisch**; sechs Menschen mußten mit Schnittwunden ins Krankenhaus eingeliefert werden.
The behaviour of the football hooligans from Liverpool was **barbarous**; six people had to be taken to hospital with cuts.
"Wir werden solche **barbarischen** Taten nicht länger hinnehmen", warnte ein Polizeisprecher im Fernsehen.
"We'll no longer tolerate such **barbarous** acts," a police spokesman warned on TV.
"Deshalb gehen wir gegen jede **barbarische** Behandlung harmloser Besucher vor", fügte der Klub-Manager von Liverpool hinzu.
"Therefore we'll take action against any **barbarous** treatment of harmless visitors," Liverpool's club manager added.

barbaric: (1) grausam, roh
(2) unzivilisiert, unkultiviert
(3) '**Barbaren-**' (in combinations)

Note: It especially refers to a foreign culture whose habits, folklore or customs seem strange (*see* Tennant, p. 12).

(1) It's unnecessary and **barbaric** to kill animals to make coats from their furs.
Es ist unnötig und **grausam**, Tiere zu töten, um Pelzmäntel aus den Fellen herzustellen.
"The slaughter of whales is without doubt the most **barbaric** form of execution," wrote a member of the Whale Club of the World in *The Times*.
"Das Abschlachten von Walen ist ohne Zweifel die **roheste** Hinrich-

tungsform", schrieb ein Mitglied des Whale Club of the World in der *Times*.
(2) "When will the regime of the **barbaric** invaders come to an end?" asked a UN representative in Namibia.
"Wann wird die Herrschaft der **unzivilisierten** Invasoren enden?" fragte ein UN-Beauftragter in Namibia.
The **barbaric** words of the tribal leader sounded in our ears.
Die **unkultivierten** Worte des Stammesführers hallten in unseren Ohren.
(3) Attila ruled over a **barbaric** empire.
Attila herrschte über ein **Barbaren**reich.

Compare: There are, however, cases in which the meaning of **barbarous** and **barbaric** overlap.
"We should pay tribute to those in positions of power who have the courage to chuck **barbarous/barbaric** planning proposals out," commented one of the journalists.
Barbarous here means hurtful to architectural taste or offensive to the eye, whereas **barbaric** means offensive and outlandish, not in keeping with local architecture.

but: In addition, a third adjective **barbarian** is the most neutral word (*see* Greenbaum/Whitcut, p. 76). If in doubt, **barbarian** [bɑːˈbeərɪən] is the safest choice.
By many Stalin is regarded as a **barbarian** dictator, although he did not see himself as a man imposing a **barbarian** culture.

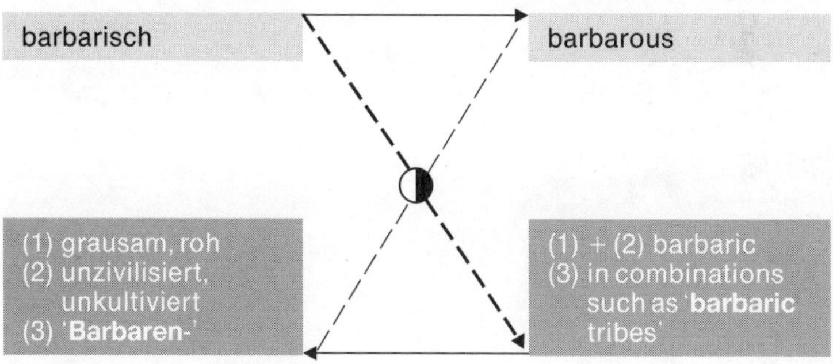

FALSE FRIENDS IN CONTEXT

A Letter to the Editor: A "Bird Festival"

Have you ever heard of the *Bird Festival*?
Well, it's the Stoning of Birds Festival in Spain, felt by many Englishmen to be the most ________ (1) festival in Europe, if not of the western world.
I can stand ________ (2) rock music and even the ________ (3) noise of football crowds, but I can't stand the ________ (4) treatment of God's feathered creatures. The Roman Catholic Church appears to tolerate such ________ (5) customs. But the enjoyment of cruelty, which has no rational basis other than a love of cruel behaviour, should be met with such measures as the boycott of Spanish imports and Spanish holiday resorts. But above all: stop this pain in Spain!

William Cooper
Hampstead, London.

SOLUTION

(1) **barbaric** festival (2) **barbarous** rock music (3) **barbarous** noise
(4) **barbarous** treatment (5) **barbaric** customs

DEFINITIV ◑ definitive

definitive [dɪˈfɪnɪtɪv] ··········► **DEFINITIV**

definite [ˈdefɪnɪt] ──────► (klar, eindeutig etc.)

DEFINITIV: (1) (klar, eindeutig, fest) definite
(2) (konkret, genau festgelegt) definite
(3) (bestimmt) definite

Note: **Definite** means clear, precise or unmistakable, not dubious or vague.

(1) Für das Arbeitslosenproblem wird es auch in den neunziger Jahren keine **definitive** Lösung geben.
There will be no **definite** solution to the unemployment problem even in the Nineties.
(2) Der deutsche Kanzler konnte noch keine **definitive** Entscheidung über die Zusammensetzung des neuen Kabinetts treffen.
The German Chancellor couldn't reach a **definite** decision on the line-up of the new Cabinet.
(3) "Es ist jetzt **definitiv**, daß Prinzessin Diana nicht nach Dubai reisen wird", kündigte der Sprecher des Buckingham-Palasts an.
"It is now **definite** that Princess Diana will not visit Dubai," announced a Buckingham Palace spokesman.
"Dieser Mini-Werkzeugkasten wird den Autofahrern **definitiv** helfen", behauptete der Repräsentant des Automobil-Clubs (etwa ADAC).
"This mini-tool kit will **definitely** help car-drivers," the AA representative maintained.

definitive: (1) entscheidend, endgültig
(2) maßgebend
(3) (wissenschaftlich) zuverlässig
(4) '**Gesamt-**' (in combinations)

Note: **Definitive** means final or unalterable, not provisional and not temporary.

(1) The **definitive** answer to this problem has to be found by the politicians.

Die **endgültige** Antwort auf dieses Problem müssen die Politiker finden.
(2) We do not regard our M. P.'s opinion on this matter as **definitive**.
Wir betrachten die Meinung unseres Parlamentsabgeordneten als nicht **maßgebend** in dieser Sache.
(3) A friend of mine is working on a **definitive** biography of John Braine.
Ein Freund von mir arbeitet an einer (wissenschaftlich) **zuverlässigen** Biographie von John Braine.
(4) A **definitive** edition of W. B. Yeats' works is to appear in the next few years.
Eine (wissenschaftliche) **Gesamt**ausgabe der Werke von W. B. Yeats soll in den nächsten Jahren erscheinen.

Compare: Sometimes **definite** and **definitive** may overlap.
'A **definite** result' is clear, but may be open to argument.
'A **definitive** result' is final and allows no room for further argument.

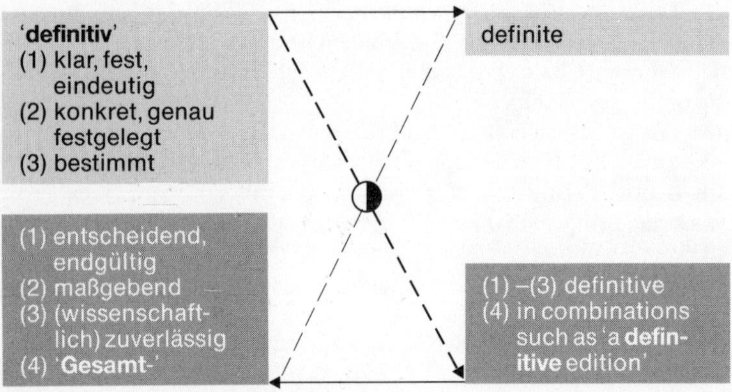

FALSE FRIENDS IN CONTEXT

The New Numbers Game

Motoring Expert (talking to a group of owners of prestigious cars): Now all drivers will have a ________ (1) choice from more than 200,000 car numbers each year sold on a first come, first served basis.

The usual pattern of registration will be ________ (2) for new car owners such as H 16 SEX, H 10 PAT.
Rolls-Royce Owner: I'm interested in attractive car numbers for rare car models. How can I buy them?
Motoring Expert: Car number plates are ________ (3) sold by the Government through the *D*river and *V*ehicle *L*icensing *C*entre (= DVLC) in Swansea at around £ 200. In addition, there are rare, high and medium value numbers which are earmarked for ________ (4) auctions.
Aston Martin Owner: What kind of auctions?
Motoring Expert: There'll be five car number auctions at Christie's for the two top categories, but I can't give a ________ (5) answer as to how many car numbers are on sale. Medium value numbers like 300 CAB, 1A CAR, C1 NDY will ________ (6) be sold through Central Motor Auctions or Phillipe Auctions.
Porsche Owner: What about the prices for plates in these categories?
Motoring Expert: Experts forecast sums of more than £ 100,000 for the most prized plates such as D1 ANA, C1 GAR, RAP 1D, MUS 1C, BUY 1T. The sell-off is expected to net £ 40 million per year.
Taxi Driver (outside): I never thought we had so many car number snobs in the country!

SOLUTION

(1) a **definite** choice (2) **definitive** (3) are **definitely** sold (4) **definite** auctions (5) **definitive** answer (6) will **definitely** be sold

DESINTERESSIERT ≠ disinterested

disinterested [dɪsˈɪntrəstɪd] .... **DESINTERESSIERT**

uninterested [ˌʌnˈɪntrəstɪd] —— (= uninteressiert)

DESINTERESSIERT: (uninteressiert) uninterested

Note: **Uninterested** simply means 'not interested'; bored and indifferent. It is the negative of 'interested'.

Unser bisheriger Geschäftspartner ist an einer weiteren Zusammenarbeit **desinteressiert**.
Our former business partner is **uninterested** in any further cooperation.
"Schau nicht so **desinteressiert** drein, Trevor", flüsterte seine Frau während des Vortrags des Psychologen. "Das Thema ist nicht so langweilig, wie du glaubst."
"Don't look so **uninterested**, Trevor," his wife whispered during the psychologist's talk. "The topic is not as boring as you seem to think."

disinterested: (1) uneigennützig
(2) unparteiisch, neutral

Note: **Disinterested** means 'without personal interest'; impartial, neutral.

(1) His **disinterested** willingness to help was recognized by Dr. Barnardo's Homes, a charitable organisation.
Seine **uneigennützige** Hilfsbereitschaft wurde von Dr. Barnardos Homes, einer gemeinnützigen Organisation, anerkannt.
(2) "Let's ask a **disinterested** solicitor what we should do in this case," suggested my aunt.
"Laß uns einen **unparteiischen** Rechtsanwalt fragen, was wir in diesem Fall tun sollen", schlug meine Tante vor.
A marriage guidance councellor is supposed to be a **disinterested** outsider who helps couples to sort out their difficulties.
Von einem Eheberater wird erwartet, daß er ein **neutraler** Außenstehender ist, der Ehepaaren ihre Schwierigkeiten lösen hilft.

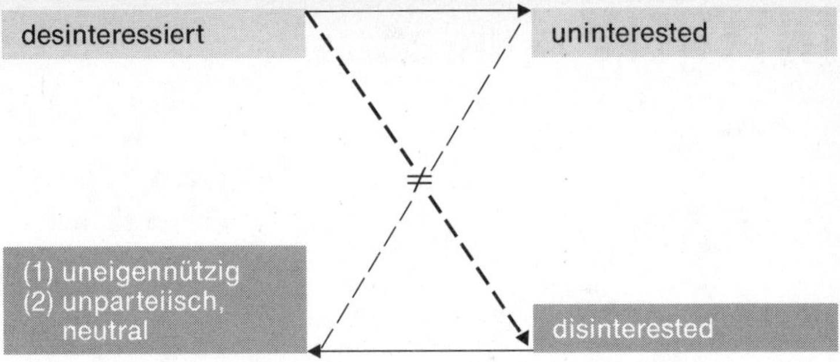

FALSE FRIENDS IN CONTEXT

My Fair Lady – A New Role

Hollywood Director: ...Don't you realize Audrey, the world still remembers your enchanting performance in the film *My Fair Lady*? One of our Hollywood producers is not ________ (1) in your return to the screen.
Audrey Hepburn: I'm sorry, but you're wasting your time. I'm perfectly ________ (2). I'm too busy saving kids.
Hollywood Director: Look, we'll send you a film script that fits your age and interests and...
Audrey Hepburn: Sorry, I've got to cut you short. At the age of nearly sixty you know what you want to do. I launched a supermarket campaign for UNICEF, the international children's charity, in London yesterday. And I will go on doing it in a ________ (3) sort of way.
Hollywood Director: Will you really, Audrey? We've much more to offer to a personality like you.
Audrey Hepburn: Listen, saving the world's starving children is far more important than acting. When you've seen children dying, the answer to any Hollywood offer can only be, "I'm ________ (4)!"

SOLUTION

(1) uninterested (2) uninterested (3) disinterested (4) uninterested

INTENSIV ◑ intensive

intensive [ɪn'tensɪv]

intense [ɪn'tens]

INTENSIV

(= sehr stark, grell etc.)

INTENSIV: (1) (Hitze, Sonnenlicht etc.: sehr stark, grell) intense
(2) (Farben, Augenfarbe etc.: lebhaft, tief) intense
(3) (Gefühle, Schmerzen etc.: äußerst stark, heftig) intense

(1) Mittags wurde die Sonne so **intensiv**, daß sie im Hause blieb.
At midday the sun became so **intense** that she stayed inside.
Sie fuhr für einige Zeit auf die Hebriden, um der **intensiven** Sommerhitze zu entfliehen.
She went to the Hebrides for a time to escape the **intense** summer heat.
(2) Er hatte schon immer das **intensive** Gelb von van Goghs *Sonnenblumen*-Bildern gemocht; jetzt war er dabei, eins zu kaufen.
He had always liked the **intense** yellow of van Gogh's *Sunflower* pictures; he was going to buy one now.
Laura hatte **intensiv** blaue Augen und ein ovales Gesicht.
Laura had **intense** blue eyes and an oval face.
(3) "Manchmal wird die Belastung so **intensiv**, daß ich lieber Kassiererin sein möchte", beklagte sich der Popstar.
"Sometimes the pressure gets so **intense** I'd rather be a check-out girl," the pop star complained.
Seit langem hatte sie **intensiv** gespürt, wie sehr er sie liebte.
For a long time she had felt **intensely** how much he loved her.
"Wie lange würden die **intensiven** Schmerzen noch andauern?" dachte der Arzt und schaute den Krebs-Patienten an.
"How much longer was the **intense** pain going to last?" thought the doctor looking at the cancer patient.

Note: (sehr) großes Vergnügen = **intense** pleasure
(sehr) starker Platzregen = **intense** downpour
eine unheimliche Sehnsucht = an **intense** longing
ein (an)gespannter Blick = an **intense** look

but: ein **intensiver** Geruch = a penetrating smell
sehr, äußerst = intensely (adv.)
The Siberian winter was **intensely** cold.
Hormonal activity can make women **intensely** miserable.

intensive: (1) gründlich
(2) konzentriert
(3) '**Intensiv-**' (in combinations)

(1) In spite of **intensive** training, he didn't succeed in his career.
Trotz einer **gründlichen** Ausbildung kam er beruflich nicht weiter.
(2) After two hours of **intensive** work my friend had solved the problem.
Nach zwei Stunden **konzentrierter** Arbeit hatte mein Freund das Problem gelöst.
(3) "The **intensive** course in London with four hours of conversation each day was very useful for me," my friend told me after his return.
"Der **Intensiv**kurs in London mit vier Stunden Konversation pro Tag hat mir sehr genützt", erzählte mir mein Freund nach seiner Rückkehr.
After three weeks I gradually got better through **intensive** treatment in an **intensive** care unit.
Durch die **Intensiv**behandlung auf der **Intensiv**station ging es mir nach drei Wochen allmählich besser.

Note: live fast, live a fast life = **intensiv** leben

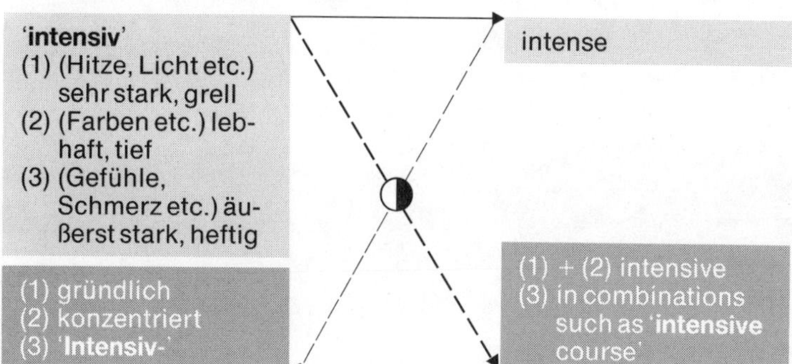

FALSE FRIENDS IN CONTEXT

A Personal Question

Interviewer: ... Your Highness, your life at this time of year must be very ________ (1). State visits, meeting people from all walks of life, opening hospitals – to name just a few of your many engagements. May I ask you a personal question?
Prince Charles: It rather depends on the nature of the question.
Interviewer: Do you like animals?
Prince Charles: I like horses, dogs and most other animals, but slithery things like lizards and snakes ... I dislike ________ (2). After a day of ________ (3) work I like to have one of my pets around, but only for half an hour at most.
Interviewer: Thank you for a most stimulating interview, Your Highness.

SOLUTION

(1) intense (2) dislike **intensely** (3) **intensive** work

KONTINUIERLICH ◑ continual

continual [kən'tɪnjʊəl]

KONTINUIERLICH
(= ununterbrochen)

continuous [kən'tɪnjʊəs]

KONTINUIERLICH: (ununterbrochen) continuous

Note: **Continuous** means without interruption; it implies an unbroken action.

Die Maschine war acht Stunden **kontinuierlich** gelaufen.
The machine had run **continuously** for eight hours.
Das neue Heizungssystem bietet Ihnen mehr als **kontinuierliche** Wärme; es bietet Ihnen kontrollierbare Wärme.
The new heating system gives you more than **continuous** warmth; it gives you controllable warmth.
Das **kontinuierliche** Trommelschlagen erfüllte nach den Zusammenstößen zwischen Hindus und Moslems noch immer die Luft.
The **continuous** beating of drums still filled the air after clashes between Hindus and Moslems.
Der Kapitän schaute auf das Meer hinaus; vor ihm lag eine **kontinuierliche** Wasserfläche.
The captain looked out at the sea; a **continuous** stretch of water lay before him.

continual: ständig, fortwährend, andauernd

Note: **Continual** means with occasional interruption; it implies an action that is regularly repeated. It often refers to unpleasant situations.

“I can’t stand these **continual** interruptions at my work any longer. Don’t put any phone calls through to me,” the boss told his secretary.
“Ich kann diese **ständigen** Unterbrechungen bei der Arbeit nicht länger ertragen. Stellen Sie keinerlei Telefonate zu mir durch”, wies der Chef seine Sekretärin an.
As a teacher you must **continually** look for ideas to hold the interest of your students.

Als Lehrer muß man **fortwährend** nach neuen Ideen Ausschau halten, um das Interesse der Schüler aufrechtzuerhalten.
Joan had become tired of his **continual** nagging over the years. "I'm going to leave him if he starts nagging once again," she decided.
Joan war seiner **andauernden** Meckereien über die Jahre überdrüssig. "Ich werde ihn verlassen, wenn er nochmals zu meckern anfängt", entschied sie.

Compare: 'He worked **continuously** for 12 hours' means he never stopped working, whereas 'He worked **continually** for 12 hours' means he worked for that time, but there were interruptions.

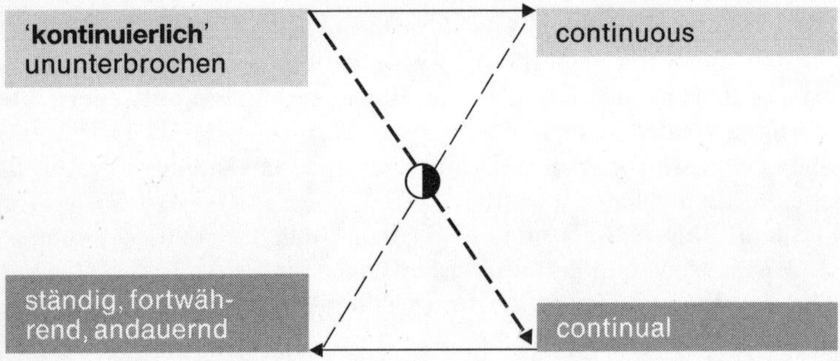

FALSE FRIENDS IN CONTEXT

A Different Kind of Catch

Manager General: Hull? That's the last town I would think of living in. ________ (1) unemployment in the seventies and now more than 20 per cent unemployed.
Project Manager: We're in the nineties now. Admittedly, the fishing industry has been ________ (2) declining, but now Hull is more than just a seagull's nesting place.
Manager General: Are you joking? Look at its history, Hull was first battered by the Vikings, then ________ (3) bombed by the Luftwaffe and more recently its industry almost died when the Cod War was lost.
Project Manager: It has seven miles of ________ (4) seafront which is being developed. Since the opening of the marina in the Old Humber

Dock, property prices have been going up rapidly. A sea view brings a £ 10,000 to 40,000 premium.
Manager General: So there's a ________ (5) boom in property prices?
Project Manager: Without a doubt.
Manager General: I'm becoming mildly optimistic, but don't want to make a decision right now.
Project Manager: The Hull area is ________ (6) catching on, and in terms of property investment we are bringing home a different kind of catch.

SOLUTION

(1) continuous (2) continuously (3) continuously (4) continuous
(5) continual (6) continually

LOSE ≠ lose

lose [lu:z] → **LOSE** (= locker, frei etc.) ← **loose** [lu:s]

LOSE: (1) (locker, frei etc.) loose (adj.)
(2) in combinations such as 'break **loose**'

(1) "Ich habe einen **losen** Zahn", sagte der kleine Junge zum Zahnarzt.
"I've got a **loose** tooth," said the little boy to the dentist.
Warum trägst du immer **loses** Geld (Kleingeld) in der Tasche? Es könnte herausfallen.
Why do you always carry **loose** change in your pocket? It might fall out.
Die alte Dame war über einen **offenen** Schnürsenkel gestolpert und hatte sich den linken Arm gebrochen.
The old lady had tripped over a **loose** bootlace and broken her left arm.
(2) Eines Tages überraschten wir auf unserer Kanu-Safari eine kleine Flottille von Nilpferden im Sambesi-Fluß, und die Hölle brach **los**.
One day on our canoe-safari we surprised a small flotilla of sleeping hippos in the Zambesi River and all hell broke **loose**.
Ihre roten Haare fielen **lose** um ihre Schultern.
Her red hair was falling **loose** around her shoulders.
Plötzlich lief ein Bulle **frei** auf dem Marktplatz herum.
Suddenly a bull was running **loose** in the market square.

Note: unüberlegtes Gerede, unverantwortliches Geschwätz = **loose** talk
lösen, (sich) lockern = **loosen**
Cliff had put on so much weight, he had to **loosen** his belt.
The brushes of the new vacuum cleaners **loosen** and lift dirt.
but: seinen Gefühlen freien Lauf lassen = let **loose** one's feelings
At the end of the film, in a domestic scene Mignon announces that she's pregnant and lets **loose** her feelings.

lose: (Verb) verlieren

Note: In contrast to the adjective **loose** the Confusible **lose** is an irregular verb.

Where did you **lose** your wedding ring?
Wo hast du deinen Ehering **verloren**?
“You can **lose** everything, but not your honour,” my father used to say.
“Du kannst alles **verlieren**, aber nicht deine Ehre”, pflegte mein Vater zu sagen.
Women can **lose** up to 7 lbs in 15 days and men 7 to 15 lbs.
Frauen können in 15 Tagen bis zu 7 Pfund Gewicht verlieren, Männer zwischen 7 und 15 Pfund.

Compare: The following **Confusibles** often cause trouble.
(adj.) loose [lu:s] = locker, frei etc.
(verb) lose [lu:z], lost, lost = verlieren
(verb) loosen ['lu:sn], loosened = lösen, (sich) lockern

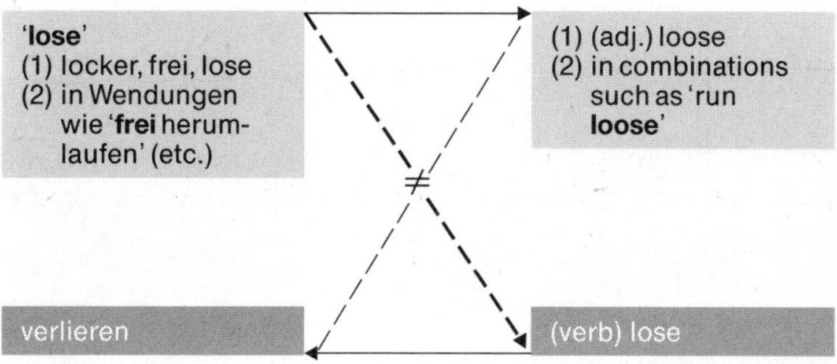

FALSE FRIENDS IN CONTEXT

Let the People Talk

Do you know what ________ (1) talk is? If not, here are four examples:
- Every day I work a 29-hour day (Craig McLachlan).
- People have been let ________ (2) for less (Jayne Irving).

– I now feel as if my film career never existed (Brigitte Bardot).
– Richard Nixon will run for President again . . . and ________ (3).
Perhaps you can add other examples of ________ (4) talk yourself.

SOLUTION

(1) **loose** talk (2) let **loose** (3) lose (4) **loose** talk

A Parking Note

A commercial traveller had parked his car in a no-parking area and left this note behind the windscreen wiper:
"Circled the office block ten times. Had to keep an appointment or else ________ (5) my job. Sorry."
On his return he found the usual parking ticket behind the windscreen wiper with an added note:
"Have been circling this office block for ten years. Had to follow my instructions or else ________ (6) my job, too. Sorry."

SOLUTION

(5) lose (6) lose

LUXURIÖS ≠ luxuriant

luxuriant [lʌgˈʒʊərɪənt]

LUXURIÖS
(= aufwendig etc.)

luxurious [lʌgˈʒʊərɪəs]

LUXURIÖS: (1) (aufwendig; prächtig etc.) luxurious
(2) ('**Luxus-**') in combinations such as 'a **luxurious** yacht'

(1) Jedes Haus wird mit **luxuriösen** Teppichen und Gardinen ausgestattet.
Each home will be fitted with **luxurious** carpets and curtains.
Dieser Fabrikbesitzer hat eine **luxuriös** eingerichtete Wohnung in Nizza.
This factory owner has a **luxuriously** furnished flat in Nice.
Die Häuser im Chalet-Stil waren nicht **luxuriös**, aber sie waren sauber und bequem eingerichtet.
The chalet-style houses weren't **luxurious**, but they were clean and comfortably furnished.
(2) Der Mercedes Benz 600 Sedan aus dem Jahre 1969 wurde als größtes **Luxus**auto seiner Zeit angesehen.
The 1969 Mercedes Benz 600 Sedan was considered to be the most **luxurious** car in its day.

Note: ein **luxuriöses** Leben führen = live **luxuriously** (or live in luxury, lead a life of luxury)

luxuriant: (1) üppig, wuchernd
(2) (Haar, Bart etc.) dicht (gewachsen)

(1) Neil enjoyed the **luxuriant** vegetation of the rain forests of Venezuela.
Neil genoß die **üppige** Vegetation der Regenwälder Venezuelas.
He had never seen so many **luxuriant** plants in his life.
Er hatte noch nie so viele **wuchernde** Pflanzen in seinem Leben gesehen.
(2) Elvis Presley's **luxuriant** black hair went well with the white colour of his limousine.

Elvis Presleys **dichtes** schwarzes Haar paßte gut zu der weißen Farbe seiner Limousine.

Note: a **luxuriant** imagination = eine blütenreiche Phantasie
luxuriant prose = blütenreiche Prosa

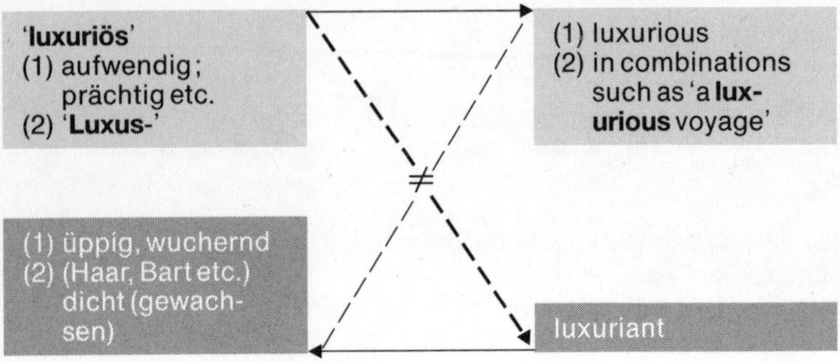

FALSE FRIENDS IN CONTEXT

A Golden Prize for Golden Days

Tourist Manager: Congratulations! You've not only won two ________ (1) weeks for two people on Queensland's sunny Gold Coast; you've also won £500 spending money.
Winning Couple: What? We can't believe it!
Tourist Manager: You'll stay at the ________ (2) Gold Coast International Hotel in Brisbane. The hotel has three restaurants, several bars and a swimming pool. You can also relax on the golden sands of Surfers' Paradise.
Winning Couple: There must be a mistake. It can't be true.
Tourist Manager: But it is true. We've made sure and you are indeed the winning couple. And in addition, you'll be able to explore the ________ (3) rain forests and the national park, the sacred Aboriginal caves and tour the Tweed River region with its plantations of sugar cane, bananas, avocados, and pineapples – all in one terrific holiday! What do you say?
Winning Couple: We'll take the golden prize and have a second honeymoon.

SOLUTION

(1) **luxurious** weeks (2) **luxurious** Gold Coast International Hotel
(3) **luxuriant** rain forests

MEISTERLICH ◑ masterful

masterful

MEISTERLICH

masterly

MEISTERLICH: (1) masterly
(2) (meisterhaft) masterly

Note: The adjective **masterly** suggests "in the manner of a master" (*see* Howard, p. 130). It is synonymous with **skilful**, **accomplished**, **expert** such as a **'masterly** touch', 'a **masterly** speech'.

(1) Der Pianist spielte einfach **meisterlich**.
The pianist's playing was simply **masterly**.
Der Chor aus Cambridge bot eine **meisterliche** Aufführung of G. F. Händels *Dies ist der Tag*.
The choir from Cambridge gave a **masterly** performance of G. F. Handel's *This is the Day*.
(2) Das **meisterliche** Timing der Schauspielerin verschaffte ihr mehr Lacherfolge als irgendeinem anderen Mitspieler im Ensemble.
The actress's **masterly** timing gained her more laughs than any other player in the cast.
Die Portraits im Museum waren **meisterlich** in der Ausführung.
The portraits in the museum had been executed in a **masterly** way.

masterful: (1) herrisch, gebieterisch, herrschsüchtig
(2) souverän, gekonnt, meisterhaft

Note: The adjective **masterful** suggests "acting like a master" (*see* Howard, p. 130). It is synonymous with **bossy**, **commanding**, **domineering** such as 'a person's **masterful** ways' (**herrische** Art).

(1) "He's too **masterful** for me," Philippa thought and decided not to marry him.
"Er ist mir zu **herrisch**", dachte Philippa und entschloß sich, ihn nicht zu heiraten.

In his **masterful** voice the king demanded that the meal be served.
Mit **gebieterischer** Stimme verlangte der König, das Essen aufzutragen.
Jane, a shy person, was attracted to her new boss, but she didn't like his **masterful** ways.
Jane, eine von Natur aus scheue Person, fühlte sich zu ihrem neuen Chef hingezogen, aber sie mochte nicht seine **herrschsüchtige** Art.
(2) The captain's **masterful** handling of the small boat in heavy seas saved a dozen lives.
Der **souveräne** Umgang des Kapitäns mit dem kleinen Schiff bei schwerem Seegang rettete ein Dutzend Menschen.

Compare: The Confusibles **masterly** and **masterful** overlap in the sense of '**meisterhaft**'.
– 'The pianist gave a **masterly** rendering of Debussy's delicate *Reflections in the Water*' meaning he gave a very skilful and expert interpretation of that work by Debussy.
– 'The pianist gave a **masterful** rendering of Beethoven's the *Appassionata*' meaning he gave a robust and forceful interpretation of this work by Beethoven.

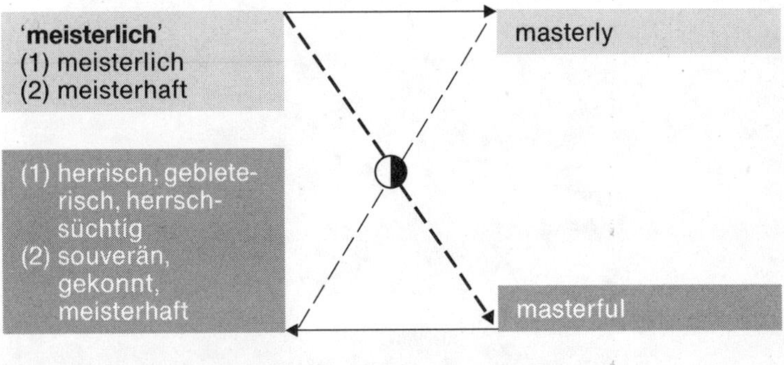

FALSE FRIENDS IN CONTEXT

The Proof of the Pudding is in the Eating

Young Lady: I've stopped drinking decaffeinated coffee since Dr. Superico showed it could lead to heart disease.
Old Lady: Then you should go to the famous Camisa Italian delicatessen in Soho. There they still cut Parma from the genuine product in a ________ (1) fashion. You can't match the flavour.

Young Lady: But hasn't medicine proved that decaffeinated coffee really causes heart disease?

Old Lady: I'm 71 and have been drinking coffee all my life. Honestly, Dr. Sinico is too ________ (2) for me. The report was based on just 100 people out of millions the world over. Why do doctors draw silly conclusions based on the wrong people?

Young Lady: The result is not a ________ (3) piece of medical research at all. Dr. Superico has imposed it on us in a rather ________ (4) way.

Old Lady: Come and visit me next week. And I'll serve you real Parma ham and a ________ (5) cup of coffee with one of Mozart's concertos as background music.

Young Lady: Oh, I can't wait.

SOLUTION

(1) in a **masterly** fashion (2) masterful (3) **masterly** piece of medical research (4) in a rather **masterful** way (5) a **masterly** cup

MOMENTAN ≠ momentous

momentous [məʊ'mentəs]

MOMENTAN
(= augenblicklich)

momentary ['məʊməntərɪ]

MOMENTAN: (1) (augenblicklich) momentary
(2) (kurz, flüchtig) momentary

(1) Dann setzte eine **momentane** Stille ein, als eine unbekannte amerikanische Stimme zu sprechen begann.
Then came a **momentary** hush as an unfamiliar American voice began to speak.
"Dein **momentanes** Zögern zeigt, daß du krank bist", bemerkte er langsam.
"Your **momentary** hesitation shows that you are ill," he remarked slowly.
(2) Lady Annes Verhalten wurde nicht durch Trunkenheit ausgelöst, sondern durch ein **momentanes** Nachlassen der Selbstdisziplin.
Lady Anne's behaviour was caused not by intoxication, but by a **momentary** lapse of self-discipline.

Note: **Momentan** kann ich Ihnen nicht weiterhelfen = At the moment I can't help you.
eine **momentane** Laune = a passing whim

momentous: (1) bedeutsam
(2) von ziemlicher Tragweite

(1) It was a **momentous** day in the history of the young African state.
Es war ein **bedeutsamer** Tag in der Geschichte des jungen afrikanischen Staates.
(2) In a **momentous** decision the Kremlin leaders reduced their arms potential.
In einer Entscheidung **von ziemlicher Tragweite** verringerten die Kremlführer ihr Waffenpotential.

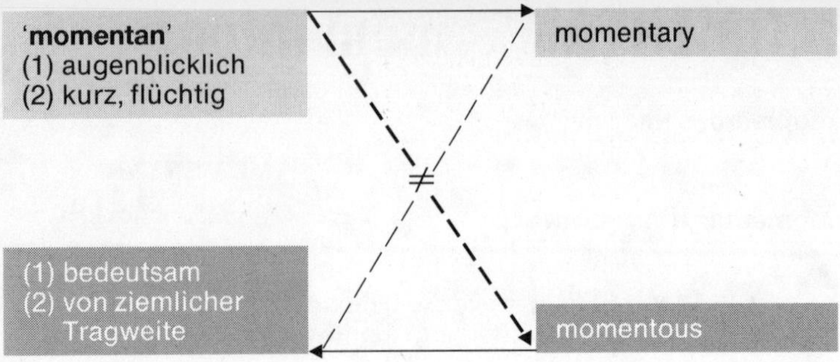

FALSE FRIENDS IN CONTEXT

The Giant Street Party
(During the night of 8th November, 1989 in West Berlin)

First East Berliner: I was just going to bed when I heard the news bulletin. "By Ministerial order all direct crossing points between East and West Germany are from now on open to anyone who chooses to pass." (Screaming) I cannot remember when I felt so excited. It was a ________ (1) decision to dress again and rush to the Wall.
Young East Berliner: All our lives we have waited for this ______ (2) day, for the border to be opened. Suddenly after 28 years when everyone had given up hope, it has happened.
First West Berliner: Look at all the little Wartburgs and Trabants all heading for the Western Sector. What a ________ (3) night!
Second West Berliner: Let's have a giant street party (handing bottles of champagne to East Germans in their cars). Welcome! Welcome to West Berlin!
Young East and West Berliners (waving their arms in victorious salute): Let's go to the Brandenburg Gate, the symbol of German unity! (Shouting) Let's make for the Gate! [amid a wave of ________ (4) jubilation]

* * *

Half an hour later at the Wall facing the Brandenburg Gate, carried away by ________ (5) emotions:
Let's sing our national anthem (they start singing while some weep

freely). Let's now go to the Street of the 17th of June and change it into Street of the 8th of November (Cheers)... (another voice) What about our welcome money?

SOLUTION

(1) **momentary** decision (2) **momentous** day (3) **momentous** night
(4) **momentary** jubilation (5) **momentary** emotions

SINNLICH ◑ sensual

sensual ··········▸ **SINNLICH** (= sinnenfreudig etc.)

sensous ◂—— **SINNLICH** (= sinnenfreudig etc.)

SINNLICH: (1) (sinnenhaft, sinnenfreudig etc.) sensuous
(2) ('**Sinnes**-') in combinations such as '**sensuous** joy'
(3) (durch die Sinne empfunden als 'weich, fein') sensuous

Note: **Sensuous** is mainly aesthetic with reference to painting, music, literature etc. It is often used in a favourable sense.

(1) In diesem Lebensstadium empfand sie eine Art **sinnliches** Vergnügen an der Dichtung.
At that stage of her life she derived a kind of **sensuous** pleasure from poetry.
(2) Aber Tanita war ja kein normaler Popstar. Manchmal sah sie wie ein gequältes **Sinnes**wesen aus, das mit einem besonders schwierigen Satz von Heidegger rang.
But then Tanita was no ordinary pop star. Sometimes she looked like a tortured, **sensuous** soul wrestling with a particularly difficult proposition from Heidegger.
(3) Eine New Yorker Modenschau hatte Petticoat-Kleider herausgebracht, die aus **feinem** Veloursleder gemacht waren.
A New York fashion show had featured petticoat dresses made from **sensuous** suede.

sensual: (1) lüstern, wollüstig, sinnlich
(2) körperlich, fleischlich

Note: **Sensual** is mainly physical with reference to food, sex etc. It is often used in an unfavourable sense.

(1) Her **sensual** lips kissed his mouth passionately.
Ihre **lüsternen** Lippen küßten leidenschaftlich seinen Mund.
"There's more to being a model than walking up and down the catwalk," the **sensual** agency owner added with a meaningful look.

“Zum Mannequin muß man mehr mitbringen als auf dem Laufsteg auf und ab zu gehen”, fügte der **wollüstige** Agenturinhaber mit einem vieldeutigen Blick hinzu.
Fashion designer Klein’s new perfume *Obsession* is described as warm, **sensual** and passionate.
Das neue Parfum *Obsession* des Modeschöpfers Klein wird als warm, **sinnlich** und leidenschaftlich beschrieben.
(2) Her dancing partner was fascinated by her **sensual** presence and her movements.
Ihr Tanzpartner war von ihrer **körperlichen** Nähe und ihren Bewegungen fasziniert.
It’s the **sensual** personality that counts in her case as she lounges on a leopard skin.
Es ist die **fleischliche** Person, um die es in diesem Falle geht, wenn sie sich auf dem Leopardenfell rekelt.

Compare: There are, however, cases in which the confusibles **sensuous** and **sensual** overlap.
‘The dolphin’s **sensuous** and loving nature offers a model of our better selves’ meaning these animals have a nice nature.
‘On the other hand, dolphins are also very **sensual**. They may turn nasty if they get too sexually excited by close contact’ meaning the physical contact could have a negative side, even to the point of aggression.

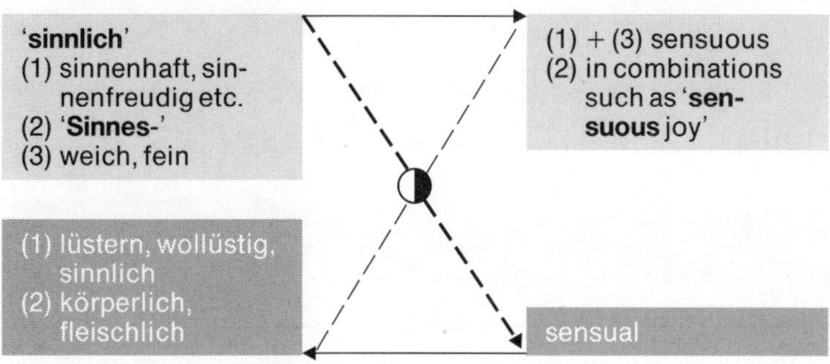

Hidden Talents

Jennifer (after entering a photographer's studio): I'd like a special photo of myself as a surprise gift for my husband.
Portrait Photographer: Why not take a boudoir portrait of yourself?
Jennifer: That sounds a good idea. But I'm a grandmother. Wouldn't it look a bit frivolous at my age?
Portrait Photographer: By no means, especially if you want to show you're still a ________ (1) woman. A boudoir portrait captures you at your ________ (2) private best.
Jennifer: Could you do one where I look soft, ________ (3) and seductive?
Portrait Photographer: You'll just have to lie back on the sofa over there and face the camera. Believe me you'll look a beauty of the boudoir, a striking example of a ________ (4) woman.

SOLUTION

(1) sensual (2) sensuous (3) sensual (4) sensuous (*see Note* on p. 270 and *compare* on p. 271)

'STATIONÄR' ≠ stationery

stationery ['steɪʃn̩ərɪ]

STATIONÄR

(= ortsfest etc.)

stationary ['steɪʃn̩ərɪ]

'STATIONÄR': (1) (ortsfest, stehenbleibend, fest verankert, stehend etc.) stationary
(2) (**stationär** behandeln) treat as an in-patient

Note: The term **stationary** is an adjective, not a noun.

(1) An einer Stelle in dem Film schien die Landschaft trotz der Geschwindigkeit des Schnellzugs **stationär** (= stehenzubleiben).
At one stage in the film the scenery, despite the speed of the express train, seemed to remain **stationary**.
"Dieses Schiff ist **stationär** (= fest verankert). Es wird als Restaurant genutzt", erklärte der Fremdenführer und wies gleichzeitig darauf hin.
"This ship is **stationary**. It's used as a restaurant," the tourist guide explained, pointing it out to us.
Die Reise im *Blue Train* zur Riviera war unterhaltsamer als **stationäre** (= haltende) Autos auf der Londoner M 25 zu zählen.
Travelling down to the Riviera on the *Blue Train* was more amusing than counting **stationary** cars on London's M 25.
(2) Der Arzt rief die Frau des Patienten an, um sie zu informieren, daß ihr Mann **stationär behandelt werden** müßte.
The doctor rang the patient's wife to inform her that her husband had to **be treated as an in-patient**.

stationery: (1) Briefpapier, Schreibpapier
(2) Schreibmaterial, Schreibwaren
(3) '(Brief- etc.)-**papier**' (in combinations)

Note: The term **stationery** is a noun, not an adjective.

(1) One practical tip for a 'greener' office is to switch to **stationery** made from re-cycled paper.
Ein praktischer Tip für ein umweltbewußteres Büro ist, auf **Schreibpapier** überzugehen, das aus wiederaufbereitetem Papier hergestellt ist.

(2) "You can fetch all our **stationery**, including paper clips and pencils, at Jasons near the post office," my boss told the new office girl.
"Sie können unser gesamtes **Schreibmaterial**, inklusive Büroklammern und Bleistifte, bei Jason gleich beim Postamt holen", sagte mein Chef zu der neuen Büroangestellten.
"We don't have any **stationery**," she explained to the customer at the counter.
"Wir führen keine **Schreibwaren**", erklärte sie dem Kunden am Tresen.
(3) "We cannot change the phone number because it is on all our business **stationery**," he told his secretary.
"Wir können die Telefonnummer nicht ändern, weil sie auf unserem gesamten Geschäfts**papier** steht", teilte er seiner Sekretärin mit.

Note: office **stationery**= Büromaterial
but: **Stationery** Office = (in etwa) Bundesdruckerei (in der BRD)
Next month the **Stationery** Office will send the new forms to British expatriates to register as overseas voters at the General Election.

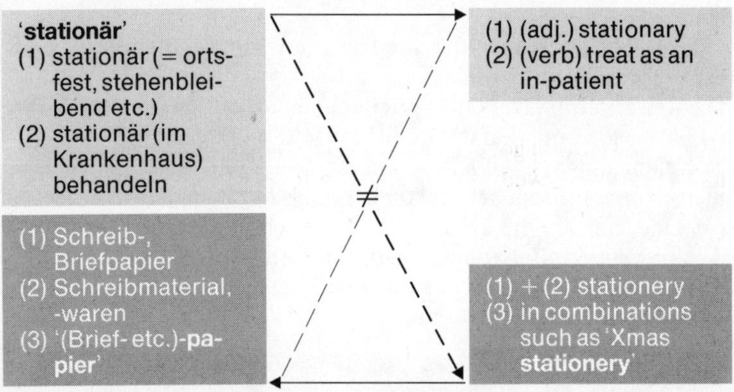

FALSE FRIENDS IN CONTEXT

In the Public Eye

Judge: What happened on May 3rd between three and four o'clock?
Manager's Wife: I was going to fetch my daughter from school. My car

was absolutely ________ (1) at the bus stop. Suddenly I felt a bump behind me. A bus had driven into my car.
Judge: What did the bus driver do?
Manager's Wife: He got out and told me he wanted to fetch the police.
Judge: The bus driver claims you ran away when he tried to call the police.
Manager's Wife: That's untrue. I went to the corner shop to buy some ________ (2) for my daughter. I bought it and returned to the bus stop.
Judge: I understand your car had a portable telephone. It would have been better to call the police that way. Why didn't you use it, especially as you were ________ (3)?
Manager's Wife: I was driving my husband's company car and I had never used the phone before. I didn't even know the company's code numbers.

SOLUTION

(1) stationary (2) stationery (3) stationary

Answering Letters

Uncle Tom was not good at answering letters. Once a friend of his who had waited for several weeks to get a reply sent him several blank sheets of paper.
A week later he received a postcard saying, "Have received ______ (4). Am being ________ (5) at Guy's Hospital. Please send envelopes and stamps now. Tom."

SOLUTION

(4) stationery (5) treated as an in-patient

TRIUMPHAL ◑ triumphal

triumphal [traɪˈʌmfl] → **TRIUMPHAL**

triumphant [traɪˈʌmfənt] ← (jubelnd; siegreich)

TRIUMPHAL: (1) (großartig; strahlend; triumphierend) triumphant
(2) (jubelnd; siegreich; triumphierend) triumphant

(1) Als Naturwissenschaftler konnte er den **triumphalen** (= großartigen) Erfolg nicht fassen.
As a scientist he couldn't believe his **triumphant** success.
Er hatte den Nobelpreis gewonnen und zeigte einen Augenblick lang das **triumphale** (= strahlende) Lächeln eines Siegers.
He had won the Nobel Prize and for a moment showed the **triumphant** smile of a winner.
Die Grünen könnten die **triumphalen** (= strahlenden) Gewinner bei den nächsten Unterhauswahlen werden.
The Greens could become the **triumphant** winners of the next General Election.
(2) Nach der Niederschlagung des Staatsstreichs stand der General inmitten loyaler Soldaten und hob **triumphal** (= jubelnd) die Faust.
After defeating the coup the general stood among loyal troops and raised a **triumphant** fist.
Etwa 200000 Menschen erschienen, um Australiens **triumphale** (= siegreiche) Kricketmannschaft bei der Heimkehr mit einem Konfetti-Umzug zu begrüßen.
About 200,000 people turned out to welcome Australia's **triumphant** cricket team home with a ticker tape parade.

triumphal: (1) überwältigend, alles in den Schatten stellend
(2) '**Triumph-**', '**Sieges-**' (in combinations)

Note: "Whether something that is **triumphal** is also **triumphant** will depend on the manner of its performance: a **triumphal** speech could be a dull and boring one, but if made exultantly it would also be **triumphant**" (*see* Room, p. 137).

(1) It is not often that business managers are met with continuous **triumphal** applause.
Es passiert nicht oft, daß Direktoren von Unternehmen anhaltenden, **überwältigenden** Beifall erhalten.
The German team was given a **triumphal** reception in Frankfurt after winning the Soccer World Cup.
Der deutschen Mannschaft wurde nach dem Gewinn der Fußballweltmeisterschaft in Frankfurt ein **alles in den Schatten stellender** Empfang bereitet.
(2) **Triumphal** arches such as Marble Arch were built to honour important persons or to commemorate an event.
Triumphbögen wie Marble Arch wurden gebaut, um bedeutende Personen zu ehren oder eines Ereignisses zu gedenken.

Compare: There may, however, be cases in which **triumphant** and **triumphal** overlap.
'England's **triumphant** march to the final was stopped by the German soccer team in the World Cup semi-final in 1990' indicating the jubilant and emotional aspirations of the team.
'France's victory in World War II was celebrated by a **triumphal** march of troops through the Arc de Triomphe in 1985' indicating a formal procession commemorating a historic triumph or victory.
'A **triumphal** welcome' has been organized and is a formal affair, whereas 'a **triumphant** welcome' would be spontaneous and jubilant.

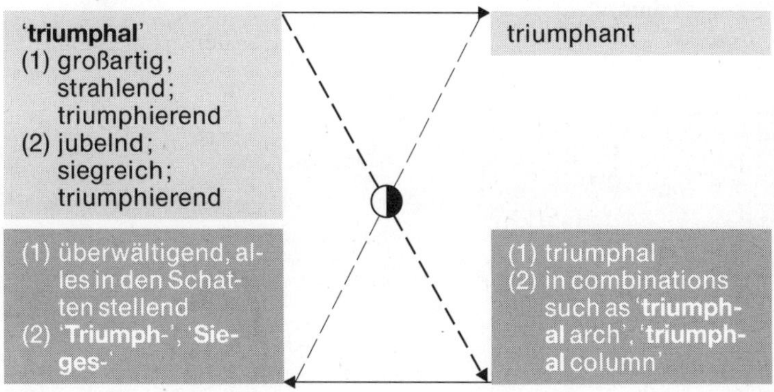

Having One Up One's Sleeve

________ (1) Father to Mother watching their teenage son mow the lawn:

Father: I told Andy I'd lost my car keys in the grass.
Mother: Why?
Father: Now you watch Andy come in and say with a ________ (2) gesture that he can't find them.

* * *

Half an hour later the teenage son comes in asking ________ (3):

Andy: About your car keys, Dad, did the nod of your head mean yes or no?

SOLUTION

(1) triumphant (2) triumphant (3) triumphantly

ZEREMONIELL ◑ ceremonial

ceremonial [ˌserɪˈməʊnjəl]

ZEREMONIELL

(= förmlich etc.)

ceremonious [ˌserɪˈməʊnjəs]

ZEREMONIELL: (1) (förmlich) ceremonious
(2) (rituell, zeremoniös) ceremonious
(3) (Verhalten etc.: umständlich, korrekt) ceremonious

Note: "People can be **ceremonious** but not **ceremonial**" (*see* Greenbaum/Whitcut, p. 121).

(1) Mit einer **zeremoniellen** Handbewegung eröffnete der Oberbürgermeister das neue Freizeitzentrum.
With a **ceremonious** gesture the Lord Mayor opened the new leisure centre.
Bei dieser **zeremoniellen** Entlassungsfeier am Semesterende sollten eure Eltern anwesend sein.
On this **ceremonious** end-of-term graduation your parents should be present.
(2) "Wenn sich zwei Messer kreuzen, müssen sie in **zeremonieller** (ritueller) Weise zu Boden geworfen werden", erläuterte mir der Zauberer.
"If two knives cross, they must be thrown **ceremoniously** to the floor," the magician informed me.
Nach dem Protokoll war der ganze Vorgang mehr eine **zeremonielle** Handlung als ein Empfang.
According to protocol the whole procedure was more of a **ceremonious** act than a reception.
(3) Die **zeremonielle** (umständliche, korrekte) Höflichkeit des alten Herrn war auffallend.
The old gentleman's **ceremonious** politeness was striking.

ceremonial: (meist von offiziellen Anlässen oder Kleidung) feierlich

Note: **Ceremonial** is used of *things* connected with ceremony, e. g. **ceremonial** mace, **ceremonial** laws (*see* Snell, p. 39).

The bearskins worn on **ceremonial** occasions by Britain's Guards' regiments date back to the battle of Waterloo.
Die Bärenfellmützen, die von den britischen Garderegimentern bei **feierlichen** Anlässen getragen werden, gehen auf die Schlacht von Waterloo zurück.
Captain Mark Phillips, Princess Anne's former husband, was dressed up in a **ceremonial** kimono as though he hadn't a care in the world.
Hauptmann Mark Phillips, der frühere Ehemann von Prinzessin Anne, hatte sich einen **feierlichen** Kimono angelegt, als ob er überhaupt keine Sorgen hätte.

Compare: There are also cases in which the two confusibles **ceremonious** and **ceremonial** overlap.
'A **ceremonial** event' indicates something large, full of colour, flags and trumpets, whereas 'a **ceremonious** event' is usually carried at a lower level and often fussily attends to the smallest detail; it hasn't the splendour and grandeur of **ceremonial**.

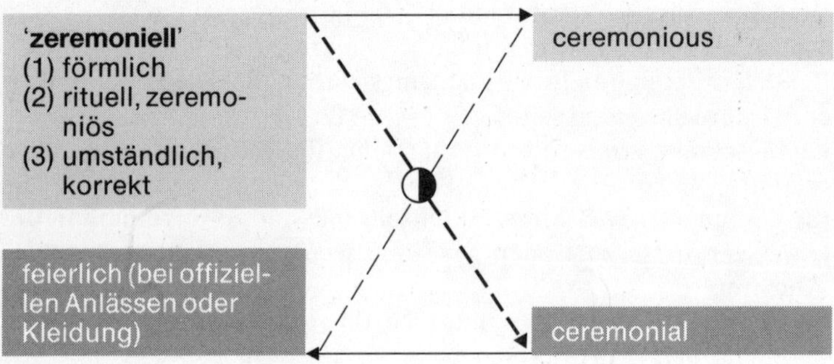

FALSE FRIENDS IN CONTEXT

The First Spaceman Joke

The following spaceman joke used to be associated with the Russian Yuri Gagarin, the first man in space:
On his return to Earth, Gagarin had to report to Khrushchev at the Kremlin.
"Tell me," Khrushchev asked in one of his ______ (1) moods, "when you were in space, did you see God?"

"Yes, I did," answered Gagarin.
"I thought so," commented Khrushchev ________ (2). "But don't tell the people. They aren't ready for it yet."

* * *

A year later, Gagarin was on a visit to Pope Paul VI.
"Tell me," asked the Pope wearing his white ________ (3) robe, "when you were in space, did you see God?"
"No, I didn't," answered Gagarin tongue in cheek.
"I thought so," commented the Pope ________ (4). "But don't tell the people. They aren't ready for it yet."

SOLUTION

(1) **ceremonious** moods (2) ceremoniously (3) **ceremonial** robe
(4) ceremoniously

FALSE FRIENDS TRAPS TEST 7

CONFUSIBLES

1.a. "But in Italy we prefer ________ suspense and thrill (**kontinuierlich ◑ continual**). That's the way we are," the stage manager kept saying.
1.b. The girl next door couldn't stand the ________ pressure at school, so she left last year (**kontinuierlich ◑ continual**).
2.a. My uncle couldn't enjoy a ________ lifestyle in his later years, even though he wanted to (**luxuriös ◑ luxuriant**).
2.b. There's still ________ vegetation in the tropical forests of Colombia (**luxuriös ◑ luxuriant**).
3.a. When I jumped into the icy Thames at Richmond Bridge to save a drowning man, I was struck by the ________ cold (**intensiv ◑ intensive**).
3.b. After two years of ________ training, the electrical technician returned to his former company in the Midlands (**intensiv ◑ intensive**).
4.a. "The Cabinet hasn't come to a ________ decision as yet (**definitiv ◑ definitive**). It'll be made after the Prime Minister's visit to the Soviet Union," the government spokesman told reporters.
4.b. Birks' book *Gentlemen of the Law* is a ________ work on the English solicitor (**definitiv ◑ definitive**).
5.a. Our headmaster has a ________, yet pleasant way with his staff and pupils (**meisterlich ◑ masterly**).
5.b. All through the concert the violinist's playing was ________ (**meisterlich ◑ masterly**).
6. Pens, ________ (**Schreibpapier**), craft work equipment and five classrooms have been destroyed by vandalism.
7. It was a ________ (**triumphal**) opening night at the Metropolitan Opera House, New York, for the English National Ballet.
8. He liked her light blue eyes and honey blonde hair. And suddenly with his ________ (**sinnlich**) lips he kissed her.
9. "Why couldn't they leave him alone on such a ________ (**bedeutsam**) day in his career?" he pondered.
10. Engineers have discovered cracks in the 15th century stonework of St. George's Chapel in Windsor Castle, near where the Queen and other members of the Royal family sit on ________ (**zeremoniell**) occasions.

ANSWER SHEET: TRUE FRIENDS TEST 7

CONFUSIBLES

1.a. "But in Italy we prefer **continual** suspense and thrill. That's the way we are," the stage manager kept saying.
1.b. The girl next door couldn't stand the **continuous** pressure at school, so she left last year.
2.a. My uncle couldn't enjoy a **luxurious** lifestyle in his later years, even though he wanted to.
2.b. There's still **luxuriant** vegetation in the tropical forests of Colombia.
3.a. When I jumped into the icy Thames at Richmond Bridge to save a drowning man, I was struck by the **intense** cold.
3.b. After two years of **intensive** training, the electrical technician returned to his former company in the Midlands.
4.a. "The Cabinet hasn't come to a **definite** decision as yet. It'll be made after the Prime Minister's visit to the Soviet Union," the government spokesman told reporters.
4.b. Birks' book *Gentlemen of the Law* is a **definitive** work on the English solicitor.
5.a. Our headmaster has a **masterful**, yet pleasant way with his staff and pupils.
5.b. All through the concert the violinist's playing was **masterly**.
6. Pens, **stationery**, craft work equipment and five classrooms have been destroyed by vandalism.
7. It was a **triumphant** opening night at the Metropolitan Opera House, New York, for the English National Ballet.
8. He liked her light blue eyes and honey blonde hair. And suddenly with his **sensual** lips he kissed her.
9. "Why couldn't they leave him alone on such a **momentous** day in his career?" he pondered.
10. Engineers have discovered cracks in the 15th century stonework of St. George's Chapel in Windsor Castle, near where the Queen and other members of the Royal family sit on **ceremonial** occasions.

PSEUDO-ANGLICISMS KURZ-EINFÜHRUNG

Was sind Pseudo-Anglizismen?

Pseudo-Anglizismen lassen sich am besten als scheinbare False Friends beschreiben. Das Besondere von Pseudo-Anglizismen vom Typ ***showmaster**, ***smoking**, ***twen** besteht darin, daß trotz ihres englischen Aussehens im Deutschen (**Showmaster**, **Smoking**, **Twen**) im Englischen **kein** entsprechender Begriff vorhanden ist; sie stehen gewissermaßen "ohne (sprachlichen) Freund" (**sans ami**; **without a friend**) da. Aus diesem Grunde spricht man bei diesem False Friends-Typ auch von Scheinentsprechungen.
Die Anzahl von Pseudo-Anglizismen ist glücklicherweise gering.

AFFEKT ◑ (*) affect

(*) affect ['æfekt] (in psychology etc.)

AFFEKT
(= starke Erregung)

anger ['æŋgə]

AFFEKT (starke Erregung; unkontrollierte Handlung):

(1) (im **Affekt**) on impulse, in the heat of the moment, in a burst of feeling; in anger, in a passion of anger

(2) ('**Affekt-**') in combinations such as 'an act of **emotion**', 'a crime of **passion**' (mainly used by lawyers and in legal terminology)

(3) ('**Affekt-**') in combinations such as '**affective** reaction' or '**emotional** disturbance' (**Affekt**störung); '**affective** blockage' or '**emotional** block' (**Affekt**stau); **affective** crisis (**Affekt-**ausbruch) (these terms are mainly used in psychology)

(1) Die Worte meines Vaters waren zwar **im Affekt** gesprochen, aber mir reichte es endgültig, und ich zog aus.
It is true that my father's words were spoken **in anger**, but I was sick and tired of it all and left home.
"**Im Affekt** griff ich mir ein Stück Rohr und schlug dem Wachhabenden auf den Kopf", gab der frühere Gefängnisinsasse zu.
"**In a passion of anger** I grabbed a piece of pipe and hit the guard over the head," admitted the former prisoner.
Tracy hatte gestern wohl **im Affekt** gehandelt. Das tat ihr jetzt leid.
Tracy had acted **on impulse** yesterday. Now she was sorry for it.
Als die Polizisten ankamen, begannen die Fußballrowdies im **Affekt** Steine auf sie zu schleudern.
When the policemen arrived, the hooligans began to hurl stones at them **in the heat of the moment**.
Im Affekt hatte mein Freund gesagt: "Ich spiele nie wieder Squash."
In a burst of feeling my friend had said, "I'll never play squash again."
(2) "Seine Tat war eine reine **Affekthandlung**", entgegnete der Direktor der überraschten Mutter.
"His deed was an **act of** pure **emotion**," the headmaster told the surprised mother.

Der Mord war schlicht ein **Affekt**delikt.
The murder was purely a **crime of passion**.
(3) "Zunächst hatte der Patient einen **Affekt**stau und dann einen typischen **Affekt**ausbruch", erläuterte der Psychologe den Zustand des Patienten.
"At first the patient had an **emotional** block and then a typical **affective** crisis," the psychologist explained the patient's condition.

Note: eine **affekt**geladene Situation = a highly **emotional** situation

(*) affect: (1) noun: — (in everyday English); as a technical term *see* Note below.
(2) verb: sich auswirken auf, schaden
(3) verb: betreffen, berühren
(4) verb: (die Gesundheit etc.) angreifen

Note: In everyday English **affect** is not used as a noun, but as a verb only. The noun **affect** exists only as a technical term in psychology, philosophy etc.
Note that the common verb **affect** [ə'fekt] differs in both pronunciation and meaning from the noun **affect** ['æfekt] which is mainly used in psychology (*see* Greenbaum/Whitcut, p. 23).

(1) **Affect** is an umbrella term for feeling, emotion and mood in psychology.
Affekt ist ein Sammelbegriff für Gefühle, Emotionen und Stimmungen in der Psychologie.
(2) Can a little more salt **affect** my diet in any way?
Kann ein wenig mehr Salz meiner Diät in irgendeiner Weise **schaden**?
Leaded petrol may **affect** the development of unborn babies.
Verbleites Benzin kann **sich auf** die Entwicklung ungeborener Babys **auswirken**.
(3) Please note that this will **affect** the interests of my firm.
Bitte beachten Sie, daß dies die Interessen meiner Firma **berührt**.
(4) If your husband's not careful, stress may **affect** his health.
Wenn Ihr Mann nicht aufpaßt, kann die Managerkrankheit seine Gesundheit **angreifen**.

Note: There are, however, two similar nouns in English which are frequently confused: affectation [ˌæfek'teɪʃn] Affektiertheit

During the interview her only **affectation** was to refer to you all the time as 'darling'.
affection [ə'fekʃn] Zuneigung
Although he tried hard, John couldn't win her **affection**.
In addition, the verb **affect** should not be confused with the noun **effect** meaning '(Aus-)Wirkung, Effekt'.
The new medicine had a good **effect** on the patient.

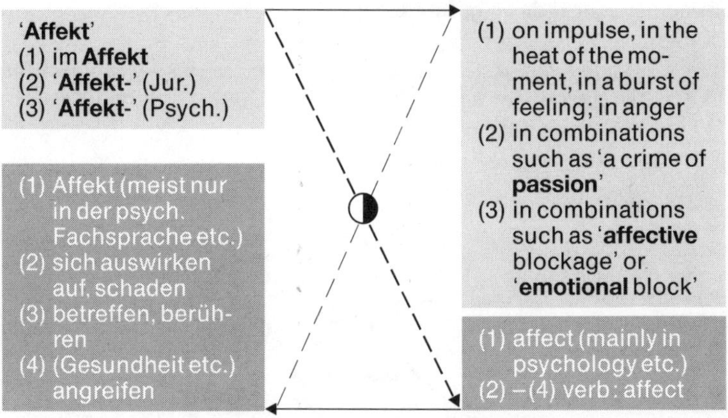

FALSE FRIENDS IN CONTEXT

A Nice Day's Outing

Jane (on holiday in Great Yarmouth, at a place overlooking the beach): What an appalling day today! Rain all the time! I hope it doesn't stay like this.
Terry, suddenly shouting in ________ (1): I can't stand it any longer! Didn't I tell you to stay at home? I'm sick and tired of it all.
Jane: Control yourself. Stop it, Terry.

* * *

Terry (an hour later): Look at that fool on the beach in the pouring rain. Must be out of his mind (starts giggling).
Jane: What is it now?
Terry: Look at the fellow! Stripped to his bathing trunks, and sitting in

a deckchair. His clothes are in a plastic bag under his deckchair.
Jane: Go and cheer him up a bit. He's being really brave.

* * *

Terry (putting on his raincoat and walking up to the lonely man on the beach): You are being very brave in this weather. I wouldn't like sitting in a deckchair all alone in the rain.
Lonely Man, speaking in ________ (2): It's no business of yours! I've come here for a day's outing to sit on the sands and that's what I'm doing.
Terry, replying on ________ (3): You must be out of your mind sitting like that in the rain for hours. The cold will ________ (4) your health. What a nice day's outing!

SOLUTION

(1) in anger (2) in a burst of feeling (3) on impulse (4) affect

BOWLE ≠ bowl

bowl → **BOWLE** (als kaltes Getränk) → **(wine) cup etc.**

BOWLE: (1) (kalte Bowle) cup (wine cup, claret cup, champagne cup etc.)
(2) (heiße Bowle) (drink with hot) punch (BE); cobbler (AE)

(1) "Habt ihr heute abend Zeit? Wir haben eine Frucht**bowle** angesetzt; es wäre schön, wenn ihr kommen würdet", sagten unsere Bekannten.
"Are you free tonight? We've mixed a fruit **cup**. It would be nice if you could come," our friends said.
"Eure **Bowle** schmeckt hervorragend, Jim." – "Das freut mich, es ist eine Sekt**bowle**."
"Your **cup** tastes superb, Jim." – "I'm pleased you like it; it's a champagne **cup**."
(2) An einem frostigen Winterabend ist ein Glas heiße **Bowle** gerade das richtige.
On a cold winter's evening a glass of hot **punch** is just the thing.

bowl: (1) Schale, Schüssel, Napf
(2) (Pfeifen-)Kopf
(3) (Toiletten-)Becken

(1) Princess Diana loves to tuck into a **bowl** of strawberries and cream while she watches Wimbledon – and don't we all?
Prinzessin Diana läßt sich gerne eine **Schale** Erdbeeren mit Sahne schmecken, während sie in Wimbledon zuschaut – und machen wir das nicht alle gerne?
Julia enjoyed the different types of fresh salad in the salad **bowls**.
Julia erfreute sich an den verschiedenen frischen Salatarten in den Salat**schüsseln**.
Before the cat came in, Roger put some food in the **bowl** for her.
Bevor die Katze hereinkam, tat Roger etwas Nahrung in den **Napf** für sie.
(2) After cleaning the **bowl** of his pipe and filling it, he began to talk.

Nachdem er den **Pfeifenkopf** gereinigt und gefüllt hatte, begann er zu reden.

(3) The maid spotted a snake in the lavatory **bowl** of her London flat; it was a python.
Eine Hausangestellte entdeckte eine Schlange im Toiletten**becken** ihrer Londoner Mietwohnung; es war eine Python-Schlange.

Note: **bowl** = **Bowlen**gefäß

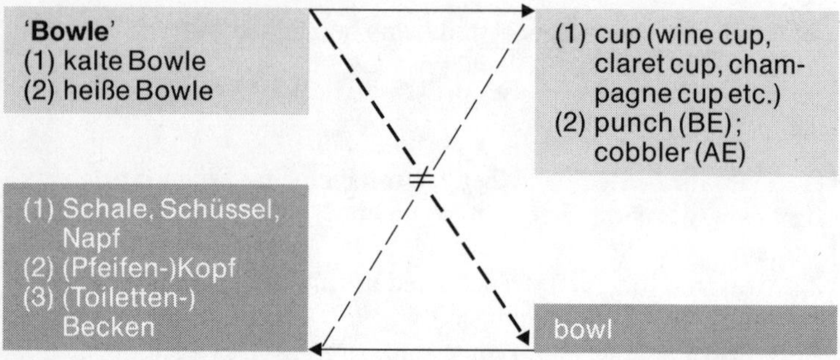

FALSE FRIENDS IN CONTEXT

Ending a Hunger Strike

After twenty days a Burma war veteran, Andy Burgess, gave up his hunger strike. He had been disgusted at Prince Philip attending the funeral of the Japanese Emperor Hirohito, whom many in Britain regard as a war criminal. The Queen had even sent Andy an appealing letter which satisfied the old soldier.
The first thing he ate after his protest strike was a ________ (1) of leek soup. Some fellow Burma war veterans had come to see their former comrade home. They cheered him up by saying, "We admire you, Andy. We've come to invite you to a fruit ________ (2) in your honour next month. Meanwhile here's a bottle of champagne, perhaps for a nice champagne ________ (3) later on. You've done well!" As Andy was too weak to speak, he simply nodded in reply.

SOLUTION

(1) **bowl** of leek soup (2) fruit **cup** (3) champagne **cup**

CHIPS ≠ chips (BE)

chips (BE)

CHIPS
(Kartoffel**chips**)

crisps

CHIPS: (Kartoffel**chips**) (potato) crisps (BE); (potato) chips (AE)

"Hör doch auf, ständig **Chips** beim Fernsehen zu essen", bat ihn Eileen. "Es stört mich."
"Stop eating **crisps** all the time while you're watching TV," Eileen told him. "It disturbs me."
Die Briten geben mehr als eine Billion Pfund im Jahr für Knabberzeug aus, und sechs Billionen Tüten **Chips** werden jährlich verzehrt.
The British spend more than £ 1 billion on snacks every year, and six billion packets of **crisps** are eaten annually.
Die Leute im Kino begannen zu zischen, als John die **Chips** hervorholte.
People in the cinema began to hiss when John got his **crisps** out.

chips (BE): Pommes (frites)

Note: *Pommes frites* are also called *French fries* in English.
Unfortunately, Sir Walter Raleigh brought the wrong potato to England 400 years ago if you like **French fries**. Russet Burbank, an American potato now grown in England and Scotland, make better **French fries** – the advertisement maintained.

More than three quarters of the 400 English schools surveyed, served **chips** more than three times a week.
Bei mehr als Dreiviertel von 400 begutachteten englischen Schulen standen mehr als dreimal pro Woche **Pommes frites** auf dem Speiseplan.
During our holiday we never even attempted to resist that famous Belgian invention – **chips**.
Während unseres Urlaubs haben wir überhaupt nicht versucht, jener berühmten belgischen Erfindung zu widerstehen – **Pommes frites**.

Note: fish and **chips** = (gebratenes) Fischfilet mit Pommes frites
a fish and **chip** shop, a **chip** shop; a fish and **chip** lunch ('chip' in these cases without an 's' at the end)
Day-trippers to Alton Towers fun park could enjoy a traditional fish and **chip** lunch.

but: a **chip** off the old block = ganz der Vater (sein)
have a **chip** on one's shoulder = Komplexe haben; eine herausfordernde Haltung einnehmen
when the **chips** are down = im Ernstfall; wenn es hart auf hart geht
When the **chips** are down, the IRA do not respect your nationality.

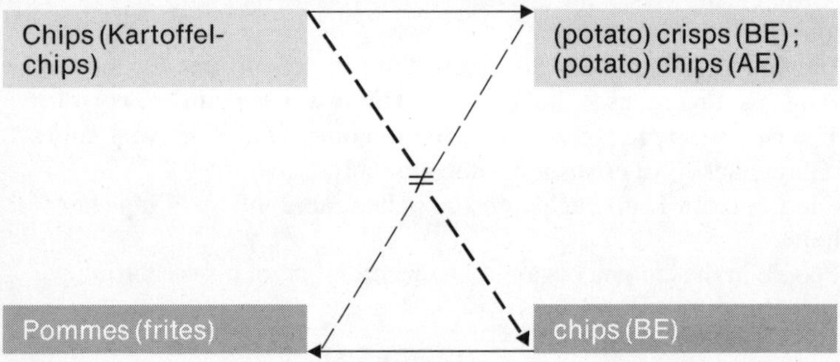

FALSE FRIENDS IN CONTEXT

Smell like a Lord

A young Scotsman was passing a ________ (1) shop in his car with his girlfriend sitting next to him.
Girlfriend: Hmm! Those ________ (2) smell good.
Scotsman: Just a minute, Carol. I'll go round the block, so you can smell them again.

SOLUTION

(1) **chip** shop (2) chips

Dirty Pie in the Sky

Young Man: I've come here to complain about the amount of litter left in our streets.
Publicity Director: We're doing what we can to keep the streets and parks tidy.
Young Man: Well, look at all that litter on the riverbank and near the harbour. In Dubai I never saw so much as a screwed-up ______ (3) packet on the pavement. As a taxpayer I keep asking myself where all our money goes.
Publicity Director: Let me just make something clear. On ______ (4) packets and drink cans, there is a picture of a person putting litter in the bin. But do they do it? People just don't take any notice.
Young Man: Yes, that's all dirty pie in the sky. That's why I keep complaining.

SOLUTION

(3) a screwed-up **crisp** packet (4) **crisp** packets

DRESSMAN ≠ *dressman

***dressman**

DRESSMAN

male model

(= männliches Mannequin)

DRESSMAN: (1) (männliches Mannequin) male model, male mannequin
(2) (Modevorführer) (male) fashion model

(1) Unter den Überlebenden bei der Schiffstragödie auf der *Marchioness*, bei der 51 junge Menschen den Tod fanden, war ein **Dressman** mit dem Namen Timo.
Among the survivors of the *Marchioness* riverboat tragedy, in which 51 young people died, was a **male model** called Timo.
Als der erste **Dressman** über den Laufsteg ging, folgten die anwesenden Damen gespannt der Vorführung der neuen Kreationen.
When the first **male mannequin** went along the catwalk, the ladies present followed his presentation of the new creations eagerly.
(2) Susan hatte zum drittenmal geheiratet, dieses Mal einen Lotto-Millionär, der ein ehemaliger **Dressman** ist.
Susan got married for the third time – this time to a pools millionaire who is a former **fashion model**.

(*dressman): –

Note: There is no such word as * **dressman** in BE or AE.

'**Dressman**'
(1) männliches Mannequin
(2) Modevorführer

(1) male model; male mannequin
(2) (male) fashion model

≠

– – –

(*dressman)

FALSE FRIENDS IN CONTEXT

Tragedy on the Thames

Danny: Hallo, Carol, I've just dropped by on my way to a riverboat party. We're going to celebrate Kenneth's 21st birthday on a pleasure boat. Why don't you come, too?
Carol (owner of the Ultra model agency in Chelsea): Sounds fun, but I'm too busy tonight preparing tomorrow's fashion show. By the way, one of our ________ (1) is stuck in Greece. Couldn't you help out?
Danny: If I'm still alive in the morning, I'll turn up. Bye, Carol.

* * *

Carol (next morning talking on the phone to Nigel Halifax, the model agent): You sound so serious. Anything wrong?
Nigel: You've got to cancel this afternoon's fashion show.
Carol: You must be mad. Why?
Nigel: There was a pleasure boat tragedy on the Thames last night. The papers say 16 or 18 models were drowned. Among them were three of our top ________ (2).
Carol: What about Danny?
Nigel: He's also among the dead. I understand he couldn't swim.
Carol: My God, Danny who so loved life . . . (starts to cry)

SOLUTION

(1) male models (2) male models/fashion models

OLDTIMER ◑ (*) old-timer

(*) **old-timer** [ˌəʊld'taɪmə]

OLDTIMER

veteran ['vetərən] **car etc.**

(= Autoveteran etc.)

OLDTIMER:	(1)	(allgemein für altes Auto, Schnauferl etc.) old car, old model; collector's car
	(2)	(Oldtimer vor 1916) veteran car, veteran (BE); antique car, antique (AE)
	(3)	(Oldtimer zwischen 1916 und 1930) vintage car, vintage (BE); classic car, classic (AE)
	(4)	(Oldtimer-Flugzeug aus der Vorkriegszeit) vintage aircraft; (Oldtimer-Militärflugzeug aus dem 2. Weltkrieg) vintage military aircraft

Note: Strictly speaking, all cars built before December 31, 1916 are **veteran cars** or **veterans** in BE; they are called **antique cars** or **antiques** in AE. Of these, all cars built before December 31, 1904 are **true veterans** in BE and **true antiques** in AE. Only **true veterans** are permitted to take part in the Brighton Run from the Hotel Metropole in London to the Hotel Metropole in Brighton.

All cars built between 1916 and 1930 are called **vintage cars** or **vintages** in BE and **classic cars** or **classics** in AE. This classification was laid down by the Veteran Car Club of Great Britain (founded in 1930) and accepted by the Antique Automobile Club of America (founded in 1935).

(1) Der Milliardär vertraute dem Autohändler an: "Ich sammle **Oldtimer** wie andere Briefmarken."
The billionaire confided to a car-dealer, "I buy **old models** as others collect stamps."
Zwei **Oldtimer** waren die Attraktion auf der Automobilausstellung.
Two **collector's cars** were the attraction at the motor show.
(2) Auf einer Tour durch verschiedene Autofabriken entdeckte der Direktor von British Heritage viele **Oldtimer** (vor 1916) unter Abdeckplanen.
On a tour of various car factories the British Heritage director discovered many **veteran cars** under dust sheets.

"Hast du die Einladung zum **Oldtimer**-Rennen von London nach Brighton schon gelesen?" rief mein Freund enthusiastisch.
"Have you read the invitation to the **(true) veterans**' race from London to Brighton?" cried my friend with enthusiasm.
(3) "Der Besitzer hat mir diesen **Oldtimer**, einen Chrysler von 1928, gestern angeboten. Er kostet nur 84000 Dollar", erzählte mir unser Manager.
"The owner offered this Chrysler 1928 **vintage** to me yesterday. It costs only $ 84,000," our manager told me.
"Ich fühle mich wie ein **klassischer Oldtimer** (**Klassiker**), der sich in tadellosem Zustand befindet", sagte die 46jährige Filmschauspielerin während des Interviews.
"I feel like a **vintage car** that's been kept in great nick," the 46-year-old filmstar said during the interview.
(4) Die größte Auktion von **Oldtimer-Flugzeugen**, die jemals stattfand, wurde 1990 in Santa Monica, Kalifornien, abgehalten.
The biggest ever **vintage aircraft** auction was held at Santa Monica, California, in 1990.

old-timer: (1) erfahrener Alter; alter, bewährter Mitarbeiter; ein altgedienter Mitarbeiter; 'einer von den Etablierten'
(2) alter Mann, ein Alter, 'alter Knabe', 'ein (ganz) alter Hase', 'einer von den ganz Alten' (coll., usually AE)

(1) You could sense that these **old-timers** valued their shared experiences more than money.
Man konnte spüren, wie diese **bewährten Mitarbeiter** Erlebnisse miteinander teilten, die mehr zählten als Geld.
Mr. McKerron is one of the **old-timers** in our firm.
Herr McKerron ist **einer von den Etablierten** in unserer Firma.
(2) It was the week before Christmas, and all the **old-timers** had come for the annual dinner again.
Es war die Woche vor Weihnachten, und all **die alten Knaben** waren wieder zum Jahrestreffen gekommen.

Note: a Vietnam War **veteran** = ein Teilnehmer am Vietnamkrieg

'Oldtimer'
(1) altes Auto, Schnauferl etc. (allgemein)
(2) Oldtimer (Automodell vor 1916)
(3) Oldtimer, Klassiker (Automodell zwischen 1916 und 1930)
(4) Oldtimer-Flugzeug

(1) old car, old model; collector's car
(2) veteran car, veteran (BE); antique car, antique (AE)
(3) vintage car, vintage (BE); classic car, classic (AE)
(4) vintage (military) aircraft

(1) erfahrener Alter; alter, bewährter Mitarbeiter; ein altgedienter Mitarbeiter; 'einer von den Etablierten'
(2) alter Mann, ein Alter, 'alter Knabe', 'ein (ganz) alter Hase', 'einer von den ganz Alten' (koll.)

old-timer (only used for male persons; coll., usually AE)

FALSE FRIENDS IN CONTEXT

The Silver Ghost and the Phantom

Car Collector (at car show): Did you know that Ayatollah Khomeni was the owner of two Rolls-Royce ________ (1)?
Vice-President of **V***eteran* **C***ar* **C***lub (VCC)*, the car collector's friend: I would never have thought a religious leader like him would have such a hobby.
Car Collector: It's not Khomeni's hobby. The matter is a bit more complicated. Both ________ (2) originally belonged to the late Shah. He had sent them for servicing to Rolls's plant in Crewe, Cheshire, in 1978 just before the revolution. After a long battle in English courts the Ayatollah's government won ownership of the two Rolls-Royces in 1988. Now Khomeni wants them back to put them into a museum.

Vice-President of VCC: What about the value of these cars?
Car Collector: Well, one, an armour-plated ________ (3), is a 1956 Phantom IV specially made for heads of state of which only 16 were produced. It's worth more than £110,000. The other, an even older ________ (4), is a 1922 Silver Ghost worth about £60,000. Both cars are very rare.
Vice-President of VCC: So the Ayatollahs have got their way at long last!
Car Collector: But what Khomeni doesn't know is how much Rolls will charge for ten years of servicing plus the shipping costs.

SOLUTION

(1) vintages (BE); classics (AE) (2) old models; old cars (3) old model/old car (4) vintage/vintage car (BE); classic/classic car (AE)

SHAKEHANDS ≠ *shakehands

***shakehands**

SHAKEHANDS
(= Händeschütteln)

shake hands

SHAKEHANDS: (1) (**Shakehands** machen) (verb) shake hands (with); shake the hand of
(2) (Händeschütteln) (noun) handshake

(1) Bei der Ankunft zu ihrer Konferenz **machten** die Staatsmänner **Shakehands** vor den Kameras.
On their arrival for the conference the statesmen **shook hands** before the cameras.
Prinzessin Diana trug dazu bei, einen Mythos zu beseitigen, als sie sich beim **Shakehands** mit AIDS-Kranken fotografieren ließ.
Princess Diana helped to explode a myth when she was photographed **shaking hands with** AIDS victims.
Die Anhänger möchten alle gerne mit Richard Corsie, dem Hallen-Weltmeister im Bowling, **Shakehands machen**.
His fans will all want to **shake the hand of** Richard Corsie, the World Indoor Bowls Champion.
(2) Alte Witze von umgekrempelten Hosenbeinen und lustigen **Shakehands** machen jedes Jahr unter den Studenten die Runde in England.
Old jokes about raised trouser legs and funny **handshakes** do the round among undergraduates in England every year.
Wie seine Art, **Shakehands** zu **machen**, war auch sein Charakter, herzlich und offen.
His character was like his **handshake**, friendly and warm.

Note: großzügige finanzielle Abfindung = golden **handshake** (for top and middle management)
The two London Underground bosses who resigned after the King's Cross fire received **golden handshakes** amounting to over £300,000.
Abstandssumme; Treueprämie = golden **handshake**
For his 25 years' service to the company he received a **golden handshake**.

(*shakehands): —

Note: In British English the term * **shakehands** does not exist.

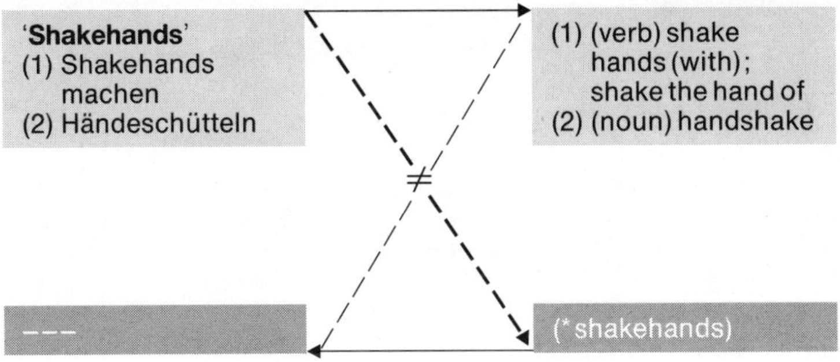

FALSE FRIENDS IN CONTEXT

Being Better Off than Before

Taxi Driver: Did you watch the railway bosses ________ (1)?
TV-Reporter: They seemed to mc a bit tense, but otherwise unconcerned.
Taxi Driver: After the Clapham train disaster all of them should be sacked. But you wait until their spokesman comes out after the meeting.
TV-Reporter (three hours later, still waiting outside the conference room): Ah, here they come at long last.
Spokesman of Railway Chiefs: Two members of the railway board are resigning at the end of next month. They'll get golden ________ (2) amounting to £120,000 each...
While the other railway chiefs ________ (3) before the TV cameras, the taxi driver says to the TV-Reporter:
Taxi Driver: So they'll get golden ________ (4). It's unbelievable! You can tell that to your viewers on TV. The tax payers will be delighted!

SOLUTION

(1) shake hands (2) golden handshakes (3) are shaking hands
(4) golden handshakes

SHOWMASTER ≠ *showmaster

***showmaster** ··········· **SHOWMASTER**

compère [ˈkɒmpeə] ——— (Unterhaltungskünstler)

SHOWMASTER:	(1)	(Unterhaltungskünstler in Radio- und Fernsehsendungen) compère (BE); presenter; show host
	(2)	(Conférencier bei Banketten, Galaveranstaltungen und Unterhaltungssendungen) master of ceremonies, M. C.; emcee (AE)

(1) Nach mehr als dreißig Jahren zog sich Kulenkampff als **Showmaster** aus dem Showgeschäft zurück.
Kulenkampff retired from show business after more than thirty years as a **compère**.
Der neue **Showmaster** Bob Wellings, der schon in einer anderen Fernsehsendung mit Erfolg aufgetreten war, wurde mit großem Beifall begrüßt.
The new **presenter** Bob Wellings, who had been a big success in another TV show, was welcomed with tremendous applause.
"Sie ist eine grundvernünftige Dame", beschrieb der **Showmaster** Johnny Carson die First Lady des Weißen Hauses Barbara Bush.
"She is a real no-nonsense lady," **show host** Johnny Carson described the First Lady of the White House Barbara Bush.
(2) Er fungierte als **Showmaster** während des Varieté-Programms.
He acted as an **M. C.** during the variety programme.
At the height of the revels, the **master of ceremonies** ordered the guests to discard their masks.
Auf dem Höhepunkt des Feierns forderte der **Showmaster** die Gäste auf, ihre Masken abzunehmen.

Note: durch eine Sendung als **Showmaster** führen = (to) compère (or host) a (TV or radio) show
It was a woman who **compèred** (or **hosted**) the Eurovision Song Contest last night.

(*showmaster): —

Note: The term ***showmaster** does not exist in British or American show business.

but: ring**master** = Manegenleiter, Zirkusdirektor
Traditionally, the person in a circus who announces the acts is called a **ringmaster**.
grand**master** (in chess etc.) = (Schach- etc.) Großmeister
"That boy may become the youngest **grandmaster** in chess history," my uncle commented.

'Showmaster' (1) Showmaster in Radio und Fernsehen (2) Conférencier bei Banketten, Galas etc.	≠	(1) compère (BE); presenter; show host (2) master of ceremonies, M. C.; emcee (AE)
— — —		(*showmaster)

FALSE FRIENDS IN CONTEXT

An Open-Air Phone-in

TV ________ (1) busily preparing his new Open-Air Phone-in Show:
Bob Wellings: Just hand me the microphone, will you?
TV Technician (handing it to him): Er...
Bob Wellings (without stopping): Rhubarb, rhubarb, rhubarb... (tapping at the microphone nervously)
TV Technician, wildly gesticulating to Wellings: We're on the air!
Bob Wellings: Hello, welcome to our Open-Air Phone-in Show. Your ________ (2) is Bob Wellings... And here's our first phone-in participant...
Furious Phone-in Voice: Why the hell did you greet us with 'rhubarb'? I want an explanation! Right now!
Bob Wellings: Oh, sorry, I didn't realise my microphone was on the

air already. Sorry, I was really caught out. Not even my own technician told me. Any other queries?

SOLUTION

(1) presenter/compère (2) presenter/compère

SLIP ≠ (*)slip

(*)**slip**

SLIP

panties

(Damen- oder Herren-**Slip**)

SLIP: (1) (beinloser Damen-**Slip**) knickers, briefs, panties
(2) (beinloser Herren-**Slip**) (under-)pants, briefs

(1) Für den Fall eines längeren Aufenthalts auf Flughäfen rät *Travel Care* weiblichen Passagieren 'Tragen Sie stets zusätzliche **Slips** bei sich'.
In case of longer delays at airports, *Travel Care's* advice to female passengers is 'Always carry spare **knickers**.'
Die meisten Männer verlieren ihre Konzentration, wenn sie einen kurzen Blick auf einen weißen Damen-**Slip** erhaschen.
Most men lose their concentration if they get a glimpse of a lady's white **briefs**.
41000 Italiener in Roms Olympiastadion waren entzückt, als Sandra Farmer-Patrick die 400 m Hürden gewann – im kurzen Seiden-**Slip**.
41,000 Italians were delighted in Rome's Olympic Stadium when Sandra Farmer-Patrick won the 400 m hurdles – in scanty silk **panties**.

Note: Nowadays **knickers** is somewhat old-fashioned; **briefs** and **panties** are generally preferred by women. In a shop a lady would ask for **briefs**.

(2) "In diesem Falle hätte ich gerne einen blauen **Slip**", antwortete der junge Mann.
"In that case I'd like to have blue **pants**," the young man replied.
Danach ging er zu Marks and Spencer und kaufte sich zwei weiße **Slips**.
Then he went to Marks and Spencer and bought two pairs of white **briefs**.

slip: (1) Unterrock, Unterkleid
(2) Zettel, Beleg
(3) Kissenbezug
(4) Flüchtigkeitsfehler

(1) Some of the curvy little dresses of the new fashion collection looked like little **slips**.
Einige der kurvenreichen kleinen Kleider der neuen Modekollektion sahen wie kleine **Unterröcke** aus.
Princess Diana wore a plain **slip** under her lace dress at the reception at the British Embassy in Paris.
Prinzessin Diana trug ein einfarbiges **Unterkleid** unter dem Seidenkleid beim Empfang in der Britischen Botschaft in Paris.
(2) "Have you got a **slip** of paper for me, otherwise I can't write down your address and telephone number," John asked her.
"Hast du einen **Zettel** für mich, sonst kann ich nicht deine Anschrift und Telefonnummer notieren", bat John sie.
All I had to do was hand my Visa card to the shop assistant and sign the sales **slip**.
Alles, was ich tun mußte, war, dem Verkäufer meine Visa-Karte zu reichen und den Kassen**beleg** zu unterschreiben.
(3) "You've got to take off your pillow**slip**; it's dirty," his mother reminded him for the second time that morning.
"Du mußt deinen Kopf**kissenbezug** abziehen; er ist schmutzig", erinnerte ihn seine Mutter an diesem Morgen zum zweitenmal.
(4) "Try to avoid any **slips** of the pen," their French teacher told them.
"Versucht **Flüchtigkeitsfehler** (beim Schreiben) zu vermeiden", sagte ihnen ihr Französischlehrer.

Note: gym**slip** = Falten-Trägerrock (besonders an englischen Mädchen-Internatsschulen)

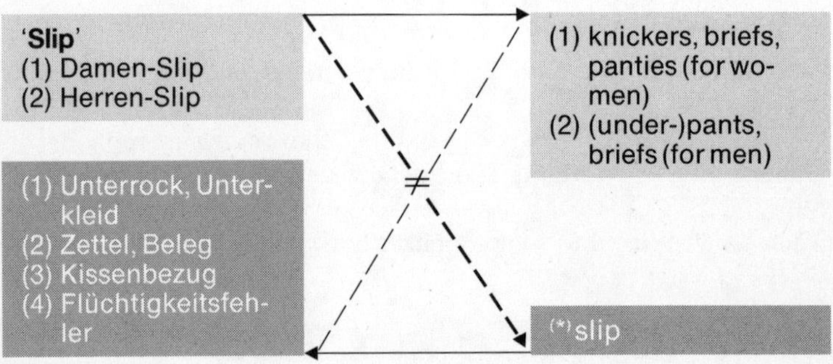

FALSE FRIENDS IN CONTEXT

Stop Worrying and Start Living

A young lady on her way to the office was standing on a crowded Chicago bus. She had got up in a hurry that morning and was worrying whether her ________ (1) was showing. So she asked a little boy standing next to her. "No, ma'am," he shook his head.
A few stops later she got off the bus and started to walk along crowded Washington Boulevard.
As the bus passed her, the little boy shouted at the top of his voice, "Your ________ (2) is showing now, lady, it is showing now!"

SOLUTION

(1) slip (2) slip

Spending an Afternoon in Class

Mother: Why are you so late back from school today?
Schoolgirl: I (half crying)... I had to spend the afternoon in class wearing a PE skirt with no ________ (3). (Bursts into tears.)
Mother: Really! That's the last straw!

* * *

Mother (on the phone): I'd like to speak to the headmaster.
Male Voice: Speaking.
Mother: I'm furious with you! Why did my daughter have to sit in class without her ________ (4) on?
Headmaster: There must be a misunderstanding. Your daughter wet her ________ (5), so I told her to change into her PE kit...

SOLUTION

(3) knickers/panties (4) knickers/panties (5) knickers/panties

Posing in Underwear

O. Stillman Rockefeller, 30, heir to the famous Rockefeller fortune, was once asked to strip off for an underwear advertisement by the Jockey Company.

Jockey Advertising Manager: ... and the Jockey Company is offering you $ 50,000 to pose in their new collection of ________ (6). You've got a fairly decent body for the job. What do you say?

O. Stillman Rockefeller: The money's good, but the job's bad. I'm afraid I've got to turn the offer down.

Instead, Stillman Rockefeller went into men's clothing himself, adapting the family crest for his own creations, ________ (7) included.

SOLUTION

(6) briefs (7) briefs

SMOKING ≠ *smoking

***smoking**

SMOKING (= Gesellschaftsanzug)

dinner-jacket

SMOKING: (Gesellschaftsanzug) dinner-jacket (BE); tuxedo, tux (AE)

"Wir gehen heute abend zur Wohltätigkeitsgala ins Grosvenor Hotel. Du mußt deinen **Smoking** anziehen", rief ihm seine Frau hinterher, als er das Haus morgens verließ.
"We're going to the charity gala in the Grosvenor Hotel tonight. You've got to put on your **dinner-jacket**," his wife called after him as he left the house in the morning.
Lord Bristol bestritt alles und behauptete, daß der **Smoking**, den er trug, seinem Chauffeur gehörte.
Lord Bristol denied everything, claiming the **dinner-jacket** he was wearing belonged to his chauffeur.
Ein Spitzen-Taschentuch, das in die Tasche eines **Smokings** gesteckt wird, verleiht einer sonst männlichen Linie Weichheit.
A lace handkerchief tucked into the pocket of a **tuxedo**, lends softness to an otherwise masculine line.

Note: **Smoking**zwang (aufgrund schriftlicher Einladung) = black tie
If a written invitation specifies '**black tie**', this indicates that a **dinner jacket** (= Smoking) should be worn with a 'black bow tie':
The Bradleys have been invited to this winter's **black tie** dinner dance.

*smoking: (1) –
(2) (das) Rauchen
(3) '(Nicht-)**Raucher**-' (in combinations)

Note: There is no such term as ***smoking** for 'Gesellschaftsanzug' in BE and AE.

(1) –
(2) **Smoking** and drinking are harmful to pregnant mothers.

Rauchen und Trinken sind für schwangere Mütter schädlich.
(3) Princess Diana revealed in the interview she kept a 'no-**smoking**' sign at home.
Prinzessin Diana enthüllte in dem Interview, daß sie in ihrem Haus einen 'Nicht-**Raucher**'-Hinweis hängen habe.

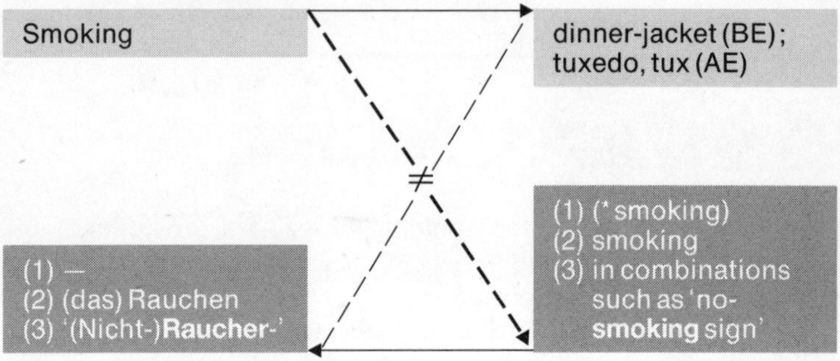

FALSE FRIENDS IN CONTEXT

Not Caring any Longer

TV Star Travanti: I'm angry. There's too much ________ (1).
Girlfriend (looking at him in surprise): I don't understand...
TV Star Travanti: ________ (2) is a killer. I'm going to scream whenever someone smokes in my presence.
Girlfriend: Think of your fans, neighbours, friends at parties etc. What'll they think?
TV Star Travanti: I don't care any longer. If I turn up at charity galas wearing a ________ (3) I look respectable. But I'm determined to fight ________ (4) because I'm right.
Girlfriend: Darling, don't work yourself up so much. Is it worth it?
TV Star Travanti: Everyone should follow the example of British Airways and ban ________ (5). I'm sick of having to ask people to put out cigarettes in no-________ (6) areas.

SOLUTION

(1) smoking (2) smoking (3) dinner-jacket (BE) (4) smoking
(5) smoking (6) no-**smoking** areas

Finding Out

Have you checked your husband is not having an affair?
Measure the length of his black tie before he goes out and when he comes back to see whether he has taken off his shirt and ________ (7).

SOLUTION

(7) dinner-jacket

TALKMASTER ≠ *talkmaster

***talkmaster** ··········► **TALKMASTER**

host ——————► (= Moderator)

TALKMASTER(IN):	(1) (Moderator) chat show host; talk show host; host (BE)
	(2) (Moderatorin) chat show hostess, talk show hostess; hostess (BE)

Note: The term **talk show** exists in English, but the word * **talkmaster** does not; **chat show** is BE for German **Talkshow**.

(1) Zu den Tanzpartnern der Prinzessin Michael von Kent zählte der Fernseh-**Talkmaster** Terry Wogan beim Portman Square Ball, einer Wohltätigkeitsveranstaltung, die 140 Pfund pro Person kostete.
Princess Michael of Kent had TV **chat show host** Terry Wogan among her dancing partners at the Portman Square Ball, a charity £ 140-a-head event.
"Könnten Sie Gast meiner nächsten Talkshow sein?" fragte der **Talkmaster** Boris Becker nach seinem Sieg beim Tennis-Masters-Turnier in New York. "Ich möchte gerne, aber ich kann zu diesem Zeitpunkt nicht", antwortete Boris.
"Could you be my guest in my next chat show?" the **chat show host** asked Boris Becker after he had won the New York Masters Tennis Tournament. "I'd like to, but I can't come on that date," Boris answered.
(2) Oprah Winfrey ist mehr als eine **Talkmasterin**. Die Leute sprechen sich gerne bei ihr aus.
Oprah Winfrey is more than a **talk show hostess**. People like to confess to her.

Note: eine **Talkshow** moderieren = (to) host a chat show; (to) host a talk show
"I've no ambition to **host a chat show**," said Julia Somerville, the first woman to have presented both Britain's top television news bulletins.

(*talkmaster): —

Note: The expression * **talkmaster** is unknown in British and American English.

'Talkmaster(in)'
(1) Moderator
(2) Moderatorin

(1) chat show host; talk show host; host (BE)
(2) chat show hostess; talk show hostess; hostess (BE)

≠

(*talkmaster)

FALSE FRIENDS IN CONTEXT

Britain's Top Chatter

Female TV Viewer: Did you read about our new chat king? Michael Aspel has been voted the best British ________ (1). I don't think that's fair.
Male TV Viewer: Mind you, Aspen is Britain's highest-paid TV star. Still, my favourite ________ (2) is Terry Wogan... and always will be! Did you know Terry won the *Favourite Male Personality Award* ten times on the trot?
Female TV Viewer: The truth is, Terry would have won the award anyway, but he stayed out of the competition this time because it had become a 'Wogan Award'. I think he just wanted to give someone else a chance.
Male TV Viewer: Look, Aspen's success is largely due to the fact that he's taken over chat shows such as *This is Your Life* and *Family Favourites*. And he's been helped by Susan who makes a competent ________ (3) in his team.
Female TV Viewer: That's right. It's not enough to be Mr. Nice Guy and spend more than £1 million on a chat show! Which Terry never did!

SOLUTION

(1) host/chat show host (2) host/chat show host (3) talk show hostess/hostess

die TEENS ≠ (*) the teens

(*) the teens .... → **die TEENS**

teenagers ← (= die Jugendlichen)

die TEENS: (1) (die Jugendlichen) teenagers; youngsters, young people
(2) in compounds such as '**teenage** star'

(1) Einer der Anrufer wollte von der Expertengruppe wissen, warum heutzutage so viele **Teens** Drogen nehmen würden.
One of the phone-in callers wanted to know from the panel of experts why so many **teenagers** were taking to drugs nowadays.
Die im Augenblick populärste Kinderband *Pünktchen, Pünktchen* besteht aus fünf **Teens** im Alter von 11–14 Jahren; sie spielte beim Bonner Kinderfest '88 im Kanzleramt. Die **Teens** kamen aus Wuppertal.
At present the most popular children's band *Pünktchen, Pünktchen* consists of five **young people** aged 11 to 14. It played at the Bonn Children's Festival '88 at the Chancellor's Office. The **youngsters** came from Wuppertal.
Bundeskanzler Kohl hatte mehrere hundert **Teens** zu dem Kinderfest '90 eingeladen, und alle waren gekommen, um dabeizusein.
Chancellor Kohl had invited several hundred **young people** to the Children's Festival '90 and they had all come in order to be there.
(2) Seine Liebesaffäre mit dem **Teen**-Modell Helen endete schon nach wenigen Wochen.
His love affair with the **teenage** model Helen ended after only a few weeks.

(1) ((*) the teens): (die Jugendlichen) —
(2) teens: Teenageralter; die Jugendjahre; Flegeljahre

Note: The term (*) **the teens** with a definite article in the sense of '**die Jugendlichen**' does not exist in English; on the other hand, **teens** without the definite article is correct, but has a different meaning '**Jugendalter**, **Teenageralter**'. In addition, the German expression '**die Teens**' refers to young people of all ages between ten and twenty whereas English **teens** is limited to the ages of thirteen to nineteen.

(1) –
(2) Tom watched her go. She was beautiful, intelligent and still in her **teens**. He was fascinated.
Tom beobachtete sie beim Weggehen. Sie war schön und intelligent und noch im **Teenageralter**. Er war fasziniert.
The way Chris behaved at school showed that he was still in his **teens**.
Die Art, wie sich Chris in der Schule benahm, zeigte, daß er noch in den **Flegeljahren** war.
When Pat had reached her **teens**, she wanted to leave school and earn money.
Als Pat das **Teenageralter** erreicht hatte, wollte sie die Schule verlassen und Geld verdienen.
The age of players at the Markson Oxford tennis camp ranged between late **teens** to late sixties.
Das Alter der Spieler am Oxforder Markson Tenniszentrum reichte von den späten **Jugendjahren** bis zu den späten Sechzigerjahren.

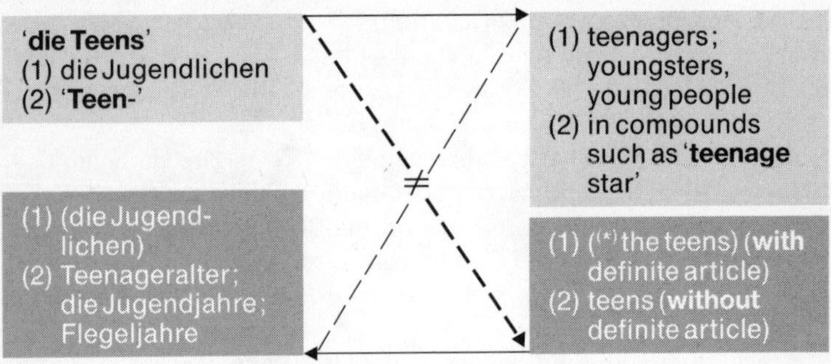

FALSE FRIENDS IN CONTEXT

In Favour of Young Offenders

Ex-Police Officer: All I can tell you is all those cars were stolen by ________ (1). This can't go on.
Scrap Dealer: Last night some ________ (2) took two car radios and smashed the dashboard in that Jaguar over there.

Ex-Police Officer: The easiest way of dealing with them is to catch them in the act and hand them over to the police.
Scrap Dealer: It doesn't solve the problem though... I've got an idea. What about giving these ________ (3) the chance to repair and race old cars? Then they won't be tempted to steal new ones.
Ex-Police Officer: And it might stop them from slipping into a life of crime. What about starting old banger racing for boys still ____ (4)?
Scrap Dealer: O.K., I'll put the ________ (5) on the right track, and you keep your eye on things. Let's give it a try.

SOLUTION

(1) teenagers/youngsters (2) young people/youngsters (3) teen-agers/youngsters (4) in their teens (5) the youngsters/the young people

TWEN ≠ *twen

***twen**

TWEN

s. o. in his (her) twenties

TWEN(S):	(1) (männlicher Twen) s. o. in his twenties; a young man in his twenties
	(2) (weiblicher Twen) s. o. in her twenties; a young woman in her twenties
	(3) (Plural: Twens) (young) people in their twenties

(1) Obwohl er noch ein **Twen** war, war er schon ein Berufsschauspieler.
Although he was only **in his twenties**, he was a professional actor.
(2) "Ich mag mich heute besser leiden als damals, als ich ein **Twen** war", gab Britt Eklund im Alter von 46 Jahren zu.
"I like myself better today than I did when I was **in my twenties**," Britt Eklund admitted at the age of 46.
Von der Art und Weise, wie sie sprach, konnte man sehen, daß sie noch ein **Twen** war.
From the way she talked you could see she was still **a young woman in her twenties.**
(3) Die Zeitschrift *Twen* war eine westdeutsche Publikation; sie wurde für **Twens** geschrieben.
The magazine *Twen* was a West German publication and was written for **people** still **in their twenties.**
Scharen von **Twens** waren zu dem Konzert angereist, aber viele verließen vorzeitig den Konzertsaal, weil sie enttäuscht waren.
Crowds of **people in their twenties** had travelled to the concert, but many left the concert hall before it had finished because they were disappointed.

(*twen): ———

Note: There is no such word as ***twen** in English. In contrast, the German term 'Teenager' has a direct equivalent in English **teenager**.

'Twen' (1) männlicher Twen (2) weiblicher Twen (3) Twens (Pl.)	(1) s. o. in his twenties; a young man in his twenties (2) s. o. in her twenties; a young woman in her twenties (3) (young) people in their twenties
— — —	(*twen)

FALSE FRIENDS IN CONTEXT

You must be Joking

Wolfram Huncke edited two volumes of jokes for ________ (1). Here is one of them:

The people of a small village were shocked at their new vicar when they saw him leave the church with a flashy tie. As none of the villagers dared to say a word, a ________ (2) walked up to him saying, "Don't you think that tie of yours is too flashy?" – "There's no harm in that," was the vicar's reply. "Your tie can be any other colour as long as your soul is black." – "Surely, you must be joking," someone replied.

SOLUTION

(1) people in their twenties (2) a young man in his twenties/a young woman in her twenties

VERKEHRSROWDY ≠ traffic * rowdy

traffic ***rowdy** (etc.)

VERKEHRS**ROWDY** (etc.)

roadhog etc.

VERKEHRS**ROWDY** (etc.):	(1)	(Verkehrs**rowdy**) road**hog**, (stronger) mad driver; (See**rowdy**) sea**hog**
	(2)	(Fußball**rowdy**, Ferien**rowdy**) soccer **hooligan**, holiday **hooligan**

(1) "Wir werden das Verhalten der Verkehrs**rowdys** nicht länger hinnehmen", kündigte der Polizeisprecher an.
"We won't tolerate the behaviour of road**hogs** any longer", the police spokesman announced.
Verkehrsrowdys sterben nie aus – dieser hier war innerhalb der Stadt mit Tempo 150 gefahren.
Mad drivers never die – this one had gone at 150 inside the town.
Wir werden einige von diesen See**rowdys** festnehmen müssen; sie stiften um die Insel Wight herum zu viel Unruhe.
We'll have to arrest some of these 'sea**hogs**'; they're causing too much trouble around the Isle of Wight.
(2) Britische Ferienveranstalter baten den Fußballverband um Hilfe gegen die englischen Fußball**rowdies**.
British holiday companies have asked the Football Association for help against English soccer **hooligans**.
Michael Simpson, 23, aus Norwich ist als Großbritanniens schlimmster Ferien**rowdy** in Griechenland bezeichnet worden, nachdem er auf Korfu zweimal ins Gefängnis wanderte.
Michael Simpson, 23, from Norwich has been described as Britain's worst holiday **hooligan** in Greece, after he was jailed twice in Corfu.

Note: **Roadhog** can also be an amusing term. An old person driving in the middle of the road may also be a **roadhog**.
His wife always nagged him for being a **roadhog**.

(traffic *rowdy, sea*rowdy, holiday*rowdy): —

Note: The compounds traffic* **rowdy**, sea* **rowdy**, holiday* **rowdy** do not exist in English. The term **rowdy** (= Krawallmacher), however, is a normal English word. 'Fußball**rowdys**' are soccer **hooligans**; in a more extreme form they may be called 'thugs' = Schläger(typen).

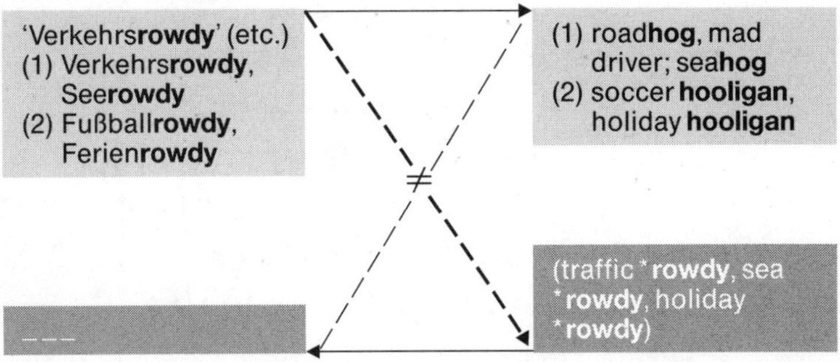

FALSE FRIENDS IN CONTEXT

The Battle of St. Tropez

Mayor of St. Tropez: Speeding by British holidaymakers has become a problem. They race like madmen through St. Tropez in their Porsches, jump in their boats and do the same thing at sea.
British Consul: I'm sorry to hear it.
Mayor of St. Tropez: They're the worst ________ (1) on land, and, what's more, they're creating havoc at sea as well.
British Consul: Could you give some details?
Mayor of St. Tropez: Only last weekend it was the *Battle of St. Tropez* for four hours with British power boats in the thick of it. More than half were driven by unlicenced boating enthusiasts.
British Consul: Hm.
Mayor of St. Tropez: The situation has developed into a big issue not only in St. Tropez and along the Riviera, but in France generally.
British Consul: It sounds serious.
Mayor of St. Tropez: Our police have fined some British holiday ________ (2) £150 on the spot and arrested others. First it was

________ (3), now it's ________ (See**rowdies**) (4), too. We don't want any more battles of St. Tropez!

SOLUTION

(1) roadhogs (2) holiday hooligans (3) roadhogs (4) seahogs

LAST NOT LEAST ≠ *last not least

***last not least**

LAST NOT LEAST
(als letztes,
aber keineswegs
Unwichtigstes)

last but not least etc.

LAST NOT LEAST: (als letztes, aber keineswegs Unwichtigstes etc.) last but not least, last but by no means least, last and certainly not least

Note: The **Duden Fremdwörterbuch** (5th ed. 1990) is wrong to put a comma after 'last' in the phrases ***last, not least** and **last, but not least**. There is no comma after 'last' in modern English. The comma in the **Duden Fremdwörterbuch** has been taken over from 16th century English (Shakespeare).

Und **last not least** beträgt Ihr Gehalt ab dem 19. Lebensjahr 8400 Pfund, wenn Sie beim Diplomatischen Dienst Großbritanniens angestellt werden.
And, **last but not least**, your salary from 19 onwards will be £ 8,400 if you become a member of Britain's Diplomatic Service.
Und **last not least** kommt es wirklich darauf an, wer was in diesem Buch sagte? Eben ja. Tschüs!
And, **last but by no means least**, does it really matter who said what in this book? Yes, it does. Bye.

*last not least: (1) —
(2) not least (nicht zuletzt); most of all (vor allem)
(3) finally, ultimately (zuletzt, schließlich)

Note: There is no such phrase as ***last not least** in BE and AE. Although the Pseudo-Anglicism ***last not least** is used in German quite frequently, the phrase **last but not least** (and its variants) are not used as often in English. Its sense is often ironical.

(1) –
(2) I'm going to India for several reasons, **not least** to see the region where my father had lived.
Ich reise aus mehreren Gründen nach Indien, **nicht zuletzt** um die Gegend kennenzulernen, wo mein Vater gelebt hatte.
Isn't this act of violence **most of all** a bad sign for the South African government?
Ist diese Gewalttat nicht **vor allem** ein schlechtes Zeichen für die südafrikanische Regierung?
(3) **"Finally** I'd like to pass on the greetings of the President of the United States," said the American ambassador, concluding his speech.
"**Zuletzt** möchte ich Ihnen noch die Grüße des Präsidenten der Vereinigten Staaten überbringen", sagte der amerikanische Botschafter am Ende seiner Rede.
The rebels want, **ultimately**, to win the war with this measure.
Die Rebellen wollen mit dieser Maßnahme **schließlich** den Krieg gewinnen.

Compare: The rendering of **zuletzt** may also be **last** or **in the end**.
Last is open-ended, whereas **in the end** is synonymous with 'finally' either concretely or figuratively.
When did you **last** see your father?
Wann haben Sie **zuletzt** Ihren Vater besucht?
In the end the old man could hardly eat anything.
Zuletzt konnte der alte Mann kaum noch etwas zu sich nehmen.

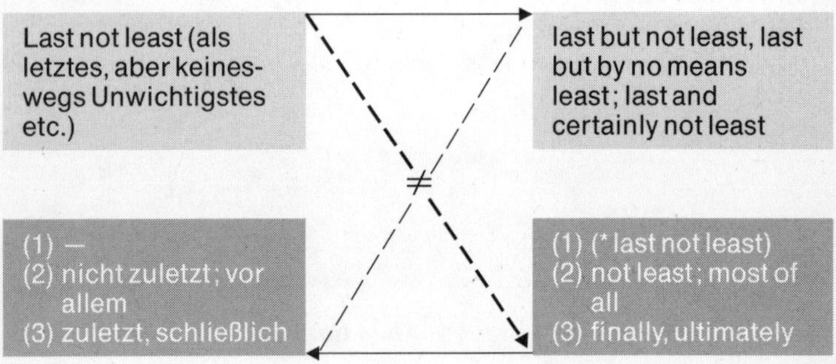

A Flourishing Finish

1. **The Follies of the Sixties** (*First Speech, final part*)
"Today Britain has to pay the price for the follies of the Sixties. The biggest folly was the exploitation of Nature; another quite different folly was the approach to politics. The Profumo Affair is a case in point. Few politicians since the war have been more severely punished than the former Minister of Defence, ________ (1) because he did not tell Parliament the truth. John Profumo was, ________ (2), punished for a single lie."

2. **The Price for going Green** (*Second Speech, final passage*)
(Minister of the Environment pausing, looking at the audience before him)
"What ________ (3) is the relevance of all this? We've got to pay the price of going green. If we are for 'eco-friendly' products then we must, ________ (4), support this campaign for the general use of unleaded petrol in Britain. Thank you."

SOLUTION

(1) not least (2) last but not least (3) finally/ultimately (4) last but by no means least

FALSE FRIENDS TRAPS TEST 8

PSEUDO-ANGLICISMS

1.a. Eight billion packets of ________ (**Chips**), nuts and nibbles were eaten in Britain last year.
1.b. British food freaks spent more than £ 1 billion on snack food last year, with ________ (**Pommes frites**) still the most popular product.
2.a. The Jockey Company had offered him to pose in their latest creation of ________ (**Slips**), but he turned the offer down.
2.b. Something had caught his eye, so he stopped to look at her. Should he tell Susan? Her ________ (**Unterrock**) was showing.
3.a. "It's amazing how many ________ (**Oldtimer**) are still on sale at more or less take-away prices in Britain. If you restore them, they can fetch enormous prices," my old friend continued.
3.b. As always, Alan had turned up for the annual candle-light dinner before Christmas. He was proud to be one of the ________ (**einer von den Etablierten; altgedienter Mitarbeiter**) who shared their professional experience of a lifetime.
4.a. Of course, they would turn up for Barnardo's charity gala, and he would put on his new ________ (**Smoking**) for the occasion.
4.b. The United States has banned ________ (**Rauchen**) on all domestic flights lasting up to six hours.
5.a. Come and see us tonight, Penny. There'll be quite an interesting lot of people around. And you'll enjoy our fruit ________ (**Bowle**) or if you don't like that, there's champagne ________ (**Bowle**) too.
5.b. In addition, you tuck into different types of delicious salads in the salad ________ (**Schalen**).
6. Teens and ________ (**Twens**) change their lifestyles a lot.
7. The most, if at all, he'll get for his brave action is a ________ (**Shakehands**) and maybe a free pint. There'll be no hugs and kisses.
8. Among the victims in the pleasure boat tragedy on the Thames was a twenty-year-old ________ (**Dressman**) known in the trade as Jarad.
9. "Being a TV ________ (**Showmaster**) is somewhat different from being a ________ (**Showmaster**) for one of the regional radio stations," he admitted in the interview.
10. "I've always found your chat show interesting and stimulating," the politician told the ________ (**Talkmasterin**). "That's why I accepted your invitation."

ANSWER SHEET: TRUE FRIENDS TEST 8

PSEUDO-ANGLICISMS

1.a. Eight billion packets of **crisps**, nuts and nibbles were eaten in Britain last year.
1.b. British food freaks spent more than £ 1 billion on snack food last year, with **chips** (or: **French fries**, **French fried potatoes**) still the most popular product.
2.a. The Jockey Company had offered him to pose in their latest creation of **briefs (pants)**, but he turned the offer down.
2.b. Something had caught his eye, so he stopped to look at her. Should he tell Susan? Her **slip** was showing.
3.a. "It's amazing how many **old models** (oder je nach Herstellungsjahr: **veteran cars**; **vintage cars**) are still on sale at more or less take-away prices in Britain. If you restore them, they can fetch enormous prices," my old friend continued.
3.b. As always, Alan had turned up for the annual candle-light dinner before Christmas. He was proud to be one of the **old-timers** who shared their professional experience of a lifetime.
4.a. Of course, they would turn up for Barnardo's charity gala, and he would put on his new **dinner-jacket** for the occasion.
4.b. The United States has banned **smoking** on all domestic flights lasting up to six hours.
5.a. Come and see us tonight, Penny. There'll be quite an interesting lot of people around. And you'll enjoy our fruit **cup** or if you don't like that, there's champagne **cup** too.
5.b. In addition, you tuck into different types of delicious salads in the salad **bowls**.
6. Teens and **people in their twenties** change their lifestyles a lot.
7. The most, if at all, he'll get for his brave action is a **handshake** and maybe a free pint. There'll be no hugs and kisses.
8. Among the victims in the pleasure boat tragedy on the Thames was a twenty-year-old **male model** known in the trade as Jarad.
9. "Being a TV **presenter** is somewhat different from being a **presenter** for one of the regional radio stations," he admitted in the interview.
10. "I've always found your chat show interesting and stimulating," the politician told the **chat show hostess**. "That's why I accepted your invitation."

FINAL TEST I

FALSE FRIENDS TRAPS

1.a. Her new summer dress looked strikingly ________ (**apart ≠ apart**).
1.b. Mind you, Jane is still an ________ woman (**apart ≠ apart**).
2.a. Scotland Yard ________ her past thoroughly (**kontrollieren ◑ control**).
2.b. Gear changing in the new VW Passat is ________ electronically rather than hydraulically (**kontrollieren ◑ control**).
3.a. The Australian ________ Robert Holmes a Court lost millions in the share crash in October 1987 (**Unternehmer ≠ undertaker**).
3.b. "Who will cover the cost of your neighbour's funeral?" the ________ asked me (**Unternehmer ≠ undertaker**). As I had only come to arrange the funeral and didn't have the money to cover the expenses, I left.
4.a. The yacht ________ with a crew of 13 after smashing into a submerged wreck off St. Catherine's Point near the Isle of Wight (**untergehen ≠ undergo**).
4.b. First the famous actor went to his dressing-room in *Her Majesty's Theatre* for the two-hour make-up he has to ________ before each performance (**untergehen ≠ undergo**).
5.a. Martina Navratilova admitted the antique Wimbledon silver fruit ________ meant much more to her than money (**Bowle ≠ bowl**).
5.b. When the hostess offered her some champagne ________, she took a cocktail instead (**Bowle ≠ bowl**).
6.a. The synthetic production of pearls in Japan deprived the traditional pearl-fishers of their ________ (**Existenz ◑ existence**).
6.b. For many years my father chose simply to ignore my ________ (**Existenz ◑ existence**).
7.a. The ________ pleasures of Mozart's *Magic Flute* have made it popular all over the world (**sinnlich ◑ sensual**).
7.b. At the church disco the vicar's son found her ________ presence and way of speaking rather embarrassing (**sinnlich ◑ sensual**).
8.a. The New Zealanders' humour is ________ and up-front, without irony (**prägnant ≠ pregnant**).
8.b. When Jane became ________ her boss sacked her. She is now seeking compensation against her former employer (**prägnant ≠ pregnant**).

9.a. Eddie Edwards, the worst ski-jumper at the Olympic Games, played the most ________ fool in a chat show in Los Angeles (**sympathisch ≠ sympathetic**).
9.b. Even the neighbours were quite ________ to the jilted bride (**sympathisch ≠ sympathetic**).
10.a. Derbyshire County Council beat off fierce ________ (**Konkurrenz ≠ concurrence**) from Japanese ________ (**Konkurrenz ≠ concurrence**) to lure more British firms to the area.
10.b. It was a strange ________ of events when the two leading racing cars fell from the bridge at the same time (**Konkurrenz ≠ concurrence**).

ANSWER SHEET

FINAL TEST I: TRUE FRIENDS

1.a. Her new summer dress looked strikingly **stylish**.
1.b. Mind you, Jane is still an **attractive** woman.
2.a. Scotland Yard **checked** her past thoroughly.
2.b. Gear changing in the new VW Passat is **controlled** electronically rather than hydraulically.
3.a. The Australian **entrepreneur** Robert Holmes a Court lost millions in the share crash in October 1987.
3.b. "Who will cover the cost of your neighbour's funeral?" the **undertaker** asked me. As I had only come to arrange the funeral and didn't have the money to cover the expenses, I left.
4.a. The yacht **sank** with a crew of 13 after smashing into a submerged wreck off St. Catherine's Point near the Isle of Wight.
4.b. First the famous actor went to his dressing-room in *Her Majesty's Theatre* for the two-hour make-up he has to **undergo** before each performance.
5.a. Martina Navratilova admitted the antique Wimbledon silver fruit **bowl** meant much more to her than money.
5.b. When the hostess offered her some champagne **cup**, she took a cocktail instead.
6.a. The synthetic production of pearls in Japan deprived the traditional pearl-fishers of their **livelihood**.
6.b. For many years my father chose simply to ignore my **existence**.
7.a. The **sensuous** pleasures of Mozart's *Magic Flute* have made it popular all over the world.
7.b. At the church disco the vicar's son found her **sensual** presence and way of speaking rather embarrassing.
8.a. The New Zealanders' humour is **pithy** and up-front, without irony.
8.b. When Jane became **pregnant** her boss sacked her. She is now seeking compensation against her former employer.
9.a. Eddie Edwards, the worst ski-jumper at the Olympic Games, played the most **likeable** fool in a chat show in Los Angeles.
9.b. Even the neighbours were quite **sympathetic to** the jilted bride.
10.a. Derbyshire County Council beat off fierce **competition** from Japanese **rival** products to lure more British firms to the area.
10.b. It was a strange **concurrence** of events when the two leading racing cars fell from the bridge at the same time.

FINAL TEST II

FALSE FRIENDS TRAPS

1.a. "We will be featuring four ________ Wimbledon Final photographs," the presenter announced (**klassisch ◑ classic**).
1.b. Ron owns a collection of 8.000 ________ records (**klassisch ◑ classic**).
2.a. Our neighbours have a ________ yacht on the Côte d'Azur (**luxuriös ≠ luxuriant**).
2.b. Jane's ________ fair hair is the most beautiful I have ever seen (**luxuriös ≠ luxuriant**).
3.a. In the film *We're No Angels* Robert de Niro's awkward grimaces are a substitute for ________ timing (**komisch ◑ comic**).
3.b. It looked rather ________, the way he ran to catch the bus and then slipped on a banana skin (**komisch ◑ comic**).
4.a. Teaching your children at home does not only mean buying books, ________ and a blackboard, but also making other sacrifices (**stationär ≠ stationery**).
4.b. The shots were fired at the president's ________ car at traffic lights near a bus depot (**stationär ≠ stationery**).
5.a. Every year *Le Piat de Beaujolais* is recognised by wine lovers as the ________ taste of that region (**definitiv ◑ definitive**).
5.b. The oil company can't take a ________ decision at the moment as the board of directors have to look into the problem of deep-sea technology first (**definitiv ◑ definitive**).
6.a. This was Ian Fleming's ________ bungalow, called *Goldeneye*, on the island of Jamaica (**magisch ◑ magic**).
6.b. At one of Blackpool's amusement arcades terrific ________ tricks were performed by a young illusionist called Russ Stevens (**magisch ◑ magic**).
7.a. A ________ stretch of water lay before him. Would he ever leave the island again? (**kontinuierlich ◑ continual**).
7.b. The ________ sound of hammering coming from the roadworks drove her to despair (**kontinuierlich ◑ continual**).
8.a. Unfortunately the ________ system of the submarine had been damaged (**elektrisch ◑ electric**).
8.b. The new Ford model has ________ windows and mud flaps – at no extra cost (**elektrisch ◑ electric**).

9.a. If you have more than a few pounds to ________, sticking to a diet is often a bigger problem than starting one (**lose** ≠ [*] **lose**).
9.b. "Wrap a ________ bandage around the wound," one of the Rover Scouts advised me (**lose** ≠ [*] **lose**).
10.a. Diego Maradona's playing in the last European Cup match was more flexible and ________ than ever (**ökonomisch ◑ economic**).
10.b. At a time of ________ overheating a new airport project can only add to inflation (**ökonomisch ◑ economic**).

ANSWER SHEET

FINAL TEST II: TRUE FRIENDS

1.a. “We will be featuring four **classic** Wimbledon Final photographs,” the presenter announced.
1.b. Ron owns a collection of 8.000 **classical** records.
2.a. Our neighbours have a **luxurious** yacht on the Côte d’Azur.
2.b. Jane’s **luxuriant** fair hair is the most beautiful I have ever seen.
3.a. In the film *We’re No Angels* Robert de Niro’s awkward grimaces are a substitute for **comic** timing.
3.b. It looked rather **comical**, the way he ran to catch the bus and then slipped on a banana skin.
4.a. Teaching your children at home does not only mean buying books, **stationery** and a blackboard, but also making other sacrifices.
4.b. The shots were fired at the president’s **stationary** car at traffic lights near a bus depot.
5.a. Every year *Le Piat de Beaujolais* is recognised by wine lovers as the **definitive** taste of that region.
5.b. The oil company can’t take a **definite** decision at the moment as the board of directors have to look into the problem of deep-sea technology first.
6.a. This was Ian Fleming’s **magical** bungalow, called *Goldeneye*, on the island of Jamaica.
6.b. At one of Blackpool’s amusement arcades terrific **magic** tricks were performed by a young illusionist called Russ Stevens.
7.a. A **continuous** stretch of water lay before him. Would he ever leave the island again?
7.b. The **continual** sound of hammering coming from the roadworks drove her to despair.
8.a. Unfortunately the **electrical** system of the submarine had been damaged.
8.b. The new Ford model has **electric** windows and mud flaps – at no extra cost.
9.a. If you have more than a few pounds to **lose**, sticking to a diet is often a bigger problem than starting one.
9.b. “Wrap a **loose** bandage around the wound,” one of the Rover Scouts advised me.
10.a. Diego Maradona’s playing in the last European Cup match was more flexible and **economical** than ever.
10.b. At a time of **economic** overheating a new airport project can only add to inflation.

FALSE FRIENDS NACH SCHWIERIGKEITSKATEGORIEN

I. GRUNDTYPEN VON FALSE FRIENDS

◑ = halbwahre (partielle) False Friends

EASY FALSE FRIENDS

(= Buch I)

älter	◑	older
Angel	≠	angle
also	≠	also
Bank	◑	bank
Baracke(n)	≠	barracks
bekommen	≠	become
borgen	◑	borrow
Braut	◑	bride
brav	≠	brave
Brust	◑	breast
dick	◑	thick
Engel	≠	angle
Fleisch	◑	flesh
Flur	≠	floor
Fotografie	◑	photography
Fotograf	≠	photograph
Golf	◑	golf
Kanal	◑	canal
Kropf	◑	crop
Mann	◑	man
Mappe	≠	map
Meinung	≠	meaning
Mörder	≠	murder
nächste	◑	next
Perle	◑	pearl
Rente	≠	rent
Sauce	◑	sauce
schmal	≠	small
Schnecke	≠	snake
schwimmen	◑	swim
See	◑	sea
Seite	◑	side
Sender	≠	sender
sparen	≠	spare
Straße	◑	street
Strom	◑	stream
Tablett	≠	tablet
wenn	◑	when
wer	≠	where
wo	≠	who

NOT SO EASY FALSE FRIENDS

(= Buch I)

Achse	◑	axis
Achsel	≠	axle
Akt	◑	act
Akte(n)	≠	act(s)
alarmieren	◑	alarm
Allee	≠	alley
Antenne	◑	antenna
Art	≠	art
ausgesprochen	≠	outspoken
blank	≠	blank
Dom	≠	dome
Fabrik	≠	fabric

familiär	≠	familiar
Flirt	≠	flirt
Gift	≠	gift
Hausmeister	≠	housemaster
Helm	≠	helm
Hose	≠	hose
isoliert	◑	isolated
Major	≠	mayor
Moral	◑	moral
Pension	◑	pension
Physiker	≠	physician
Plastik	◑	plastics
Politik	◑	politics
Preis	◑	price
Prospekt	≠	prospect
Rate	◑	rate
Salat	◑	salad
Schal	≠	shawl
Schatten	◑	shade
Schellfisch	≠	shellfish
selbstbewußt	≠	self-conscious
spenden	≠	spend
Stadium	≠	stadium
Technik	◑	technique
Transparent	≠	transparency
Ventilator	◑	ventilator
Vikar	≠	vicar
Warenhaus	≠	warehouse
Zylinder	◑	cylinder

DIFFICULT FALSE FRIENDS

(= Buch II)

Akkord	≠	accord
Aktion	◑	action
aktuell	≠	actual
Allüren	≠	allure
Ambulanz	◑	ambulance
apart	≠	apart
Artist	≠	artist
Basis	◑	basis
Chef	≠	chef
delikat	◑	delicate
Dessert	≠	desert
dezent	◑	decent
engagiert	◑	engaged
eventuell	≠	eventual
Existenz	◑	existence
famos	≠	famous
fatal	◑	fatal
Fraktion	≠	fraction
genial	≠	genial
graziös	≠	gracious
human	◑	human
Kaution	◑	caution
Konfession	≠	confession
Konkurrenz	≠	concurrence
konsequent	◑	consequent
kontrollieren	◑	control
Konzept	◑	concept
Menü	≠	menu
mondän	≠	mundane
ordinär	≠	ordinary
pathetisch	≠	pathetic
prägnant	≠	pregnant
Prozeß	◑	process
rentabel	≠	rentable
Rezept	≠	receipt
sensibel	≠	sensible
seriös	≠	serious
spendieren	≠	spend
Stipendium	≠	stipend
sympathisch	≠	sympathetic
temperamentvoll	≠	temperamental
Trakt	≠	tract
transpirieren	≠	transpire
unsympathisch	≠	unsympathetic

II. SONDERTYPEN VON FALSE FRIENDS

◑ = halbwahre (partielle) False Friends

PARTICULARLY DIFFICULT FALSE FRIENDS

(= Buch II)

TERRIBLE TWINS

elektrisch	◑ electric
historisch	◑ historic
klassisch	◑ classic
komisch	◑ comic
Kritik	≠ critic
kritisch	≠ (*)critic
magisch	◑ magic
ökonomisch	◑ economic
politisch	≠ politic
zynisch	≠ (*)cynic

TRICKY OVER/UNDER-COMPOUNDS

überblicken	◑ overlook
Überfluß	≠ overflow
überhören	≠ overhear
übernehmen	≠ overtake
überreichen	≠ overreach
überschlafen	≠ oversleep
übersehen	≠ oversee
Übersicht	≠ oversight
überwinden	≠ overwind
Unterarm	≠ underarm
untergehen	≠ undergo
unterliegen	≠ underlie
unternehmen	◑ undertake
Unternehmen	◑ undertaking
Unternehmer	≠ undertaker
unterschreiben	≠ underwrite

CONFUSIBLES

barbarisch	◑ barbaric
definitiv	◑ definitive
desinteressiert	≠ disinterested
intensiv	◑ intensive
kontinuierlich	◑ continual
lose	≠ (*)lose
luxuriös	≠ luxuriant
meisterlich	◑ masterly
momentan	≠ momentous
sinnlich	◑ sensual
stationär	≠ stationery
triumphal	◑ triumphal
zeremoniell	◑ ceremonial

PSEUDO-ANGLICISMS

Affekt	◑ (*)affect
Bowle	≠ bowl
Chips	≠ chips (BE)
Dressman	≠ *dressman
last not least	≠ *last not least
Oldtimer	◑ (*)old-timer
Shakehands	≠ *shakehands
Showmaster	≠ *showmaster
Slip	≠ (*)slip
Smoking	≠ *smoking
Talkmaster	≠ *talkmaster
die Teens	≠ (*)the teens
Twen	≠ *twen
Verkehrs**rowdy**	≠ traffic ***rowdy**

FALSE FRIENDS: LITERATURHINWEISE

1. Literatur zum False Friends-Phänomen (mit Fehlerbeispielen)

Alfes, Leonhard. "**Falsche** und **halbehrliche** Freunde. Ein Problem der Wortschatzdidaktik". **Englisch** 20 (1985), 140–145.

Barnickel, Klaus-Dieter. "Trügerische Verwandte: Überlegungen zu einem vergleichenden Fehlerwörterbuch Deutsch–Englisch". **Erlanger Anglistik und Amerikanistik in Vergangenheit und Gegenwart**, hrsg. von U. Bertram und D. Petzold. **Erlanger Forschungen**, Reihe A, Bd. 52 (Erlangen 1990), 153–174.

Breitkreuz, Hartmut. "Arbeitsformen des differenzierten **Notebook**". **Englisch** 7 (1972), 120–122.

Breitkreuz, Hartmut. "**False Friends** und ihre unterrichtliche Behandlung". **Die Neueren Sprachen** 72, 22 N. F. (1973), 70–74.

Breitkreuz, Hartmut. "Pseudo-Anglizismen – Ein Beitrag zur Fehlerforschung". **Grazer Linguistische Studien** 3 (1976), 5–27.

Breitkreuz, Hartmut. "Pseudo-Anglizismen im Englischunterricht. Ein Beitrag zur Fehlerforschung". **Error Analysis. Proceedings of the Fourth International Congress of Applied Linguistics**, ed. by G. Nickel (Stuttgart 1978), 9–35.

Breitkreuz, Hartmut und Wiegand, Nicole. "Zur Problematik gemein- und fachsprachlicher **False Friends**". **Fremdsprachenunterricht im Wandel. Lieselotte Weidner zum 65. Geburtstag**. Schriftenreihe zur Lehrerbildung, Lehrerfortbildung und pädagogischen Weiterbildung, Bd. 13 (Heidelberg 1989), 94–110.

Breitkreuz, Hartmut. "Typen von **False Friends**". **Ein Europa – Viele Sprachen**. Kongreßbeiträge zur 21. Jahrestagung der Gesellschaft für Angewandte Linguistik, hrsg. von Klaus J. Mattheier. **Forum Angewandte Linguistik**, Bd. 22 (Frankfurt 1991), 224–225.

Fanning, Hiltgunt. "Falsche Freunde in zweisprachiger Erziehung (Englisch/Deutsch)". **Studien zur Sprachdifferenzierung**. Roland Arnold zum 60. Geburtstag. **Wissenschaftliche Beiträge der Ernst-Moritz-Arndt-Universität Greifswald** (Greifswald 1990), 47–51.

Höfler, Manfred. "Zum Problem der *Scheinentlehnung*". **Archiv** 142 (1990), 96–107.

Perl, Matthias, und Winter, Roger. "Zum Problem der **False Friends**". **Fremdsprachenunterricht** 16 (1972), 183–185.

Siegrist, Ottmar K. "**False Friends** im Bereich Aussprache und ihre unterrichtliche Behandlung". **Erziehungswissenschaft und Beruf** 27 (1979), 93–98.

Siegrist, Ottmar K. "'England' und 'English'. Zwei **False Friends** hinsichtlich ihrer Aussprache?" **Praxis des Neusprachlichen Unterrichts** 31 (1984), 286–288.

Siegrist, Ottmar K. "Idiomatische **False Friends**". **Ein Europa – Viele Sprachen**. Kongreßbeiträge zur 21. Jahrestagung der Gesellschaft für Angewandte Linguistik, hrsg. von Klaus J. Mattheier. **Forum Angewandte Linguistik**, Bd. 22 (Frankfurt 1991), 242.

Thiemer, Eberhard. "Die 'falschen Freunde' als Erscheinung zwischensprachlicher und innersprachlicher Interferenz". **Fremdsprachen** 23 (1979), 263–271.

Wandruszka, Mario. "Falsche Freunde: Ein linguistisches Problem und seine Lösung". **Lebende Sprachen** 24 (1979), 4–9.

2. Sprachpraktische Literatur und False Friends-Sammlungen

Dretzke, Burkhard und Nester, Margaret I. **Student's Guide to False Friends, New Friends and Old Friends**. Berlin: Cornelsen, 1990.

Greenbaum, Sidney, and Whitcut, Janet. **Longman Guide to English Usage**. Harlow: Longman Group, 1988.

Hawkes, Harry. "**-ic** and **-ical**: The Terrible Twins". **Lenguaje Y Ciencias** 16 (1976), 91–99; leichter zugänglich in **English Teaching Forum** 16 (1978), 27–29.

Helliwell, Margaret. **Can I Become a Beefsteak? Trügerische Wörter zum Nachschlagen und Üben**. Berlin: COUP, 1989.

Howard, Godfrey. **A Guide to Good English** in the 1980s. London: Pelham, 1985. (Sonderausgabe München: Orbis, 1990).

Parkes, Geoff, and Cornell, Alan. **German–English False Friends. Reference and Practice**. Book 1. Southampton: England, 1989.

Pascoe, Graham, and Pascoe, Henriette. **Sprachfallen im Englischen. Wörterbuch der falschen Freunde**. München: Hueber, 1985.

Room, Adrian. **Dictionary of Confusing Words and Meanings**. London: Routledge, repr. 1986.

Snell, Mary. **German Thought in English Idiom.** Exercises in Translation and Style for Final Year Students. München: Hueber, 1967.

Tennant, John. **A Handbook of English Usage**. London: Longmans, 1964.

Treble, H. A., and Vallins, G. H. **An ABC of English Usage.** Oxford: OUP, repr. 1965.

Woulfe, Patrick. "Exploiting **False Friends**". **Modern English Teacher** 9 (1981), 2, 14–16.

FALSE FRIENDS INDEX: ENGLISCH A–Y

Der englische Index erfaßt die in diesem Band behandelten False Friends-Paare (vgl. hierzu die Übersicht "False Friends nach Schwierigkeitskategorien" für Band II auf den Seiten 335–336) und weitgehend die Wortkombinationen (Kollokationen), soweit sie mit den ausgewiesenen False Friends in direkter Verbindung stehen.
Die Seitenzahlen in Fettdruck geben den Haupteintrag des jeweiligen False Friend bzw. True Friend an, die Seitenzahlen in Normaldruck liefern dem Benutzer weitere Belegbeispiele an die Hand. In bestimmten Fällen wie *deposit, economic, fashionable* etc. wurde aus Gründen der Eindeutigkeit eine Bedeutungszuordnung vorgenommen. Einträge in Klammern wie (*showmaster), (*twen) stellen Begriffe dar, die es im Englischen in dieser Form nicht gibt (Pseudo-Anglizismen).

abstract **209**, 209, **210**
abundance **190**, 190, **192**, 192
action **18**, 18, 19, **20**, 20, 21, 46, 47, 222; *action* committee 19, *action* group 19; disciplinary *action* 19, industrial *action* 19, legal *action* 19, 20, 21; libel *action* 19, take *action* (against) (jur.) **225**, 225, **226**, 240, 242
actual 11, **22**, **23**, 23, 46; actually **23**, **24**, 24, 25
adopt (an idea, a plan etc.) **197**, 197, **198**, 198, 199
*affect (noun, only in psychology, philosophy etc.) **286**, 286, **287**
affect (verb) 79, 80, 91, **286**, 286, **287**, 287, 288; be affected 230
affluence **190**, 190, **192**, 192
agreeable **133**, 133, **134**
airs **26**, 26, **27**, 27, 28; airs and graces 26, **27**, 27, 28
allure 8, 14, **26**, 26, **27**, 27, 28, 46, 47
ambulance **29**, 29, **30**, 30, 31, 46, 47
in anger 213, **285**, 285, **287**, 287, 288
any ... may/might (in questions or negative sentences) **58**, 58, **59**, 59
apart **32**, 32, **33**, 34, 67, 328; *apart* from **33**, 33, 34, 65, 140; be *apart* **33**, 33; fall *apart* **33**, 33; joking *apart* 33; live *apart* **33**, 33, 34
artist **35**, 35, **36**, 36, 46, 47, 54, 72, 139, 203, 204; woman artist 36
artiste **35**, 35, **36**, 36; circus *artiste* **35**, 35, **36**, 47; trapeze *artiste* 36; variety *artiste* **35**, 35, **36**
assess (fig.) **187**, 187, **188**, 188, 189, **205**, 205, **207**, 207, 208, 242
attractive **32**, 32, **33**, 34, 47, 330
awkward **66**, 66, **67**

bail **81**, 81, **82**, 115
barbarian 245; *barbarian* culture 245, *barbarian* dictator 245, *barbarian* tribes 245
barbaric **244**, 244, **245**, 245; *barbaric* customs 246, *barbaric* festival 246, the most *barbaric* form of execution 244, *barbaric* invaders 245
barbarous **244**, 244, **245**, 245; *barbarous* acts 244, *barbarous* noise 246, *barbarous* rock music 246, *barbarous* treatment 244, 246
base **37**, 37, **38**, 39, 47; *base* camp 37, 39; research *base* 39
basis 37, **38**, 38, 39, 249; endowment *basis* 38
behaviour: eccentric *behaviour* **26**, 26, **27**, 47
boss (1) (der Chef) 32, **40**, 40, **41**, 42, 56, 77, 134, 146, 147, 205, 328, 330; union boss 138 (2) (the bosses = die Unternehmer) **232**, 233, **234**

bowl (1) (Schale etc.) **289**, 289, **290**, 290; salad *bowl* 327; silver fruit bowl 330
(2) (Pfeifenkopf) **289**, 289, **290**, 290
(3) (Toilettenbecken) **289**, **290**
briefs **305**, 305, **306**; (1) (for men) **305**, 305, **306**, 308, 327
(2) (for women) **305**, 305, **306**
bring o. s. to **212**, **213**, 213, 214, 242
bursary **130**, 130, **131**
burst: in a *burst* of feeling **285**, 285, **287**, 288
business **228**, 228, **230**, 230, 231; businessman 233, **234**, businesswoman **232**, **234**; family *business* 230, 231, (own) *business* **61**, 61, 62
buy s. o. sth. **127**, 127, 128

campaign **18**, 18, **20**, 20, 21, 47, 165, 200, 251, 325
careful **43**, 44
carrier (1) (by air) **232**, 233, **234**
(2) firm of carriers **228**, 229, 230
case (jur.) 24, **111**, 111, **112**, 115, 180, 222; divorce *case* 111
caution **81**, 81, **82**, 83, 114; word of *caution* 82, 83
ceremonial **279**, 279, **280**, 280, 281, 283
ceremonious **279**, 279, **280**, 280, 281
chat show host(ess) **312**, 312, **313**, 313, 314, 327
check **93**, 93, **94**, 95, 115, 120, 153, 311, 330; double check **93**, 93, **94**
charming **32**, 32, **33**, 34
chef **40**, 40, **41**, 41, 42, 46, 47; *chef* de cuisine 40; banqueting *chef* 41, breakfast *chef* **41**, 41; head *chef* 41, master *chef* 41, mini-*chefs* 211
(very) chic **101**, 101, **102**
chief **40**, 94; *chief* constable 40, *chief* editor **40**, 40, **41**; *chief* pilot 37; fire *chief* 40, 41; police *chief* 41, 42; railway *chiefs* 301
chips (BE) **291**, 291, **292**, 292, 327
classic (1) (adj.) 9, 159, **160**, 160, **161**, 161, 162, 184, 185, 331, 333; a *classic* case 9, 160, 185, classic example 160, 185
(2) (noun) **160**, 160, **161**, 161, 162
classical 9, **159**, 159, 160, **161**, 161, 162, 333; *classical* music 9, 76, 159, 161, 162, 185
coarse **104**, 104, **105**; *coarse* woman 104
collapse **218**, 218, **219**
collector's car **296**, 296, **298**
come within **221**, 222, **223**
comic (1) (adj.) 49, **163**, 163, **164**, 164, 165, 333
(2) (noun) 164
comical **163**, 163, **164**, 164, 165, 333
commissioned (to do sth.) **54**, 54, 55, **56**
committed (to do sth.) **54**, 54, **56**, 56
common **104**, 104, **105**, 105, 115; *common* people 115, *common* person 105
company 22, 38, 184, 185, **228**, 228, **230**, 240, 242; film *company* 228, insurance *company* 238, 240, 242; Stock Exchange *companies* 237, tourist company 124, 229
compère (in BE) 172, **302**, 302, **303**, 303, 304
competition **87**, 87, **88**, 88, 89, 115
competitive **87**, **88**; *competitive* markets 88, *competitive* price(s) 87
concept 96, **97**, 97, 98, 114; *concept* of freedom 97, *concept* of society 97
concern **228**, 228, **230**
concise **109**, 109, **110**; *concise* style 109
concurrence 87, **88**, 88, 89, 329, 330; *concurrence* of events 88, 89, 330, *concurrence* of factors 88, 89
confession **84**, 84, 85; *confession* box 85, 86, *confession* calls 85, 86; false *confessions* 85, 86
congenial **133**, 133, **134**, 134
conquer **212**, 212, **213**
consequent (adj.) **90**, 90, **91**, 91
(be) consequent on/upon sth. (verb) **90**, **91**, 91
consequently (adv.) **90**, **91**, 91, 92, 166
considerate **77**, 77, **78**, 78
consistent **90**, 90, **91**; consistently **90**, 90, 91
contest: beauty *contest* 87
continual **255**, 255, **256**, 256, 257, 283, 331, 333
continually 199, 255, 256, 257
continuous 91, **255**, 255, 277, 283, 333

continuously 255, 256, 257
contractor **228**, 229, **230**, 230, 231; building *contractor* **228**, 229, 230; cleaning *contractor* **228**, 229; heating *contractor* **228**; holiday *contractor* 230, 231
control (o. s.) **93**, **94**, 94, 95, 287, 328, 330
copy: rough *copy* **96**, 96, **97**
(potato) crisps (BE), (= chips in AE) **291**, 291, 292, 293, 327; *crisp* packet 293
critic (noun) 65, 150, **166**, **167**, 167, 168, 170, 171; art *critic* 167, 169; literary *critic* 167, theatre *critic* 167, 168, 170
critical (adj.) 150, **169**, 169, **170**, 170, 171
(be) critical of **169**, 169, **170**, 170, 171, 184, 185
criticism 136, **166**, 166, **167**, **185**
critique **166**, 166, **167**
cup (= kalte Bowle) **289**, 289, **290**, 327, 330; champagne *cup* **289**, 289, **290**, 290, 327, 330; claret *cup* **289**, **290**; fruit *cup* 289, 290, 327; wine *cup* **289**, **290**
cure **119**, 119, 120, 147
current **22**, 22, **24**, 47, 166, 180
cynic (noun) **182**, 182, **183**, 183
cynical (adj.) **182**, 182, **183**, 183, 185

decent **51**, 51, **52**, 79, 80, 308
defeated **221**, 221, **223**, 223, 224
definite **247**, 247, **248**, 249, 283, 333; definitely 72
definitive **247**, 247, **248**, 248, 249, 283, 331, 333
delicate **43**, 43, **44**, 44, 45
delicious **43**, 43, **44**, 44, 45, 46, 326, 327
delightful **32**, 32, **33**, 34
denomination **84**, 84, **85**, 85, 86, 115
deposit 74, **81**, (1) (returnable deposit) **81**, 81, **82**, 115
(2) (Vertragskaution) **81**, 81, **82**
(3) (Anzahlung) 81, 82
(4) (Flaschenpfand) 81; bottle *deposit* 81
desert **48**, 48, 50, 67, 80; *desert* adventure **49**, 49, 50; *desert* heat 141, *desert* sand 49, *desert* sun 49; but: *desert* island 49
dessert **48**, 48, **49**, 49, 50, 80; *dessert* spoon 48, **49**; *dessert* wine **48**, 48
dinner-jacket (BE) (= tuxedo/tux in AE) **309**, 309, **310**, 310, 311, 327
disagreeable **144**, 144, 145, 147
disapproving **169**, 169, **170**
disastrous **66**, 66, **67**, 67, 68, 80
discreet **51**, 51, **52**
disinterested **250**, 250, **251**, 251
distinctive **32**, 32, 33
do nothing (etc.) **225**, 225, **226**
do sth. 37, **225**, 225, **226**, 227, 242
draft: final *draft* 115, first *draft* **96**, 96, **97**; rough *draft* **96**, 96, **97**
(*dressman) **294**, 294
drive **18**, 18, **20**, 20, 21
dislike **144**, 144, **145**, 145
economic (1) (= wirtschaftlich) 9, 88, **176**, 176, **177**, 179, 185, 187, 332
(2) ('*Wirtschafts-*') **176**, 176, 184, 185; *economic* adviser 177; *economic* agreement 176, *economic* miracle 177, *economic* policy 88, 177, 178
(3) (= konjunkturell) 9, 77; *economic* situation 178, 333
(4) ('*Konjunktur-*') **176**, **177**, 177; *economic* cycle 177, *economic* decline 177, *economic* outlook 177
economical 9, **176**, 176, **177**, 178, 185, 333; an *economical* heating system 9
electric (1) (elektrisch) 9, 150, **151**, 151, 152, **153**, 153, 154, 184, 185, 331, 333; *electric* blanket 9, 152; *electric* clock 152, *electric* current 152, *electric* light 152, 153, 154; *electric* motor 152, *electric* razor 152
(2) ('*Elektro-*') *electric* shock 152
(3) (elektrisierend) *electric* atmosphere 152, *electric* effect 152
electrical (1) (elektrisch) 150, **151**, 151, 152, **153**, 153, 154, 185, 333; *electrical* energy 151, *electrical* discharge 153, 154; *electrical* unit 151
(2) ('*Elektro-*') 9, **151**, 151, **153**; *electrical* engineers 151, 153, 154; *electrical* fault 9, 153, 154; *electrical* fitters 151, *electrical* industry 151, *electrical* store 151, 185
(extremely) elegant **101**, 101

embarrassing **66**, 66, **67**, 67, 68
emergency ward **29**, 29, **30**
(over-) emotional **106**, 106, **107**, 108
the employers **232**, **234**
engaged **54**, **55**, 55, **56**, 56, 57
enterprise **228**, **230**
eventual (adj.) 9, 58, **59**, 60, 79, 80
eventually (adv.) **59**, 59, 60, 80, 193, 221
eye: turn a blind *eye* to **205**, 205, **207**, 207, 208; *see magic* eye 173
excellent (1) (= delikat) **43**, **44**, 44, 45
(2) (= famos) **64**, 64, 65, 80
existence **61**, **62**, 62, 63, 184, 185, 328, 330
exquisite **43**, 43, **44**

faction **69**, 69, **70**
fail: (1) *fail* to hear (= unabsichtlich überhören) **194**, 194, 195
(2) *fail* to see (= unabsichtlich übersehen) **205**, 205, **207**
fall within **221**, 222, **223**
famous 27, **64**, 64, **65**, 65, 80, 291, 308, 328, 330; famous for **64**, 64, **65**, 65
fashion: (male) fashion model **294**, 294, 295
fashionable (1) (= aktuell) **22**, 22, **24**
(2) (= mondän) **101**, 101, **102**, 103; *fashionable* club 103, *fashionably* dressed 103
fatal **66**, 66, **67**, 67, 68, 79, 80; *fatal* diseases 80, *fatal* shot 66, *fatal* smash 67
(be) *fed* up with **206**, 206, 207
fellowship **130**, 130, **131**
finally **323**, **324**, 324, 325
fine **64**, 64, **65**, 65
firm (noun) 116, **228**, 228, **230**, 328, 330; investment *firm* 240, 242
flirt with 65
forearm **215**, 215, **216**, 216, 217
foresee **205**, 205, 207
fraction 9, **69**, 69, **70**,70, 71, 79, 80
funeral director (AE funeral man, AE funeral-home man) **233**, **234**
funny **163**, 163, **164**

genial **72**, 72, **73**, 73
genius: full of *genius* **72**, 72, **73**
gentle **43**, 43, **44**, 44, 45
get: (not) *get* enough of **206**, 206, **207**; *get* over **212**, 212, **213**; *get* the better of **212**, 212, **213**, 213, 214
go: *go* down (= sinken, untergehen) **218**, 218, **219**, 220, 242; *go* down (to) (Sport: verlieren) **221**, 221, **223**; *go* under (= untergehen fig.) **218**, 218, **219**
graceful **75**, 75, **76**, 76, 80
gracious **75**, 75, **76**, 76
(state) grant **130**, 130, **131**, 132; maintenance *grants* 132
grasp sth. **187**, 187, **188**, 190
great **64**, 64, 65
group **69**, 69, **70**, 70; parliamentary *group* **69**, 69, **70**, 70; political *group* **69**, 69, **70**

hand over (to) **200**, 200, **201**, 201
handshake **300**, 300, **301**, 327; golden handshake 300, 301
haulage contractor **232**, **234**
haulier (by road), AE hauler (= Transportunternehmer) **232**, 233, **234**
hauliers (by road), firm of hauliers (= Transportunternehmen) **228**, 229, **230**
hear: *hear* enough of **194**, 194, **195**
heat: in the *heat* of the moment **285**, 285, **287**
historic 92, **155**, **156**, 156, **157**, 157, 158, 184, 185
historical **155**, 155, **156**, 156, **157**, 157, 158, 185, 209
hooligan 285; holiday *hooligan* **320**, 320, **321**, 321, 322; soccer *hooligan* 212, 244, **320**, 320, **321**
host/hostess **312**, 312, **313**, 313, 314
human (1) (= human) **77**, 77, 79, 80, 223
(2) ('*Menschen-*') 77; judge of *human* character 77, *human* rights 78, 226
humane **77**, 77, **78**, 78, 79, 80

idea(s) (1) (= Konzept) **96**, 96, **97**, 98
(2) (= Übersicht, allgemein) **209**, **210**, 210
ignore (1) (= überhören) **194**, 194, **195**, 242
(2) (= absichtlich übersehen) **205**, 205, **207**, 207, 208
impassioned **106**, 106, **107**
on impulse **285**, 285, **287**, 288
industrialist **232**, 232, 234

ingenious **72**, 72, **73**, 73, 80
inspect **93**, 93, 94
inspired **72**, 72, **73**
intense **252**, 252, **253**, 283; intensely 253, 254
intensive (1) (= intensiv) 252, **253**, 253, 254
(2) ('*Intensiv-*') 253, 283; *intensive* care (unit) 125, 253; *intensive* course 253, *intensive* treatment 253
involved (in sth. or with s. o.) **54**, 54, **56**

knickers **305**, 305, **306**, 307

(*last not least) **323**, 323, **324**
last but not least **323**, 323, **324**, 325; last but by no means least **323**, 323, **324**, 325; last and certainly not least **323**, 323, **324**
latest (1) (= aktuell) **22**, 22, **24**, 24, 25, 47
(2) (= neu, neueste) 96, 101, 125, 211; the *latest* technology 125
lawsuit **111**, 111, **112**, 112, 113
lethal 24, 67, 126; *lethal* weapon 67, *lethal* overdose 68
(be) liable to **221**, 222, **223**
(new) life **61**, 61, **62**
like (a person) **133**, 133, **134**
likeable **133**, 133, **134**, 135, 147, 330
list **209**, 209, **210**
livelihood **61**, 61, **62**, 62, 63, 80, 330
lively **136**, 136, **137**, 137
living **61**, 61, **62**
logical **90**, 90, **91**, **92**; logically **90**, 90, **91**
loose [lu:s] (1) (locker, frei etc.) **258**, 258, 259, 260, 333
(2) (in combinations) break *loose* 258, fall *loose* 258, run *loose* 259
lose [lu:z] (verb) (1) (verlieren) 61, 75, 112, 114, 115, 212, 258, **259**, 259, 260, 305, 331, 332, 333
(2) (in combinations) *lose* height 67, be *lost* for words 169, *see* lose *track* of 209
(3) (*lose* or *lose to* = unterliegen) **221**, 221, **223**, 223
lucrative **116**, 116, **117**, 117, 118
luxuriant **261**, 261, **262**, 262, 263, 283, 331, 333
luxurious **261**, 261, **262**, 262, 263, 283, 333
luxury **190**, 190, **192**, 192

mad: *mad* driver **320**, 320, 321
magic (1) (adj.) **172**, 172, 173, **174**, 174, 175, 184, 333; *magic* art 172, 174, 175; *magic* eye 173, *magic* numbers 173, *magic* powers 172, 185; *magic* square 173
(2) ('*Zauber-*') **172**, 174; *magic* formula 173, 185; *magic* ring 173, 185; *magic* wand **172**, 173, **174**
(3) (noun) 172, 173
magical **172**, 172, 173, **174**, 174, 175, 185, 333; *magical* effect 172, 174, 175
make: *make* an attempt etc. **225**, 225, **226**; *make* every effort 38
(male) mannequin **294**, 294
marvellous (1) (= famos) **64**, 64, **65**
(2) (= großartig) 109
master of ceremonies (AE emcee) **302**, 302, 303; M. C. **302**, 302, 303
masterful **264**, 264, **265**, 265, 266, 283
masterly **264**, 264, **265**, 265, 266, 283
may/might (in affirmative sentences) **58**, 58, **59**
maybe **58**, 58, **59**
menu **99**, 99, **100**, 100, 114, 115
miss (1) miss hearing sth. (etwas unabsichtlich überhören) **194**, 194, **195**, 196
(2) miss (unabsichtlich übersehen) **205**, 205, **207**
(male) model **294**, 294, 295, 327
momentary **267**, 267, **268**, 269, 269
momentous **267**, 267, **268**, 268, 269, 283
monitor (verb) **93**, 93, **94**
most: *most* of all **323**, **324**, 324
mundane **101**, 101, **102**, 103; *mundane* matters 101, 103

name: put one's *name* (to) **236**, 236, **238**
nice (= sympathisch) **133**, 133, **134**, 135
not: *not* hear **194**, 194, **195**, 196; *not* least **323**, **324**, 324, 325; *not* like **144**, 144, **145**
notes **96**, 96, **97**

odd **163**, 163, **164**
old: *old* car **296**, **298**, 298, 299; *old* model **296**, 296, **298**, 298, 299, 327

* old-timer 296, **297**, 297, **298**, 327
operation **18**, **20**; rescue *operation* **18**, 18, **20**
opulence **190**, 190, **192**
ordinary **104**, 104, **105**, 105; *ordinary* family 104, *ordinary* folk 105, *ordinary* paper 104, *ordinary* party 105, *ordinary* place 105, *ordinary* sit-down affair 105
outline **209**, 209, **210**
out-patients' clinic **29**, 30; out-patients' department **29**, 29, **30**, 31, 47, 128
overcome **212**, 212, **213**, 213, 214
overflow (noun) **190**, 190, 191, **192**, 193; *overflow* of applicants 191, *overflow* of library books 191, *overflow* meeting **192**, *overflow* pipes 191, **192**; *overflow* room 191
overhear 186, **195**, 195, 196, 242
overlook (1) (unabsichtlich übersehen) **205**, 205, **207**, 242, 287
(2) (Fehler etc. übersehen) **187**, 187, **188**, 188, 189
overreach (o. s.) **200**, 200, **201**, 201
oversee (= beaufsichtigen, überwachen) 205, **206**, 206, **207**
oversight 209, **210**, 210, 211
oversleep 186, **202**, 202, **203**, 203, 204
overtake 186, **197**, 197, **198**, 199, 240, 242
overwind 212, **213**, 213, 214, 240, 242

panties **305**, 305, **306**, 307
(under-) pants **305**, 305, **306**, 327
party: parliamentary *party* **69**, 69, **70**, 70, 80; socialist *party* 71
passionate **106**, 106, **107**, 108
passion: in a *passion* of anger **285**
pathetic **106**, 106, **107**, 107, 108
paying **116**, 116, **117**, 117, 118; a *paying* firm 116, a *paying* venture 117
people: (young) *people* in their twenties **318**, 318, **319**, 327
performer (on radio, TV) **35**, 35, **36**
perhaps **58**, 58, **59**, 60, 80
perish (also fig.) **218**, 218, **219**, 220
personnel manager 40, 77, 202
perspire **141**, 141, **142**
pithy **109**, 109, **110**, 110, 115, 330; *pithy* remarks 110
plan **96**, 96, **97**, 98
pleasant **133**, 133, **134**
politic **179**, 179, **180**, 180, 181
political 22, 77, 79, 80, **179**, 179, **180**, 180, 185, 187; *political* group 69, 70
possible **58**, 58, **59**; possibly **58**, 58, **59**, 60
pregnant (1) (schwanger) 9, 98, **109**, 109, 110, 114, 115, 309, 328, 330; become *pregnant* 110, be eight months pregnant 110
(2) (bedeutungsvoll etc.) *pregnant* phrase 109, a *pregnant* silence 109
prescription **119**, 119, **120**, 121, 128, 147; *prescription* charges 121
present (adj.) **22**, 22, **24**, 24, 25, 134
present (verb): (1) present s. o. with **200**, 200, **201**
(2) present sth. (to) **200**, 200, **201**
presenter 24, 25, 136, 165, 184, 185, **302**, 302, **303**, 303, 304, 327, 331, 333; radio *presenter* 27, 28
process **111**, 111, **112**, 112, 113, 114, 115
professional: *professional* jealousy **87**, 87, 88, 89, 115
profitable **116**, 116, **117**, 117, 118, 147
profusion **190**, 190, **192**
programme: aid *programme* **18**, **20**
pudding **48**, 48, 49, 178
punch (AE cobbler) (= heiße Bowle) **289**, 289, **290**
purge **18**, 18, **20**

rate: piece-*rate* **16**, 16, 47
receipt 9, 11, 119, **120**, 120, 146, 238
recent **22**, 22, **24**, 24
recipe 100, **119**, 119, **120**, 121; *recipe* leaflets 100
reliable **124**, 124, **125**
remarkable **32**, 32, **33**
remedy **119**, 119, **120**, 147
renowned **124**, 124, **125**
rentable **116**, 116, **117**, 117, 118
reputable **124**, 124, **125**, 126, 147
respectable **124**, 124, **125**
restrained **51**, 51, **52**
review **166**, 166, **167**, 167, 168
reviewer 167
rival (in combinations) 88, 330; *rival* firms 89, *rival* product 88, 330
recover from **212**, 212, **213**, 213, 214

(be) reluctant to **212**, 212, **213**, 213
roadbog **320**, 320, **321**, 321, 322
rude **104**, 104, **105**, 105, 114, 115; *rude* person 105, *rude* words 104

scholarship **130**, 130, **131**, 132, 147; maintenance *scholarships* 132
seahog **320**, 320, **321**, 322
section (of a building etc.) **138**, 138, **139**, 139, 140, 147
sensible **122**, 122, **123**, 146, 147
sensitive 93, **122**, 122, **123**, 123, 147
sensual 243, **270**, 270, **271**, 271, 272, 283, 328, 330
sensuous 243, **270**, 270, **271**, 271, 272, 330
serious 62, **124**, 124, **125**, 125, 126, 146, 147, 295, 321
set dinner **99**, 99, **100**, 100; *set* lunch **99**, 99, **100**, 100; *set* meal **99**, 99, **100**, 100, 115
select **43**, 43, **44**
set (sun etc.) **218**, 218, 219
(*shakehands) **300**, 301, 326
shake hands (with) **300**, 300, **301**, 301
shake the hand(s) of **300**, 300, **301**
show host **302**, 302, **303**
(*showmaster) 284, **302**, **303**, 303
sign **236**, 236, **238**, 238, 306
sink (verb) **218**, 218, **219**, 220, 242, 330
sleep on sth. **202**, 202, **203**, 203, 204
slip **305**, **306**, 306, 307, 327; sales *slip* 306
smart **32**, 32, **33**, 34
(*smoking) (= der Smoking) 284, **309**, 309, 310
smoking (= das Rauchen) 79, 80, **309**, 309, **310**, 310, 327; no-*smoking* sign **310**, 310; no-*smoking* areas 310
soft **51**, 51, **52**
solemn **106**, 106, **107**
sound (= solide, reell) **124**, 124, **125**
spend: (1) spend (on) (= ausgeben für) **127**, 127, **128**, 128, 129, 165, 291, 313
(2) (Urlaub etc. verbringen) 85, 127, **128**
splendid **64**, 64, **65**
stand s. o. sth. **127**, 127, **128**, 147
stationary **273**, 273, **274**, 275, 333
stationery **273**, 273, **274**, 274, 275, 283, 333
stipend (1) (Gehalt für Geistliche etc.) 130, **131**, 131, 132, 146, 147
(2) (AE Sportlergehalt) **131**, 131, 146
strange **163**, 163, **164**
striking **32**, 32, **33**
stylish (1) (= apart) **32**, 32, **33**, 34, 330
(2) (= mondän) **101**, 101, **102**, 102, 103
subdued **51**, 51, **52**, 52, 53
(be) subject to **221**, 221, **223**, 223, 224
subscribe to (fig.) **236**, 236, **238**, 239
subtle **51**, 51, **52**, 80
succinct **109**, 109, **110**; succinctly 109
succumb to (fig.) **221**, 221, 223, 242
suit (jur.) **111**, 111, **112**, 112, 113
summary **209**, 209, **210**, 211
survey (= Landschaft etc. überblicken) **187**, 187, **188**
survey (= Überblick) **209**, 209, **210**, 211
sweat **141**, 141, **142**, 142, 143
sweet: sweet course/sweet **48**, 48, **49**
sympathetic: (1) (adj.) **133**, **134**, 134, 146, 329
(2) (be) sympathetic to **133**, **134**, 134, 135, 147, 330
synopsis **209**, 209, **210**

table **209**, **210**, 210
table d'hôte **99**, 99, **100**
talk show host(ess) **312**, 312, **313**, 313, 314
take: *take* a call **197**, 197, **198**; *take* a trip (etc.) **225**, 225, **226**; *take* sth. on **197**, 197, **198**; *take* sth. over **197**, 197, **198**, 199; *take* to a person **133**, 133, **134**
taste: in perfect *taste* **32**, 32, **33**
teenage (in combinations): *teenage* model 315, *teenage* star 315; *see model*
teenagers **315**, 315, **316**, 316, 317
teens **315**, 327; in her *teens* 316, in his *teens* 316, late *teens* 316, in their *teens* 317
(* *the* teens) **315**, 315, **316**
temperamental **136**, 136, **137**, 137
tired: be *tired* of sth. **206**, 206, **207**
topical **22**, 22, **24**, 24, **25**
track: lose **track** of **209**, **210**, 210, 211
tract (1) (Traktat) **138**, 138, **139**, 139, 140
(2) (Landstrich etc.) **138**, **139**, 139, 140

(traffic* rowdy) **320**, 320, **321**
transpire **141**, 141, **142**, 142, 143, 147
treat: *treat* as an in-patient **273**, 273, **274**, 275; *treat* s. o. to sth. **127**, 127, **128**, 128, 129
trial (jur.) **111**, 111, **112**; kidnapping *trial* 111, murder *trial* 111
triumphal (1) (= überwältigend) **276**, 276, **277**, 277
(2) ('*Triumph-*', '*Sieges-*') **276**, **277**; *triumphal* arch **277**, 277; *triumphal* column **277**
triumphant **276**, 276, **277**, 277, 278, 283
trustworthy **124**, 124, **125**
(*twen) 284, **318**, **319**
twenties: s. o. in his (her) *twenties* **318**, 318, **319**; *see* people

ultimately **323**, **324**, 324, 325
underarm (1) 186, **215**, 215, **216**, 217; *underarm* bowling 217
(2) ('*Achsel-*') underarm odour 216
undergo 218, **219**, 219, 220, 240, 242, 328, 330
underlie 221, **222**, 222, **223**, 223, 224
undertake (1) (= Aufgabe etc. übernehmen) **197**, 197, **198**, 198, 199, 240, 242
(2) (= etwas wahrnehmen, auf sich nehmen) **225**, 225, **226**, 226, 240, 242
undertaker (AE mortician) 186, 232, **233**, 233, **234**, 234, 235, 330; undertakers, firm of undertakers **233**, **234**, 234
undertaking (= Unternehmung, Unternehmen allg.) 228, **229**, 229, **230**, 230, 231
underwrite 186, **236**, 236, 237, **238**, 238, 239
unfortunate **66**, 66, **67**, 67, 68, 122
uninterested **250**, 250, **251**, 251
unobtrusive **51**, 51, **52**, 52, 53
unpleasant **144**, 144, **145**, 145, 147
unremitting(ly) **90**, 90, **91**, 92, 115
unsympathetic (1) (adj.) **144**, 144, **145**; *unsympathetic* attitude 145, *unsympathetic* doctors 145, *unsympathetic* treatment 144
(2) (verb) be unsympathetic to **144**, 144, **145**
unusual **32**, 32, **33**
up-to-date **22**, 22, **24**, 24, 25

veteran: veteran car/veteran (BE); antique car/antique (AE) **296**, 296, 297, **298**, 327; *see* Note p. 296
view: have a clear *view* of **187**, 187, 188; (overall) *view* (of) **209**, **210**, 210, 211
vintage: vintage aircraft **296**, **297**, 297, **298**; vintage car/vintage (BE); classic car/classic (AE) **296**, **297**, 297, **298**, 298, 299, 327; *see* Note p. 296
vivacious **136**, 136, **137**, 137
vulgar **104**, 104, **105**, 115; *vulgar* language 104, *vulgar* people 115

way (of doing sth.) (= Rezept fig.) **119**, 119, 120
weird **163**, 163, **164**
wing (of a building etc.) (= Trakt) **138**, 138, **139**, 139, 140, 147
wonderful **64**, 64, **65**, 65, 203

yield (to sth.) **221**, 221, **223**, 223, 224
young: a *young* man/woman in his/her twenties **318**, 318, **319**, 319; *young* people **315**, 315, **316**, 316, 317
youngsters **315**, 315, **316**, 316, 317

FALSE FRIENDS INDEX: DEUTSCH A–Z

Der deutsche Index erfaßt im wesentlichen die behandelten False Friends-Paare und berücksichtigt weitgehend die eingebrachten Wortkombinationen (Kollokationen).
Fettgedruckte Seitenzahlen beziehen sich auf die Haupteinträge der False Friends, normalgedruckte Seitenzahlen geben weitere Belegstellen an. In bestimmten Fällen wie *Rezept, stationär, überhören, Unternehmen, Unternehmer* erfolgte eine Bedeutungsdifferenzierung, um das Auffinden des englischen Begriffs gezielt zu ermöglichen.

(Versicherungen etc.) abschließen **236**, 237, **238**
sich abspielen **141**, **142**, 142
Achsel: (unter der) *Achsel, Achsel*(höhlen)-bereich **215**, 215, **216**
'*Achsel-*': *Achsel*geruch 215
Affekt (in Psychologie, Philosophie etc.): (1) **285**, 285, 286, **287**
(2) ('*Affekt-*') *Affekt*ausbruch 286, *Affekt*delikt 286, *Affekt*handlung 285
Akkord **16**, 16, 46
Aktion **18**, 18, 19, **20**, 20, 46, 200; *Aktions*komitee 19, Hilfs*aktion* 18, Rettungs*aktion* 18, Säuberungs*aktion* **18**, **20**
aktuell 11, **22**, 22, **24**, 46; aktuell sein **22**, 22; nicht mehr aktuell sein **22**, 22
alltäglich **101**, 101, **102**
Allüren 9, 14, **26**, 26, **27**, 46
Alter: ein *Alter* **297**, **298**; erfahrener *Alter* **297**, **298**; 'einer von den ganz *Alten*' **297**, **298**
Ambulanz **29**, 29, **30**, 46
sich anbahnen **141**, **142**, 142
andauernd **255**, **256**, 256
Andrang **190**, **192**
angenehm **72**, **73**, 73
(Gesundheit etc.) angreifen **286**, 286, **287**
anpacken **225**, **226**, 226
Anspruch: in *Anspruch* genommen **55**, 55, **56**
anständig **51**, 51, **52**
Ansturm **190**, 191, **192**
anteilnehmend **133**, **134**; anteilnehmend sein gegenüber **133**, **134**
Antrieb: aus eigenem *Antrieb* 16
Anziehungskraft **26**, 26, **27**, 27
apart **32**, 32, 33, 46, 328
Artist **35**, 35, **36**, 46
aufziehen: (eine Uhr) zu weit *aufziehen* **213**, 213
'*auseinander-*': *auseinander*fallen **33**, *auseinander*liegen **33**, 33
außer **33**, 33
Aussicht: *Aussicht* haben auf **187**, **188**, 188
auswirken: sich auswirken auf **286**, 286, **287**
banal **101**, **102**, 102
'*Barbaren-*' **244**, **245**, 245; *Barbaren*reich 245
barbarisch **244**, 244, **245**
Basis **37**, 37, **38**; Abschuß*basis* **37**, 37, **38**; Erb*basis* 38
beaufsichtigen **206**, 206, 207
Becken: Toiletten*becken* **289**, **290**, 290
bedeutungsvoll **109**, 109, **110**
sich beherrschen **93**, **94**, 94
bedeutsam **267**, 267, **268**, 282
(Allgemein-, Gesamt-) Begriff **97**, 97
Beichte **84**, 84, **85**
beiseite **33**, 33
bekannt: bekannt werden **141**, **142**, 142
Bekenntnis **84**, 84, **85**
Beleg **305**, **306**, 306; Kassen*beleg* 306
bemitleidenswert **106**, 106, **107**
berühmt **64**, 64, **65**, 79, 291
berühren **286**, 286, **287**
beschäftigt **55**, **56**
(Telefon) besetzt **55**, 55, **56**

Besoldung (für Geistliche) **131**, 131
*Bestattungs*institut **233**, **234**, 234; *Bestattungsunternehmer* **233**, **234**, 234
Bestehen **61**, **62**, 62
betreffen **286**, **287**
Blick: einen *Blick* bieten auf 187, **188**, 188
Bowle **289**, 289, **290**, 326, 328; Frucht*bowle* 289, 327; heiße *Bowle* 289; Sekt*bowle* 289, 327
Briefpapier **273**, **274**
Bruch **69**, **70**, 70; *Bruch*teil **69**, 69, **70**, 70; Knochen*bruch* 70, Stein*bruch* 70, Vertrags*bruch* 70
bürgen (für) **236**, 237, **238**

Chef 32, **40**, 40, **41**, 41, 46, 77, 94, 134, 205
(1) *Chef*arzt 40; *Chef*pilot 37; Personal*chef* 40, 77, 202
(2) *Chef*koch 41; Küchen*chef* **40**, **41**, 41
Chips **291**, 291, **292**, 326

Dasein **61**, **62**, 62
definitiv **247**, 247, **248**, 282, 331
delikat **43**, 43, 46
desinteressiert **250**, 250, **251**; desinteressiert sein (an) **144**, **145**, 145
Dessert **48**, 48, **49**, 79; *Dessert*löffel 48
dezent **51**, 51, **52**, 79, 105
(Bart, Haar etc.) *dicht* (gewachsen) **261**, **262**, 262, 263
Dressman **294**, 294, 326
(Tests etc.) durchlaufen **219**, 219
durchmachen **219**, 219
'*Durchschnitts-*': **104**, **105**; *Durchschnitts*mensch 104
durchstehen **219**, 219

(Vertrag etc.) eingehen **225**, **226**, 226
eigentlich (1) (Adj.) **23**, 23, 24
(2) (Adv.) **23**, 23, **24**
Eingreifen **18**, 19
Einverständnis **88**, 88
elektrisch (1) (elektrisch betrieben) 150, **151**, 152, **153**, 184, 331
(2) (allgemein) **151**, 151, 152, **153**, 331
elektrisierend (fig.) **151**, 152, **153**
'*Elektro-*': **151**, 151, 184;
(1) (*electric*) *Elektro*generator 153, *Elektro*schock 152
(2) (*electrical*) *Elektro*abteilung 151, *Elektro*-Industrie 151, *Elektro*-Installateure 151, *Elektro*-Technik 151
empfindlich 93, 122, 123
Ende: am Ende (Adv.) **59**, 59
endgültig **247**, **248**, 248
engagiert **54**, 54, 55, **56**, 56; sich engagieren für 54, **56**
entscheidend **247**
ergeben **75**, **76**
sich ergebend (aus) **59**, 59
ergreifend **106**, **107**
ernst **124**, 124, **125**, 125
ernsthaft **124**, **125**, 125
erregend **151**, 152, **153**
erschütternd **106**, **107**, 107
'einer von den *Etablierten*' **297**, 297, **298**, 326
eventuell 9, **58**, 58, **59**, 59
Existenz **61**, 61, **62**, 79, 328
famos **64**, 64, **65**, 79, 156
Faszination **26**, 26, 27
fatal **66**, 66, **67**, 79, 80, 122
feingliedrig **43**, 43, **44**
Ferienrowdy **320**, 320, **321**
Flegeljahre **315**, **316**, 316
fleischlich **270**, **271**, 271
Flüchtigkeitsfehler **305** **306**, 306
(kleine) Flugschrift **138**, **139**
Folge: als *Folge* von **59**, 59
fortwährend **255**, **256**, 256
Fraktion 9, **69**, 69, **70**, 79; parlamentarische *Fraktion* 69
freundlich (1) (genial) **72**, 72, **73**
(2) (gracious) **75**, 75, **76**
Fuß **37**, **38**
Fußballrowdys 212, 244, 285, **320**, 320, **321**

finanziell *garantieren* **236**
Gebiet **138**, **139**, 139
gebieterisch **264**, **265**, 265
gefühllos **144**, 144, **145**
Gehalt (für Geistliche) **131**, 131
vor sich gehen **141**, **142**
gekonnt **264**, **265**
genial **72**, 72, **73**, 79
'*Gesamt-*' **247**, **248**; *Gesamt*ausgabe 248
geschichtlich bedeutsam **155**, 156, **157**
geschichtsträchtig **155**, 156, **157**
Geständnis **84**, 84, **85**
getrennt: *getrennt* leben **33**, 33; *getrennt* sein **33**, 33

gewichtig (fig.) **109**, 109, **110**
gewöhnlich **104**, 104, **105**
gleichgültig **144**, **145**
grausam **244**, 244, **245**
graziös **75**, 75, **76**, 79
grazil **43**, 43, **44**
Griff: in den *Griff* bekommen **93**, **94**, 94
großartig **160**, 160, **161**
gründlich **253**, 253
'*Grund-*': *Grund*lage **37**, **38**, 38; *Grund*linie **37**, **38**; *Grund*prinzip **37**, **38**, 38
gütig **75**, 75, **76**

Handeln **18**, 19, 222
'ein (ganz) alter *Hase*' **297**, **298**
Hauptbestandteil **37**, **38**
heikel **43**, 43, **44**
sich herausstellen **141**, 141, **142**, 146
hereinbrechen (über) **197**, **198**, 198
herrisch **264**, 264, **265**
herrschsüchtig **264**, **265**, 265
herzlich **72**, 72, **73**
herzlos **144**, **145**
historisch **155**, 155, 156, **157**, 184
historisch bedeutend **155**, 156, **157**
huldvoll **75**, 76, 76
human **77**, 77, 79

intensiv **252**, 252, 282
'*Intensiv-*' **253**, 253; *Intensiv*behandlung 253, *Intensiv*kurs 253, *Intensiv*station 253

die Jugendjahre **315**, **316**

Kanone: 'unter aller *Kanone*' (koll.) **106**, **107**, 107
Kaution **81**, 81, 114; *Kaution* als gerichtliche Sicherheitsleistung **81**, Miet*kaution* 81, Vertrags*kaution* 81
Kissenbezug **305**, **306**, 306
Klage (jur.) **18**, 19
Klassiker (1) (Sport) **160**, 160, **161**
(2) (Lit.) **160**, 160, **161**
klassisch **159**, 159, **160**, 160, **161**, 184, 321
Knabe: 'alter Knabe' **297**, 297, **298**
Koch: Bankett*koch* 41, Frühstücks*koch* 41, Meister*koch* 41, Ober*koch* **40**, **41**
körperlich **270**, **271**, 271
komisch (1) (unbeabsichtigte Komik) **163**, 163, **164**, 164, 331
(2) (beabsichtigte Komik) **163**, 163, **164**, 164, 331
Konfession **84**, 84, **85**, 114
'*Konjunktur-*' **176**, **177**, 177; *Konjunktur*rückgang 177
konjunkturell **176**, **177**, 177; *konjunkturelle* Lage 177
Konkurrenz **87**, 87, **88**, 114, 329; *Konkurrenz*firma 87, *Konkurrenz*neid 87, *Konkurrenz*preise 87, Schönheits*konkurrenz* 87
kontrollieren **93**, 93, **94**, 114, 328
konsequent **90**, 90, **91**, 91, 114
kontinuierlich **255**, 255, **256**, 282, 331
konzentriert **253**, 253
Konzept (1) **96**, 96, **97**, 114
(2) (fig.) **96**, 96, **97**
Konzeption **97**, 97
Kopf: Pfeifen*kopf* **289**, **290**, 290
Krankenwagen **29**, 29, **30**
Kritik 136, **166**, 166, **167**, 184
Kritiker(in) 150 (1) **166**, **167**, 167, **169**, 169, **170**; Kunst*kritiker* 167, Literatur*kritiker* 167; (Rezensent) 167
kritisch 150, **169**, 169, 170; *kritisch* anmerken 206; *kritisch* (sein) gegenüber 169, **170**, 184
Künstler (1) (Maler) **35**, 35, **36**, 54, 72
(2) (z. B. als Pianist) **35**, **36**, 36
kultiviert **75**, **76**, 76

lächerlich **106**, **107**, 107
Landstrich 138, **139**, 139
langweilig **101**, 101, **102**

Last not least **323**, 323
launenhaft **136**, **137**
launisch **136**, 136, **137**
Leben **61**, **62**, 62
Leichenbestatter **233**, 233, **234**
letztendlich **59**, 59
liebenswürdig **75**, 75, **76**
liegen unter (geol. etc.) **222**, 222, **223**
lose, **258**, 258, 259, 331
lüstern **270**, 270, **271**
luxuriös **261**, 261, **262**, 282, 331

Magie **172**, 173, **174**
magisch **172**, 172, 173, **174**, 184, 331; *magisches* Auge 173; *magische* Kräfte 173, *magische* Kunst 173, *magisches* Quadrat 173, *magische* Zahlen 173
(Kunst-)Maler **35**, 35, **36**
Mann: alter Mann **297**, **298**

maßgebend **247**, **248**, 248
Maßnahmen: Arbeitskampf*maßnahmen* **18**, 18
meisterhaft 264, **265**, 265
meisterlich **264**, 264, 265, 283
'*Menschen-*' 77, 78; *Menschen*kenner 77, *Menschen*rechte 226
menschlich **77**, 77, 78
Menü **99**, 99, 114
mietbar **116**, 116, **117**
(Klima etc.) mild **72**, **73**
alter, bewährter *Mitarbeiter*; ein altgedienter *Mitarbeiter* **297**, 297, **298**, 326
mitfühlend **133**, **134**, 134; mitfühlend sein gegenüber **133**, **134**, 134
mitleiderregend **106**, **107**, 107
'*Modell-*' **160**, 160, **161**; *Modell*fall 160, **161**
momentan **267**, 267, **268**
mondän **101**, 101, **102**

Nachweis: den *Nachweis* liefern (für) **236**, **237**
Napf **289**, 289, **290**
neben **33**, 33
'*Neben-*' **190**, 191, **192**; *Neben*saal 191
nehmen: auf sich *nehmen* **225**, **226**
neutral **250**, 250, 251
nicht: *nicht* zuletzt **323**, 323, **324**; *nicht* zuverlässig (vom Auto etc.) **136**, **137**
normal **104**, 104, **105**, 270
'*Notfall-*': *Notfall*-Flugzeug **29**, **30**, 30

ökonomisch **176**, 176, **177**, 184, 332
Oldtimer **296**, 296, **298**, 326
ordinär **104**, 104, **105**, 114, 270

pachtbar **116**, 116, **117**
'*Parallel-*' **190**, **192**
passieren **141**, **142**
pathetisch **106**, 106, **107**
*Personal*chef 40, 77, 202; *see* Chef
politisch 22, 77, **179**, 179, **180**, 184
Pommes (frites) **291**, 291, **292**, 326
prägnant 9, **109**, 109, 114, 328
Prozeß (jur.) **111**, 111, **112**, 114, 180; Mord*prozeß* 111, Scheidungs*prozeß* 111

(das) Rauchen **309**, 309, **310**, 310, 326
regeln **93**, **94**
Reiz **26**, 26, **27**, 27
rentabel **116**, 116, **117**, 146
'*Rettungs-*': *Rettungs*fahrzeug **29**, 29, **30**, 30
richtig (koll.) **51**, 51, **52**
Rezept 9, 11, **119**, 119, **120**, 146; (1) Koch-, Back*rezept* **119**, 119, **120**
(2) Arzt*rezept* **119**, 119, **120**
(3) *Rezept* (fig.) **119**, 119, **120**
roh **244**, 244, **245**

Sanitätsauto **29**, 29, **30**
schaden **286**, 286, **287**
Schale **289**, 289, **290**, 326
Schatten: alles in den *Schatten* stellend **276**, **277**, 277
schließlich **59**, 59; **323**, **324**, 324
*Schreib*material **273**, **274**, 274; *Schreib*papier **273**, 273, **274**, 282; *Schreib*waren **273**, **274**, 274
Schrift **133**, 138, **139**
Schlüssel **289**, 289, **290**, 290
schwächlich **43**, **44**, 44
'schön' (ironisch) **51**, **52**, 52
schwanger **109**, 109, **110**
schwierig **43**, **44**
Seerowdy **320**, 320, **321**
sensibel **122**, 122, **123**, 146
seriös **124**, 124, **125**, 146
Shakehands **300**, 300, 326
Showmaster 172, 284, **302**, 302, **303**, 326
'*Sieges-*' (in combinations) **276**, **277**
sinnlich (1) (sensual) **270**, 270, **271**, 328
(2) (sensuous) 243; **270**, **271**, 271, 282
Slip **305**, 305, **306**, 326; Damen-*Slip* **305**, 305, **306**; Herren-*Slip* **305**, **306**, 326; Seiden-*Slip* 305
Smoking 284, **309**, 309, **310**, 326
Sockel **37**, **38**
souverän **264**, **265**, 265
spannungsgeladen **151**, 152, **153**
Speisekarte **99**, 99, **100**, 100
spendieren **127**, 127, **128**, 146
ständig **255**, 255, **256**
Standquartier **37**, **38**
stationär (1) (ortsfest etc.) **273**, 273, **274**, 331
(2) (stationär behandeln) **273**, 273, **274**
'im *Stich* gelassen' **136**, 136, **137**
Stipendium **130**, 130, **131**, 146; Begabten*stipendium* 130, Forschungs*stipendium* 130

aus freien *Stücken* 16
Stützpunkt **37**, 38, 46
sympathisch **133**, 133, **134**, 146, **327**

Talkmaster(in) **312**, 312, **313**, 326, **327**
Tat **18**, 18, **20**
tatsächlich **23**, 23, **24**
'*Teen-*' (in combinations) **316**; *Teen*-Modell 315, *Teen*-Star 315
Teenageralter **315**, 315, **316**, 316
die Teens **315**, 315, 316
teilnahmslos **144**, 144, **145**
temperamentvoll **136**, 136, **137**
tödlich **66**, 66, **67**, 67
todbringend **66**, 66, **67**
'*Todes-*' **66**, 66, **67**; *Todes*schuß 66
tragen: finanziell (mit-) tragen **236**, 236, **238**
Tragweite: von ziemlicher *Tragweite* **267**, 267, **268**
Trakt **138**, 138, **139**, 146
Traktat **138**, 138, **139**
transpirieren (1) **141**, 141, **142**
(2) *see* sweat
traurig (machend) **106**, **107**, 107
'*Triumph-*' **276**, **277**, 277
triumphal **276**, 276, 277, 282
Twen 284, **318**, 318, **319**, 326
(arche-) typisch **160**, 160, **161**

Überbestand **190**, 191, **192**
überblicken **187**, 187, **188**
überdrehen: (ein Uhrwerk) *überdrehen* **213**, 213
Übereinkunft **16**, 16
Übereinstimmung **88**, 88
Überfließen **190**, **192**
Überfluß **190**, 190, **192**
Überflutung **190**, 191, **192**
überhaupt **23**, 23, **24**
über'hören (1) (absichtlich oder unabsichtlich über'hören) 186, **194**, 194, **195**, 240
(2) (akustisch nicht verstehen) **194**, 194, 195, 196
'überhören (sich etwas 'überhören) **194**, 194, **195**
überholen (im Verkehr etc.) **197**, **198**, 198
Überlauf (tech.) **190**, 191, **192**
'*Überlauf-*' **190**, 191, **192**; *Überlauf*rohre 191
(jdn.) überlisten **200**, 200, **201**
übernehmen (1) (= sich übernehmen) 186, **197**, 197, **198**, **200**, 200, 201
(2) (Aufgabe etc. übernehmen) **225**, 225, **226**, 240
überraschen (fig.) **197**, **198**, 198
überreichen **200**, 200, 201
überschlafen 186, **202**, 202, **203**
Überschuß (fig.) **190**, 191, **192**
Überschwemmung **190**, 191, **192**
über'sehen **205**, 205, **207**, 240; (Fehler etc.) über'sehen **187**, 187, **188**
'übersehen **205**, 205, **206**, 206, **207**
Übersicht **209**, 209, **210**, 210
jdn. übervorteilen **200**, **201**
überwachen **93**, **94**, 94, **206**, 206, 207
überwältigend **276**, **277**, 277
überwinden **212**, 212, **213**, 213, 240
üppig **261**, 261, **262**
Umsicht **81**, **82**, 82
uneigennützig **250**, 250, 251
uninteressiert sein (an) **144**, **145**
unkultiviert **244**, **245**, 245
unparteiisch **250**, 250, 251
unsympathisch **144**, 144, **145**, 146; unsympathisch sein **144**, 144, **145**, 145
von unten: (1) (den Ball) *von unten* werfen **215**, 215, **216**
(2) (den Ball) *von unten* aufschlagen **215**, **216**, 216
Unterarm 186, **215**, 215, **216**
untergehen **218**, 218, **219**, 240, 328
Unterkleid **305**, **306**, 306
unterliegen **221**, 221, 222, **223**, 240
untermauern: (eine Leistung etc.) eindrucksvoll *untermauern* (Sport) **236**, 237, **238**
unternehmen 37, 38, **225**, 225, **226**, 240
(das) Unternehmen: (1) (*Unternehmung* allg.) 20, 22, 38, 116, 124, **229**, 229, **230**
(2) (*Unternehmen* in Industrie, Wirtschaft etc.) **228**, 228, 229, **230**
(3) (Vertrags*unternehmen*) **228**, 228, 229, **230**; Bau*unternehmer* **228**, 229; Reinigungs*unternehmen* **228**, 228
(4) (spez. Dienstlei-

stungs*unternehmen*) **228**, 228, 230; Luftverkehrs*unternehmen* 229, Speditions*unternehmen* **228**, Transport*unternehmen* **228**, 229
Unternehmer (1) (allg.) 87, 186, **232**, 232, **234**, 241, 328
(2) (Bau*unternehmer*) **232**, 241; (Sub*unternehmer*) **232**, 232
(3) (Industrieller, Industrie*unternehmer*) **232**, 232, **234**
(4) (Transport*unternehmer*) **232**, 233, **234**
(5) (Geschäftsmann/-frau) **232**, 233, **234**
(6) (die *Unternehmer* allg.) **232**, 233, **234**
Unterrock **305**, **306**, 306, 326
unterschreiben 186, **236**, 236, **238**, 306
sich (einer Sache) *unterziehen* **219**, 219
unzivilisiert **244**, **245**, 245

Veranlagung: von der *Veranlagung* her **136**, 136, **137**
sich verbürgen **225**, **226**, 226
Verfahren **111**, 111, **112**; Disziplinar*verfahren* **18**, 19; Gerichts*verfahren* **18**
vergessen 187, **188**, 188
Verkehrsrowdy **320**, 320, **321**
Verlauf **111**, **112**, 112
verlieren (1) (lose) 61, 212, **259**, 259
(2) (go down to) **221**, 221, **223**
verlobt **55**, 55, **56**
Verlockung **26**, **27**, 27
vermietbar **116**, 116, **117**
vernünftig **122**, 122, **123**, 123
sich verpflichten **225**, **226**, 226
Verpflichtung (auch jur.) **229**, 229, **230**
Versäumnis **210**, 210
Versehen **210**, 210
Versprechen (formell, auch jur.) **229**, 229, **230**
versichern (gegen) **236**, 237, **238**; sich versichern lassen **236**, 237, **238**
verständnisvoll **133**, **134**; verständnisvoll sein gegenüber **133**, **134**, 134
Verwarnung (meist jur.) **81**, **82**, 82
vor allem **323**, **324**, 324
Vorgang **111**, 111, **112**
Vorsicht **81**, 81, **82**
(Allgemein-, Gesamt-) Vorstellung **97**, 97

wahrnehmen **225**, 225, **226**, 226
Warnung **81**, 81
Wasser: ausströmendes *Wasser* **190**, 191, **192**
weit: zu *weit* gehen **200**, 200, **201**
wirklich **23**, 23, **24**
wirtschaftlich **176**, 176, **177**, 179, 184, 187
'*Wirtschafts-*' (in combinations) **176**, **177**, 177; *Wirtschafts*politik 90
wohltuend (Klima etc.) **72**, **73**, 73
wohlwollend **133**, **134**; wohlwollend sein gegenüber **133**, **134**, 134
wollüstig **270**, **271**, 271
wuchernd **261**, 261, **262**
Wüste **48**, 48, 79; *Wüsten*hitze 141, *Wüsten*sonne 49

zart **43**, **44**, 44
Zauber (fig.) **172**, 173, **174**
'*Zauber-*' (in combinations) **172**, 173, **174**; *Zauber*formel 173; *Zauber*ring 173, *Zauberstab 173*
Zauberei **172**, 173, **174**
zeitlos **160**, 161
zeremoniell **279**, 279, **280**, 282
Zettel **305**, **306**, 306
Ziel: über das *Ziel* hinausschießen **200**, **201**
zugrunde liegen **222**, 222, **223**
zuletzt **323**, **324**, 324
sich zusammenreißen **93**, **94**, 94
Zusammentreffen (von Ereignissen etc.) **88**, 88
Zustimmung **16**, 16
(wissenschaftlich) zuverlässig **247**, **248**, 248
zynisch **182**, 182, **183**, 184

rororo sprachen

Herausgegeben von Ludwig Moos

Gunther Bischoff
Speak you English?
Programmierte Übung zum Verlernen typisch deutscher Englischfehler (6857)
Managing Manager English
Gekonnt verhandeln lernen durch Üben an Fallstudien (7129)
Better times
Programm zum Gebrauch der englischen Zeiten (7987)

René Bosewitz/Robert Kleinschroth
Joke Your Way Through English Grammar
Wichtige Regeln zum Anlachen (8527)

René Bosewitz/Hartmut Breitkreuz
Do up your Phrasals
Fünfhundert Wendungen wichtiger Verben (8344)

Claire Bretécher/Isabelle Jue/Nicole Zimmermann
Le Français avec les Frustrés
Ein Comic-Sprachhelfer (8423)

Ahmed Haddedou
Questions Grammaticales de A à Z
Tout ce que vous avez toujours voulu savoir sur la grammaire sans jamais oser le demander (8445)

Hans-Georg Heuber/Marie-Thérèse Pignolo
Ne mâche pas tes mots
Nimm kein Blatt vor den Mund! Französische Redewendungen und ihre deutschen Pendants (7472)

C 2199/6

Hans-Georg Heuber
Talk one's head off
Ein Loch in den Bauch reden
Englische Redewendungen und ihre deutschen «opposite numbers» (7653)

Emer O'Sullivan/Dietmar Rösler
Modern Talking
Englisches Quasselbuch mit Sprüchen und Widersprüchen (8427)

Mario Parisi/Liborio Pepi
Parole Espresse
Italienisches Quasselbuch mit Sprüchen und Widersprüchen (8434)

Ernest Pasakarnis
Grammar Questions from A – Z
Everything you always wanted to know about Grammar but were afraid to ask (8359)
The Word Lover's Guide to How Words Work
Ein moderner Vokabeltrainer (8426)
Master your Idioms
Der Schlüssel zu den englischen Redewendungen (8491)

Senzaparole
Finalmente in Italia
Italienischkurs für wenig und weiter Fortgeschrittene (8471)

Jacques Soussan
Pouvez-vous Français?
Programmierte Übung zum Verlernen typisch deutscher Französischfehler (6940)

Lernprogramme

Eine Auswahl

Georg R. Bach/Laura Torbet
Ich liebe mich – ich hasse mich
Fairness und Offenheit im Umgang mit sich selbst (7891)

Maren Engelbrecht-Greve/Dietmar Juli
Streßverhalten ändern lernen
Programm zum Abbau psychosomatischer Krankheitsrisiken (7193)

Wayne W. Dyer
Der wunde Punkt
Die Kunst, nicht unglücklich zu sein. Zwölf Schritte zur Überwindung der seelischen Problemzonen (7384)

G. Hennenhofer/K. D. Heil
Angst überwinden
Selbstbefreiung durch Verhaltenstraining (6939)

Rainer E. Kirsten/Joachim Müller-Schwarz
Gruppentraining
Ein Übungsbuch mit 59 Psycho-Spielen, Trainingsaufgaben und Tests (6943)

Gerhard Krause
Positives Denken – der Weg zum Erfolg
13 Bausteine für ein erfülltes Leben (7952)

Walter F. Kugemann
Lerntechniken für Erwachsene
(7123)

Michael P. Nichols
40 werden
Die zweite Lebenshälfte als Chance zur Veränderung (8425)

Lernprogramme

Eine Auswahl

Hans-Peter Nolting
Lernfall Aggression
Wie sie entsteht - wie sie zu verhindern ist. Ein Überblick mit Praxisschwerpunkt Alltag und Erziehung (8352)

Friedemann Schulz von Thun
Miteinander reden
Band 1
Störungen und Klärungen. Allgemeine Psychologie der Kommunikation (7489)
Miteinander reden
Band 2
Stile, Werte und Persönlichkeitsentwicklung. Differentielle Psychologie der Kommunikation (8496)

L. Schwäbisch/M. Siems
Anleitung zum sozialen Lernen für Paare, Gruppen und Erzieher
Kommunikations- und Verhaltenstraining (6846)

Martin Siems
Dein Körper weiß Antwort
Focusing als Methode der Selbsterfahrung. Eine praktische Anleitung (7968)

F. Teegen/A. Grundmann/A. Röhrs
Sich ändern lernen
Anleitung zu Selbsterfahrung und Verhaltensmodifikation (6931)

Hobby und Freizeit

Eine Auswahl

Norbert Golluch/Eckhard Klötzer
Das Sperrmüll-Buch
(8757)

Eva C. Huvos
Im Notfall Petersilie
Tips und Tricks einer chaotischen Hausfrau (8366)

Hans-Eberhard Lessing
Das Fahrradbuch
Radfahren mit Know-how (8339)

Raimund Pousset (Hg.)
Der erste Urlaubskoffer
222 Ferienspiele: Rätselhaftes, Witziges, Spannendes und Kriminalistisches für jung und alt (7914)
Der zweite Urlaubskoffer
Das große Schmöker- und Spiele-Buch (7990)

Jürgen Stark/Klaus Farin
Das Fußball Lesebuch
(8596)

Kristine Steinhilber/Cornelius Siegel
Danke, ich schaff's alleine!
Das Autobuch für Frauen (7423)

Helmut Steuer/Claus Voigt
Das neue rororo Spielbuch
(handbuch 6270)

G.J.F. van Tuil/E.R.A. van Heerde
Wünschelruten-Gehen
Eine neue Einführung in eine alte Technik (8751)

SACHBUCH rororo

C 2121/4

Herausgegeben vom Katholischen Institut für Medieninformationen e.V. und der Katholischen Filmkommission für Deutschland

Lexikon des internationalen Films

21000 Filme auf 5000 Seiten in 10 Bänden.
Das komplette deutschsprachige Angebot im Kino und Fernsehen seit 1945.
Jeder Film wird mit Inhalt, künstlerischer Wertung seiner Form und seiner filmhistorischen Einordnung vorgestellt.
Mit einem Registrierband, der zu einer schnellen und gründlichen Orientierung verhilft.
rororo handbuch 6322

Ergänzungsband 1
Das komplette Angebot in Kino,
Fernsehen und auf Video 1987/1988
rororo handbuch 6325

Ergänzungsband 2
Das komplette Angebot in Kino,
Fernsehen und auf Video 1989/1990
rororo handbuch 6326

rororo

C 2315/2

A·N·D·E·R·S·R·E·I·S·E·N

Herausgegeben
von
Ludwig Moos

rororo SACHBUCH

C 2400/1

STÄDTE

Roland Günter
Amsterdam (7506)

zitty-Illustrierte Stadtzeitung
Berlin (9061)

Manfred Waffender/Jonathan Walters
London (7502)

Werner W. Wille
New York (7512)

Günter Liehr
Paris (7509)

Peter Kammerer/Henning Klüver
Rom (7514)

Manfred Waffender
San Francisco (7507)

Frida Bordon
Venedig mit Venetien (7570)

Herausgegeben von Falter
Wien (7563)

A·N·D·E·R·S·R·E·I·S·E·N

Herausgegeben von Ludwig Moos

LÄNDER

Christof Kehr
Andalusien (7575)

Dirk Wegner
Australien (7598)

Roland Motz
Balearen/Barcelona (7579)

Petra Schaeber/Martin Wilke
Brasilien (7594) Oktober '91

Hartiwg Bögeholz
China (7580)

Per Ketman/Andreas Wißmach
DDR (7568)

Dagmar Beckmann/Ulrike Strauch
Elsaß (7585)

Günter Liehr
Frankreich (7519)
Südfrankreich (7582)

Ingrid Backes/Gabriela Daum
Griechenland (7508)

Michael Kadereit
Großbritannien (7530)

Christoph Potting/Annette Weweler
Irland (7525)

SACHBUCH rororo

C 2400/1 a

A·N·D·E·R·S·R·E·I·S·E·N

Herausgegeben von Ludwig Moos

PRAKTISCHE REISEBÜCHER

Ingrid Backes
Das FrauenReiseBuch
(7572)

Hartwig Bögeholz/Werner Radasewsky
Almanach 90/91
Adressen, Infos & Ideen
Der Kompaß durch den Reisedschungel
(7587)

Helmut Hermann
Das ReiseFotoBuch
Ausrüstung, Technik, Praxis und Gespür (7589)

Isabelle Jue/Nicole Zimmermann
Sprachbuch Frankreich
(7520)

Christoph Kehr/Ana Rodriguez Lebrón
Sprachbuch Spanien
(7588)

Johannes Müller/Peter Müller
Gesund unterwegs
Medizinisches Reisehandbuch
(7583)

Emer O'Sullivan/Dietmar Rösler
Sprachbuch Großbritannien / Irland
(7564)

Sprachkollektiv Senzaparole
Sprachbuch Italien
(7571)

SACHBUCH rororo

C 2400/1 c

C 2092/11 a

rororo computer

Hans Herbert Schulze
Das rororo Computer-Lexikon
Schwierige Begriffe einfach erklärt (8105)
Computer-Englisch
Ein Fachwörterbuch (8177)
Computer-Enzyklopädie
Lexikon und Fachwörterbuch für Datenverarbeitung und Telekommunikation. 6 Bände (8141)

Sherry Turkle
Die Wunschmaschine
Der Computer als zweites Ich (8135)

Martin F. Wolters
Einführung in die elektronische Datenverarbeitung
Eine strukturierte Unterweisung:
Der Schlüssel zur Computer-Praxis (8111)
Der Schlüssel zur Computer-HARDWARE (8112)
Der Schlüssel zur Computer-SOFTWARE (8113)
Der Schlüssel zur Computer-ORGWARE (8114)

C 2092/11 b